The LOGOS of God is the Tree of Life

Tree of Life

Copyright © 2010 by James Curtis.
All rights are reserved.
Limited extracts from this book may be reproduced,
provided the source is acknowledged.
Extensive reproduction is prohibited without the
written permission of the author.
http://www.hecomesfirst.net

His Word Publishing
P. O. Box 141
Washington, Me 04574

Scripture quotations taken from the
NEW AMERICAN STANDARD BIBLE®,
Copyright © 1960, 1962, 1963, 1968, 1971,
1972, 1973, 1975, 1977, 1995 by the
Lockman Foundation. Used by permission.
A Corporation Not for Profit
900 S. Euclid St., La Habra, California 90631
http://www.lockman.org

Explanations of the names of God were taken from the Preface to the New American Standard Bible, Principles of Translation, The Proper Name of God in the Old Testament *The New American Standard Bible, 1995 Update*, (La Habra, California: The Lockman Foundation) 1996.

Thomas, Robert L., Th.D., General Editor, *New American Standard Hebrew-Aramaic and Greek Dictionaries, Updated Edition*, (Anaheim, CA: Foundation Publications, Inc.) 1999, c1998.

The LOGOS of God is the

Tree of Life

A Journey to Discover the Heart of God

By James Curtis

His Word Publishing

Tree of Life

To Tony & Dad

To the Brethren,
who showed Love
and were glad is see
what God did in my heart.

Tree of Life

Table of Contents

Introduction	1
A Note about Names of God	10
Part 1 A Choice between Two Trees	13
1) In the Beginning, it was in His Heart.	15
2) What Would You Exchange for Your Soul?	26
3) Jesus is True Life	34
4) Adam's Legacy	40
5) We Must Agree with God	50
6) Eat From the Wrong Tree and Believe a Lie	61
7) Entangled in a Spider's Web	68
8) Righteousness, by what Law?	75
9) Righteousness by Obeying the Law of Love	88
10) We Can Trust the God of Love	98
Part 2 In the Beginning was the LOGOS of God	109
11) The Meaning behind the Words	111
12) In the Beginning Was Jesus	118
13) Jesus Christ is the True Meaning	125
14) The Holy Spirit is Our Teacher	133
15) Scripture Comes with its Own Meaning	140
16) God so Loved the World	147
17) No Longer I, But Jesus Christ Lives in Me	154
18) God Cannot Ignore Sin	162
19) A Perfect Life is Ours	170
20) Pointing to the Right Source	178
21) We Can Know Who the False Teachers Are	184
Part 3 Walking in the Fellowship of Love	189
22) The Goal of God's Instructions is Love - I	191
23) The Goal of God's Instructions is Love - II	200
24) Relationship between Yahweh and His People	207
25) Christ's Relationship with His Bride	217
26) Jesus says, "My Sheep Hear My Voice."	231
27) Sharing the Yoke of His Fellowship	240
28) The Yoke of His Fellowship is Love	250
29) Following LOGOS is Not Easy	257
30) Jesus Says, "To Follow Me is Like Taking up a Cross"	267
31) Oh Death, Where is Thy Sting?	273
32) The Modern Day Martyrs	279
33) Treasure the Right Things in Your Heart	289

Tree of Life

A Journey to Discover the Heart of God

Introduction

I pray that you read this book. It's not important that you buy this book, but that you read this book. It is natural that I'd want you to read this book because I wrote it. But I want you to read this book for another reason. My desire is that as you read, you will find you are listening to the heart of God. As a people, we need a change in our thinking. In my observation, the pollution of worldly thinking is spoiling our spiritual environment. I feel compelled to write this book because we need spiritual teachings that point us to the right thinking. I will not try to tell you what the right thinking is. I will only to point to the source of right thinking, the heart of God. We need the thinking that cleanses our spiritual environment. I pray this book is different in that it points to what the Creator thinks and not what any man – including me - thinks.

I pray you join me in a journey to find a treasure more precious than our own life. Everyone has the opportunity to realize this treasure, but not everyone takes the time to find it. I pray that you embrace this opportunity to discover the treasure of God's thinking. If you look you will find; if you take the time to look with all your heart, you will find His. How you react to God's handiwork around you is the most important choice you make.

The marvelous treasure we find in Him is that He takes what is not right about us and He replaces it with what is right about Himself. He is Light in the darkness. He is Love amid the hate. We come to better know Him as we fellowship with Him. Knowing Him sets us free from sin. We do not depend on our own understanding of right and wrong. Instead we rely on His wisdom to keep us upright as He works to transform us into His likeness (Pro. 3:5, 2 Cor. 3:18).

There are those who have the name Christian and count themselves as one of His people yet do not value knowing Him as their treasure. They know of Him, but do not know Him. If they knew Him, they would value Him above all else. They believe they know the truth and refuse to recognize the touch of God in their lives. The result is that their hearts remain in darkness.

I want you to read this book. Yet, I feel vulnerable from the idea that you might read this book, for it exposes my thoughts which

Tree of Life

in turn expose the essence of who I am. When I started writing this book, I did not think I was opening a window into my soul. But when one writes a book, one reveals themselves in a way they would not otherwise.

I fear you'll misunderstand me when I say I am free from attempting to gain righteousness by my own efforts and I am free from the slavery of sin. I fear you will take that to mean that I think I am perfect or that it is "OK" for me to continue in sin (1 John 1:5-2:1) In a conversation, I can see your body language and I can stop and clear up a misunderstanding. In a book, you will know what I have written but maybe not what I think. I cannot correct your misinterpretation and that makes me feel vulnerable. You can see all the words of my thoughts, but perhaps not understand enough of my intended meaning to know what I am saying. Therefore I feel unprotected.

Our God also wrote a book and exposed His thinking and the essence of who He is. We can misinterpret the words He used and lose His true meaning. So He did more than write His thoughts down. He embodied His thinking into a human life by becoming a man, Jesus Christ, the Messiah (John 1:1-3 and 1:14). Jesus Christ lived according to the intent that God expressed in His book, the Bible. He gave a real-life example of what He intended to be the Bible's true meaning. After Jesus Christ finished writing His thoughts into humanity, He offered to share this perfect Life with whoever would accept Him. With His Life in us, we can better understand God's heart. When we discover His heart, we fall in love with Him. What God communicates to us is not just a nice idea. It is the essence of who He is and the deep inner part of His being. Our life comes from His Life as we becomes apart of His Life.

What the book is about

This book is about True Life. It is about the One who makes True Life possible. It is about knowledge made available to us by the One who has all knowledge. It is about discovering the heart of God. Does my writing mean I have all knowledge or that I know more than anyone else? No. I only know what He gives me. But I know the source of all knowledge and intend to point to the true source. You see, we have a Teacher who searches the heart of God and makes

A Journey to Discover the Heart of God

Him known to us (Rom. 8:27, 1 Cor. 2:10, Rev. 2:23). We are not alone in our search. The Holy Spirit explains the example lived out by Jesus Christ (Rom. 5:5-11).

This book is about God's Love. It is about sharing an everlasting Love. It is about giving Love in accordance with the character of the one giving love and not based on the goodness of the receiver of love. It is about loving those who refuse to receive the love offered and continuing to love those who hate in return. This book is about the Message of Love the Godhead displayed at Calvary, while nailed to a cross, for those who rejected Him. Imagine, the all-powerful Creator of Mankind hanging on a cross declaring forgiveness! (1 Cor. 1:18). The Message of Love says, "If I will do this for you while you reject and oppose me, what will I do after we are one in the same Spirit?" (Rom. 5:10).

This book is also about you. It is about the most important questions you face as a human. Which road are you on? In whom do you believe? Will you accept this testimony of Love or reject it for selfish reasons? I do not ask, "Do you accept with what your mind understands?" I ask, "Do you accept it in a way that changes the way you live?" Even if you "claim" to be one of God's people, ask yourself: Have I listened to hear His testimony as delivered on the cross?

Some readers have already stopped reading because they either do not want to discuss these questions or they believe they already know the answers. Most set the book down because they do not understand the questions or their importance. If you are wondering, "Should I read this book?" The answer is, "You should read this book!" The discussion within is about your spiritual life or death, and that is important. Most think the deep question is about gaining a spiritual "good life" (Heaven) and avoiding a spiritual "bad life" (Hell). How one spends eternity is important. Its importance decreases when one knows Jesus Christ in an intimate way. Then, being where He is and enjoying His friendship becomes the treasure. The verse about storing up treasure in heaven takes on a whole new meaning when Jesus Christ is the treasure we are storing (Matt. 12:30-37 and 6:19-21). I believe the treasure we store is the time we spend with Him.

Tree of Life

Where the book starts

I wish you to remember that this subject is a multifaceted truth. It may appear I am repeating myself over and over. What I am doing is connecting the dots. I will follow the branches and try to show the relationship of the current topic to a pervious part of the book. Truth is linear, so we build one precept upon another. It is also like a multipoint star. We start at the middle, travel to the end point, back to our beginning, and then take it out to another point. As we travel to each point, we keep building one precept on another, looking at the truth as a whole. Therefore, we will need to repeat the central idea as we add relevant things. We will look at many facets of the Truth. But we cannot cover all facets of this truth in one book.

Every book must have a starting point. The starting point often takes certain points for granted and uses them as a foundation to build on. As we continue our discussion, I will, in no way, try to prove or disprove basic ideas such as "the existence of God." So, this book references the Bible as the true written declaration of God and references Jesus Christ as fulfilling that declaration. Throughout the book, I hold the principle there is an Intelligent Designer of the heavenly, spiritual, and physical planes.

I believe the Creator proposed in His heart to create according to a design, which achieves the "Law of Love" (Rom. 8:1-3). He created everything according to, and through, that design. Everything that happens is a part of and not in conflict with the design (John 1:1-3, Col. 1:15-17 and 19-20). I believe the Creator of the Universe is close to each of us and is interactive in our lives. He is not sitting in heaven waiting to see what is going to happen as if we were a TV show. Every action He takes has a purpose that He planned to achieve for His people's benefit (Rom. 8:26-31). We will have an ongoing discussion about Jesus Christ being the Blueprint of Life.

Another foundation of this book is the nature of evil. The Bible speaks of Satan and Satan personifies evil. I will not argue about His existence. The beginning of the struggle between good and evil was the result of God creating His Creation. The God of the Bible does not sin, period! Even so, as long as God remained alone and did not create creatures able to sin, there was no conflict. If He did not remain alone and created creatures able to sin, the conflict would begin. Satan sinned against God by wishing to sit on the

A Journey to Discover the Heart of God

throne of the Creator and to be like a god, which was what he tempted Eve with (Gen. 3:5). He convinced her to eat fruit from the wrong tree, thus introducing his destructive thinking to humanity. He continues to introduce his lies to us every day. The Tree of the Knowledge of Good and Evil represents Satan's thinking. The human race continuously chooses to eat from it. They feast their minds on the mix of good and evil. Thus they corrupt themselves with each bite. They mix evil thinking with good.

    We will also discuss the nature of man, which opposes God's teaching. We will talk about how men teach using God's name and how they claim to come from Him, but teach contrary to His thinking and to His Message. They confuse and contradict the Word of God while quoting its passages. They do not know the Author of the Scriptures and He did not teach them. Their words are words of death, because they are about man and not God. They misinterpret His words.

    We will talk about the darkness of evil teachings that dull men's minds and lead them to spiritual death. Darkness cannot exist where Light exists. Also, evil cannot stand in the presence of God. For the darkness to survive, it must destroy the Light. The conflict between darkness and Light existed before man's creation and will play out to its fullest, even to complete destruction. Man's destruction would be a done deal except God said He will put a stop to it (Matt. 24:21-22).

    For Satan to win, he must destroy the Light. Otherwise it will destroy him. He must prove there is darkness in God by showing Him to be unrighteous in some way. Satan has already lost the battle in heaven and God restricts his activities to this planet (Luke 10:18, Rev. 12:10-12). His Blueprint has allotted a time for evil to reign. Then, He will put evil away and Satan knows his time is short. The Creator does not do evil but did account for evil in His design and will use the results of evil to perform good for those who belong to Him. All belong to Him for He created all, but there are those He has separated and called His, for these He will make everything work out for their good according to His purposes (Rom. 8:24-32).

Tree of Life

The Workman is still working and battles for the hearts of men

The Workman is still working. Therefore another foundation is this: the purpose of Creation remains unaccomplished. People witness the skill of the Creator's craftsmanship. The "Citizens of Heaven" eagerly watch and learn from our experiences (1 Peter 1:12, 1 Cor. 4:9 and 11:10). The experiences we face during our struggles are for their benefit also. The Creator will not allow the forces of evil to work in Heaven. The Citizens of Heaven must learn by watching the proceedings as they happen on earth.

The Workman of Creation is working from a perfect Blueprint. Our understanding of what happens around us must conform to this truth. We must accept that we work with flawed interpretations. We misunderstand the intent of the Workman's labors. God's methods are perfect because He is without fault. He does not make mistakes. If the Creator had a fault, then the conflict would turn into a battle pitting one form of darkness against another - evil vs. evil.

We will not spend much time discussing why God allows evil to exist or why He allows the results of sin to pile up. Instead, we will discuss why our participation as humans is a unique opportunity. We are participants in the struggle while also being the prize of the combatants. Only members of the human race can enter this struggle based solely on faith. **No matter which side we choose to believe, we must do so based solely on faith.**

The debate about what comprises good and what comprises evil will continue to rage. The proof that we need to settle the debate is being withheld until the end. Therefore, the faith of a human being is valuable because he trusts in someone he cannot prove exists. Angels and demons believe in what they know. You are a prize, highly desired by both sides but valued by only one. The battle is not out there somewhere between two supernatural forces struggling to see who will rule Creation. That battle is finished and Satan lost. The battle is in the spiritual realm and it involves you. It takes place in the depths of your being. Satan wants to be equal to God and the only place he can accomplish that is in your mind. This is the only battleground left. It is a spiritual battle for your devotion and plays out in every human being, resulting in either spiritual life or spiritual death.

A Journey to Discover the Heart of God

Each person must choose between God's thinking and Satan's thinking. Those who agree with the Creator must travel along the path He has provided, walking by the Light He has provided. They must believe that He is the only Truth, the only Light, and the only source of Life. Some will believe the lie and say, "Satan's thinking is equal to God's thinking." They enter an agreement with Satan, which causes them to oppose the Creator. Currently, the thinking of this world is a reflection of Satan's thinking and comes from the Tree of the Knowledge of Good and Evil, which I also call the Tree of Death.

If you make no choice, you accept the choice made for you by Adam in the Garden of Eden. Be warned: you cannot declare your choice by mouthing a confession. You declare it by the thoughts you allow in your mind and the actions you take daily. The thoughts you willingly feed on become the thinking of your soul. The thinking of your inner person becomes the actions of your outer person (Luke 6:43-45). If you make yourself one with the thinking of darkness, the Truth of the Light will make you uncomfortable. Allowing the Light of Jesus Christ to influence your thinking creates a new life. You will have no reason to fear the Light. Then you will have the freedom you seek.

The stage is set with two trees

This book uses the tree of the Knowledge of Good and Evil to symbolize all teachings that are contrary to the Blueprint, by which God created the Universe. Satan uses the Tree of the Knowledge of Good and Evil to spread his lie. His teachings take on many forms for they do not need to conform to any standard. The lie of Satan can be disgustingly undesirable in its error and appear evil, or be attractively desirable in its error and appear virtuous. Its character is still wrong and unhealthy. To lead men astray, Satan's teachings only need to be believable. They do not need to be effective. Satan wants to hide Truth in a fog of knowledge by focusing on a myriad of teachings from the Tree of Death.

This book uses the Tree of Life to symbolize all the teachings that make the Blueprint knowable and understandable. The teachings of the Tree of Life must remain true to the design. Truth must carry out its task (Isaiah 55:6-11). Truth can never change or turn apart from itself. Any deviance from God's original thinking will change

Tree of Life

the underlying character of its nature. Therefore Truth, as taught by the Tree of Life, can never fail or change, because it will stop to be true if it does. Our Creator can never fail, else all will become a lie and nothing can be true. Seekers of the Truth can fail, for they are not the Truth. They are only the seekers of the Truth. The messengers of the Message can fail, for they are only the messengers and not the Message. But God cannot fail for He is both the Truth and the Message (Luke 16:15-17, Hab. 2:3, Heb 2:1-4). He is what we search for. It is our journey to follow the path that discovers Him.

Summary

This book speaks of two opposing points of view. The Tree of Life represents all that is good. The Tree of the Knowledge of Good and Evil represents all that would destroy the good by mixing evil with it. Evil wants to trick us into eating what is poisonous to our soul and can represent itself any way it wants. The Tree of Life can have only one Image, one Purpose, one Method, one Mediator, one Path, one Spirit, and one Mind. (Eph. 4:1-7) One of these trees alternatively condemns us and excuses us of sin; while the other cleans us of sin (1 John 1:6-2:1).

The Tree of Life teaches us the truth about our sin and sets before us, for our examination, a life that is without sin. The Tree of Life is about entering a partnership with the God of Love. It is about a Teacher who personally teaches about God's heart to those who will listen. It is about His teaching us about sin. Jesus Christ explained the meaning of the words of Love, on a Cross of hate. In doing so, He turned an instrument of death into an instrument of spiritual life.

I ask that you read at least the first chapter of this book before you make up your mind about the rest of the book. Then I pray that you read the next chapter also, for it asks an important question. I continue to pray that you find the book helpful in finding the Tree of Life and that you eat its fruit. May you discover the treasure buried in the heart of the Creator. His Spirit is love issued from a pure heart, given to those who do not deserve it.

A Journey to Discover the Heart of God

But the fruit of the Spirit is love, joy, peace, patience, kindness, goodness, faithfulness, gentleness, self-control; against such there is no law. (Gal. 5: 22-23)

May the Life which gives meaning to the Word of God be as a Tree of Life to you.

Tree of Life

A Note about the Names of God

[1]It is inconceivable to think of spiritual matters without a proper name for the Supreme Deity. Thus, the most common name is simply God; a translation of the original Elohim. One of the titles for God is Lord; a translation of Adonai. There is yet another name for God which is particularly assigned as His special or proper name. That is, the four letters YHWH יהוה **Yhvh**2 (That is. הוָיָה **Yehovah** or וַהֲיֹעַ: **Yahveh**) The Jews have not pronounced this name because of their reverence for the great sacredness of the divine name. Therefore, it has been consistently translated LORD. For many years now YHWH has been transliterated as Yahweh, however, no complete certainty attaches to this pronunciation

In Exodus 3:14, Moses asked God what His name was. He answered, "I AM WHO I AM" The Hebrew word for "I AM" is יָהָה **hayah** (Strong's Number 1961), which is a primary root word, meaning to fall out, come to pass, become, be. It is related to the name of God, YHWH, (Strong's Number 3068) rendered LORD," which is derived from the verb, הָוָה **havah** to be.

In this book, I constantly refer to the person of God. He has several names and they all have meaning to me. I think He will answer to "I AM", "HE IS," and YOU ARE. I don't think of Him the same way every time I use His name. He is my Father and the Creator of the Universe. He is also my Savior and the Great Shepherd of the flock. Yahweh, the Creator of the Universe, and God are names I use when writing about the Godhead collectively. Elohim and Adonai are equally good names, but I have never got into the habit of using them. I write "Yahweh" instead of referring to Him as "God" all the time because I like it and it breaks the text up pleasingly. Yahweh is not a religious teaching or a something I do to

---

1. Portions were taken from the Preface to the New American Standard Bible, Principles of Translation, The Proper Name of God in the Old Testament, *The New American Standard Bible, 1995 Update*, (La Habra, California: The Lockman Foundation) 1996.
2Thomas, Robert L., Th.D., General Editor, *New American Standard Hebrew-Aramaic and Greek Dictionaries, Updated Edition*, (Anaheim, CA: Foundation Publications, Inc.) 1999, c1998.

A Journey to Discover the Heart of God

follow a code. I would like writing "YHWH" more, which is truer to what I know - but how would one pronounce it - Yehovah, Jehovah, Yahveh, Yahweh? I use Yahweh.

The Greek word translated into English as Jesus is ʼΙησοῦς Iēsous; (Strong's Number 2424) and is of Hebrew origin, which in the Old Testament is the Hebrew word שְׁוּיה **Yehoshua** or שְׁוִיהָ **Yehoshua**. (Strong's Number 3091). It is translated Jeshua (28) and Joshua (219). Most likely, Jesus' parents called Him Yeshua, the Hebrew version of His name, as He walked on the earth. I will not be calling Him Yehoshua Mashiach (Savior, the Anointed One) in this book, mostly because, after 30 plus years, it does not feel natural for me to do so, but it would not bother me to do so. Those who refer to Him as Yeshua the Messiah are technically more correct than me.

How does Jesus feel about which name I use? I believe His concern is with the way I use His name more than which name I use. You can call me James, Jimmy, or Jim. I am called Daddy, husband, and late for supper. I do not prefer one to the other as long as you use my name as my friend. How you treat me is more important than the name you use. Yahweh, Lord, Lord Jesus, the Holy Spirit, the Father, the Son, the Messiah, the Creator, my Friend, the Light, Love, and my Husband are all terms of endearment for God.

I will capitalize the first letter when I use a word that is also a reference to God's nature, teachings, or purpose, such as the words *Light* and *Love* that are pictures of whom God is. One such name for Jesus Christ is the "Logos of God" (Word of God). I also call Him the Message and Blueprint. The concept behind Jesus Christ being the Word of Yahweh is the reason behind my writing this book. When the Holy Spirit revealed the meaning of this name to me, it changed my life and my thinking. I hope it will change yours also. We will talk further about the Greek word for Logos in Part Two, Chapter 12.

When I talk about God's names, it causes me to think of Him as a person and not an entity or spiritual force. Take time to think of why He called Himself "I AM," for, in doing so, He established the first truth we must accept: "HE EXISTS." It is impossible to please God if you do not believe "HE IS" (Heb. 11:5-6). How can you please someone who is not there? How can you please someone you ignore as if He was not there?

Tree of Life

The problem that divides man from God is not with God receiving man. It is with man receiving God as God (Rom. 1:18-23).

May a personal knowledge of Yahweh be a Tree of Life to you.

The LOGOS of God is the

Tree of Life

A Journey to Discover the Heart of God

Part One

Eating From the Wrong Tree

A choice we must make, a question we must answer.

So this I say, and affirm together with the Lord, that you walk no longer just as the gentiles also walk, in the futility of their mind, being darkened in their understanding, excluded from the life of God because of the ignorance that is in them, because of the hardness of their heart; (Ephesians 4:17-18).

A Choice between Two Trees

Chapter 1

In the Beginning, it was in His Heart

An old, old story

On the stage of mankind's history, an undeniable theme has been playing, the classic tale of good versus evil. Every civilization on earth has taken part in its telling by passing numerous fairy tales, myths, legends, storybooks, and history books from generation to generation. Throughout the ages, man's thinking about religion and politics has revolved around various man-centered characterizations of the struggle.

The God of Creation has an exclusive understanding of this struggle. His understanding comes from a time before there was a struggle, a time in the forever past when there was only good. There was only good because there was only Yahweh. He fully understands the dynamics of good and evil. So, when He created the universe He did so to reflect His perspective and He created light to symbolize good and darkness to symbolize evil.

Yahweh teaches what is good to those who will listen. His teachings are like a tree bearing good fruit that gives spiritual life to those who are spiritually dead by giving them victory over evil. All teachings that do not align with Yahweh's teachings are like a tree bearing fruit of spiritual death. It is full of wrong thinking that poisons the soul.

Yahweh communicates through the words of the Bible, through the example of His Son, and through the workings of the Holy Spirit. The Bible verbalizes what the Godhead of Creation spiritually communicates. Jesus Christ fulfills the Bible, giving the words a clearer meaning. The Holy Spirit is a Tutor of Righteousness who makes the communication in Jesus Christ's life understandable. The Holy Spirit uses the Word of God to express the Godhead's thoughts that He interweaves with the deeper meaning of God's intent. We find His intent in the life, death, and resurrection of Jesus the Christ. Together, they explain the heart of the Father and make known His mind to those who believe that "He is." We need the Holy Spirit's help to study what Jesus Christ came to communicate. When we incorporate Yahweh's view of good versus evil into our thinking,

Tree of Life

it causes us to gain True Life. The thoughts of God are true. Any thinking that does not match His thinking is false and misleading. Who else can know what is truth like the one who is Truth?

Throughout history, human beings have defined the conflict between good and evil as light versus darkness or right versus wrong. In truth, it is mostly a conflict between love and hate. Humankind explains the battle inaccurately as spiritual good opposing spiritual evil, as if evil came first and good is trying to overcome it. The Bible tells us that good existed at a time when there was no evil. Therefore, the forces of evil are attacking the dominion of what is good. The conflict is not about someone who is good focusing His intent on evil's destruction. Instead, evil cannot continue to exist in the presence of what is good, just as darkness cannot survive the presence of light.

The God of Creation stands for all that is good. The forces of evil are trying to overcome Him. It is His virtue and leadership that evil is challenging. The Bible tells us that, in the dominion of Heaven, the battle has taken place and is finished. Good defeated evil. But the battle continues in the domain of men's hearts. The battle rages because of the darkness of men's hearts. Evil can only exist where ignorance limits the Light. As soon as the Light of God's Love becomes known within a man's soul, the darkness of hate weakens.

Purity can only be pure if it is 100 percent without defilement. Even a little evil will compromise what is good. Therefore, the essence of good cannot receive the essence of evil into its company. Teachings contrary to God's thinking brought evil into man's thinking. It broke our fellowship with God and caused us to die spiritually. The Tree of Life drives evil thinking out of our minds again. The Tree of Life gives us new life by reuniting us with God, restoring the companionship He originally intended.

His thinking is a new way of thinking and as old as the beginning

<u>Now to the one who works</u>, his wage <u>is not</u> reckoned as a <u>favor</u>, but as <u>what is due</u>. But to the one <u>who does not work</u>, but <u>believes in Him</u> who justifies the ungodly, <u>his faith is reckoned as righteousness</u>, for the Law brings about wrath, but where there is no law, neither is there violation. (Romans 4:4-5, and 15)

A Choice between Two Trees

One of them, a lawyer, asked Him a question, testing Him, "Teacher, which is the great commandment in the Law?" And He said to him, "'YOU SHALL LOVE THE LORD YOUR GOD WITH ALL YOUR HEART, AND WITH ALL YOUR SOUL, AND WITH ALL YOUR MIND.' This is the great and foremost commandment. The second is like it, 'YOU SHALL LOVE YOUR NEIGHBOR AS YOURSELF.' <u>On these two commandments depend the whole Law and the Prophets</u>" (Matt. 22:35-40).

Owe nothing to anyone except to love one another; for <u>he who loves his neighbor has fulfilled the law</u>. For this, "You shall not commit adultery, you shall not murder, you shall not steal, you shall not covet," and if there is any other commandment, it is summed up in this saying, "You shall love your neighbor as yourself." <u>Love does no wrong to a neighbor; love therefore is the fulfillment of the law</u> (Romans 13:8-10).

Beloved, I am <u>not writing a new</u> commandment to you, but an old commandment which you have had from the beginning; the old commandment is the word which you have heard. <u>On the other hand, I am writing a new commandment to you</u>, which is true in Him and in you, because the darkness is passing away and the true Light is already shining. <u>The one who says he is in the Light and yet hates his brother is in the darkness until now</u> (1 John 2:7-9).

These verses are only a taste of what the Bible has to say about justification by the Law (Rom. 9:30-33) and justification by the Law of the Spirit of Life in Christ Jesus, which is the Law of Love (Rom. 8:2). Today, much is written about a type of love that is not from Yahweh's way of thinking. What does Yahweh mean when He speaks of Love? How is His thinking different from the flood of man's thinking? The difference is that God's love is based on who He is and not on those He loves. God has long desired to help us discover what has been on His heart from the beginning. But since Yahweh's thoughts of Love still sound like a new idea, people must not have listened well. One would think that, after 6,000 years of the Creator interacting with His people, there would be more peace on earth and not less. Two thousand years after the birth of Jesus Christ, worldwide Christ-like love and happiness is as elusive as ever.

Tree of Life

For many, Christmas brings thoughts of a general good feeling men have toward one another. They remember how people treat one another a little better during that time of year. The idea of peace and goodwill toward all men is synonymous with the Christmas holidays because the Message was communicated through the life of a baby born in Bethlehem (Luke 2:8-14, Isa. 9:1-7). The promise of peace and goodwill declares the love that Yahweh has for His creation and those who please Him. The birth, life, and death of the Son of God fulfilled everything He intended. His love performed the greatest act of self-sacrifice ever committed on earth that resulted in peace on earth between God and His people. This peace takes place deep inside in the hearts of men and not everyone enjoys it.

The promise of His coming, His birth, His life, His teachings, His death, His resurrection, and His return for His people all point toward the Love Yahweh has for humans. The peace Jesus Christ offers is between the Creator and each one of us. When accepted, the offer of peace also affects the interactions individuals have with each other.

We must choose between two trees and their teachings

We have been discussing two choices. Each of us must decide between them and the schools of thought each represents. I say there are only two choices. One must choose to believe or disbelieve Yahweh's Message. The thesis of this book claims that choosing not to believe God Almighty, by rejecting His claims of Love, leaves the Tree of Death as the only other choice. It no longer matters what the other theoretical choices are, for they all end in the choice to believe a lie and by eating from the wrong tree.

We all begin with the school of thought Adam and Eve received from the Tree of the Knowledge of Good and Evil. For many, it is all they know. Adam and Eve ate from the wrong tree and, by so doing, received the thinking of the Serpent. Their companionship with the Creator gave them knowledge of good, which was all they needed. Eating from the wrong tree added knowledge of evil. The knowledge of evil instantly placed them in opposition to their Maker and spiritual death was the result.

The Tree of Life, which is the knowledge of Yahweh, is not available to those who are without Him. No one can know the

A Choice between Two Trees

pathway to the Tree of Life without Yahweh because Yahweh is the Tree of Life. We discover the Tree of Life when we fellowship with the Person of the Eternal God who gives everlasting life. Therefore, we need Him to make known the path that guides us to Him that we might have friendship.

Men who claim to have found the Tree of Life are confused about which tree they are feeding from. It is the wrong tree, for it denies their Creator. The teachings that come from the Tree of the Knowledge of Good and Evil appear enlightened but bring spiritual poison to any who eat from it. They cannot mature spiritually. It is spiritual junk food with little nutritional value for the soul and many harmful ingredients.

We begin life in disagreement with the Creator. This fact leaves us ill-prepared to fit into the pattern that He designed for us. The story is in Genesis, when Adam and Eve made the choice to believe Satan instead of God. They decided to disbelieve Yahweh, who created them. The two choices before us are mutually exclusive. You cannot believe what the one is saying without disbelieving the other.

We write our own story about the everyday choices we make and how they affect our eternity. Most of us ensnare ourselves with selfish, hateful, and self-righteous thinking that opposes what is good for us and embraces our devastation. We need freedom from our old way of thinking. We need the better way of thinking that Yahweh provides us through the Fellowship of Love.

In everything, therefore, treat people the same way you want them to treat you, for this is the Law and the Prophets. Enter through the narrow gate; for the gate is wide and the way is broad that leads to destruction, and there are many who enter through it. For the gate is small and the way is narrow that leads to life, and there are few who find it.

Beware of the false prophets, who come to you in sheep's clothing, but inwardly are ravenous wolves. You will know them by their fruits. Grapes are not gathered from thorn bushes, nor figs from thistles, are they? Even so, every good tree bears good fruit; but the bad tree bears bad fruit. A good tree cannot produce bad fruit, nor can a bad tree produce good fruit. Every tree that does not bear good

Tree of Life

fruit is cut down and thrown into the fire. So then, you will know them by their fruits (Matt. 7:12-20).

Here is the Golden Rule! Everyone knows the Golden Rule. Who practices the Golden Rule? Jesus Christ describes the choice that we must make. It is a choice between entering a narrow gate that allows us to travel a lesser-used road and a broad gate that gives us the right to travel the highway leading to destruction. Notice that Jesus links our treatment of others to the choices we make between these two roads. If we treat others the way we want them to treat us, we will travel a lesser-known path and will fulfill the Message of God. The lesser-known path leads to everlasting life, but it is a difficult path to walk and we cannot succeed alone.

All men start life on the pathway to destruction. They look for Truth leading to Life on the path that leads to destruction. The path to destruction is so wide, it will at times look like many paths. It is wide enough to hold large volumes of people who never find the narrow pathway. The majority will not find the narrow path and will travel a path that looks good to them but is wrong (Pro. 14:12). The path that leads to life is not wide because few travel it. Since many believe they travel the path of life and few are they who travel it, the traveler must take serious inventory of their spiritual walk.

Traveling the right path is all about the communication we have between our human soul and the one true God. It is also about our contacts with other human souls. The question is, "Are we putting into practice the Golden Rule?" Jesus attaches our treatment of others to the path of Truth. These are strong, unacceptable words to someone who wants to travel any spiritual path he chooses by believing whatever is pleasing to his ears.

The truth about "the Truth" is Jesus Christ walked the pathway of truth successfully. He is the only one to complete the course and the only one who can avoid all the pitfalls. That means that He is the only one qualified to be a guide. Those who join Him in His Life have already completed the course by association and He guarantees they will arrive at the correct location (Matt. 7:13-14). Knowledge of what is right is not the narrow path. The Person of Jesus Christ is.

A Choice between Two Trees

These verses also warn about false prophets or teachers that travel the path of destruction. They will come looking like someone holding onto truth but will offer an imitation truth. They will mix lies with truth and poison it. Jesus is the Way, the Truth, and the Life. He says no one can enter the presence of God if they do not come through Him (John 14:5-15). This is a stumbling block for many who have built religions based on man-centered works. They want to think of Jesus Christ as just another man, teaching about one of many correct paths to follow. They do not want to think of Jesus Christ as God, the Creator, visiting His creation for the purpose of being the correct path.

There are those who say, "Jesus lied. There is more than one path man can traverse to get to God. There is more than one right way of thinking." They do not know that what appears diverse and varied is really the same path leading them to the same destruction. They ask, "Why should all Christians be right and all Hindus be wrong?" and "What about the savages who live out in the outermost jungle who have never heard these things?" They bring up fairness as an issue, forgetting the Creator of all is also Owner of all and has the right to do as He wishes with what is His.

"Woe to the one who quarrels with his Maker. An earthenware vessel among the vessels of earth! Will the clay say to the potter, 'What are you doing?' Or the thing you are making say, 'He has no hands'? (Isaiah 45:9).

Any artist or furniture maker has rights to what they create, just as I have certain rights concerning this book. This book has no say about the cover or if I publish it or how I publish it. You might say there is a huge difference between an inanimate object and a human being, but the difference between a book and a human being is not as great as the difference between Yahweh and a human being (Jer. 18:1-10; Rom. 9:1-23; Isa. 64:1-9, 29:14-16, 41:21-42:6, and 45:7-12).

The Holy Spirit said through Paul the Apostle that God created man with enough knowledge of his Creator to honor Him (Romans 1:18-22, 2:14-15, and 2:23-27). That means God created all men with the knowledge necessary to choose the right course. From the day of their birth, every person has within him enough knowledge of the Godhead to honor Him as God. He has left everyone without excuse.

People will argue "What about the savages?" Those arguments will not help them if they are on the wrong road and end in the wrong location. God the Father will ask, "What did you do with the Light I gave you?" Honor God for who He is, the "I AM". He will not hold people accountable for an understanding they don't have. He holds them accountable for their reaction to the Truth they do have.

Oh, by the way, all Christians are not right just because they call themselves Christians. Many people make the claim but do not live the life. Be careful you do not judge a Holy God who, because of kindness, brought into His house a sinful people. He transforms those who walk with Him but not all mature fully before meeting Him! (Matt. 7:15-23, 25:1-13). I do not believe I have ever met a true follower of Jesus Christ who was right in every respect. We are all a work in progress and I advise you not to judge the Workman until He finishes His work. If you judge the work you also judge the Workman's skill.

A choice between two trees is a choice about sin

Naturally, when we companion with a Holy God, we should expect the issue of sin to come up. Sin is important to Yahweh but it is not His main focus. The true motive for every action He takes is the welfare of His people. It might be hard to hear, but dealing with our sin is an expression of His Love. Our God watches over us for our good and not for our injury, much like parents who guide their children with kindness and severity, depending on the circumstance, because they want the best for them.

We think of sin as OK when we do it to others and something harmful when done to us. But it is always harmful to us even when we do it to others. Why should a God of Love allow something that is harmful go unchecked and unchallenged? Why should we expect Him to sit by idly while danger lurks at our doorstep to attack us? It is for our well-being that He confronts us with our sin, so we may have peace with Him and with all men. If everyone responded to Him as they should, there would be no danger on our doorstep.

A Choice between Two Trees

Mankind tries to deal with sin by gaining more knowledge about sin. The Tree of the Knowledge of Good and Evil provides teachings that measure things and labels them, "This is right" or "This is wrong." Many believe the study of right and wrong will lead to their overcoming sin by overcoming the results of sin, therefore erasing evil. They create standards of right and wrong that they use to decide what is evil. Then they try to remove sin by enforcing their standard on others. This requires an enforcer who executes a negative response when faced with noncompliance. The one being evaluated finds his acceptance withheld depending on his compliance with the standard. Failure to earn acceptance causes feelings of inadequacy.

Poorly defined standards create confusion and hypocrisy among those trying to keep them. They make sense in one situation and no sense at all in another. People commit actions that are clearly wrong by one group's standard but are accepted by another group. Society ties its own hands in the face of obvious hate with competing definitions of right and wrong. This thinking allows injustices to continue for centuries before figuring out why it was wrong. When we finally set the record straight, we condemn the wrongs of the past, while committing an equally unacceptable wrong in our own day. By condemning those who lived before us, we prove ourselves guilty as charged. For example, those who teach about the injustice of slavery or the tragedy of the Holocaust find no problem with abortion, which history will one day view as a horrible destruction of innocence on a scale greater than the Holocaust.

The Tree of Life deals with sin by studying the God of Love and His expression of Love. The Tree of Life provides access to an example of True Love lived out by Jesus Christ. He trains us by showing why Love is the power of righteousness. The Tree of Life overcomes evil by taking away our motives to do evil. Unlike the thinking of Satan, the thinking behind Yahweh's Love has no evil in it. Feeding from His thoughts causes His Love to grow within the deepest parts of our nature. Once filled with a thinking that is only good, there is no room for evil.

The two opposing natures of good and evil

There are only two ways of thinking and their natures are as opposite as night and day. While one promotes thoughts that achieve

Tree of Life

another's benefit, the other promotes self-centered thoughts for one's own benefit. Good is other-centered, forgiving, and generous. Its emotions flow outward to others. Evil is its opposite. It is self-promoting, uncaring, preoccupied, and cares only to the limit of its influence. Its emotions flow inward toward self.

When we see self-sacrifice in others, we find it attractive. While this is true, it is also true that when circumstances require us to promote another's well-being to our own, it becomes unattractive. Men cherish the thought of others seeing them as other-centered, as long as it costs them little. Those who start out with good motives find the temptation to excuse their selfishness irresistible, particularly as the personal cost goes up. Self-sacrifice is an expression of Love, and Love cannot continue to the end without it. This is where man's ability to be good departs significantly from the God of the Universe. The truth we deny is that Love obligates the giver to sacrifice, even when the price to them is costly.

Love is the Message found in Jesus Christ. It came at a great personal price for Him, which includes much more than His physical sufferings. The Message of Love has given peace to those who have listened and have put it into practice. It gives them the power to become God's children (John 1:9-13), not by their own ability but by the Creator's skill. Love brings a peace that does not come to the world at-large. It is only available at an individual level. Not all receive His call. Many reject His message and remain on the pathway of destruction. The way of the world results in hate, selfishness, and a great deal of anger toward others. Where the heart rejects the Message, the darkness of hate prevails.

Man has mistakenly believed that he is in control of his own destiny. Knowledge of evil only leads him to tremendous suffering. Man ate from the wrong tree and lost the right to the Tree of Life. True Love is not in control of the world because its residents chose the wrong tree. Humanity accepted a diluted watered-down message of love, one that allows them to love some and hate others. They will continue to refuse the Message of Love, which can set them free from the horrors of sin. Therefore human beings continue to lose the good available from the Tree of Life. We must ask, how long will man continue to refuse the only message that brings True Life? How

A Choice between Two Trees

about your own life? Are you eating from the wrong tree? How do you know?

Many ask, "With so many religions saying so many different things, why should we believe you?" The answer is, "You shouldn't believe me!" This is not about what I believe or about what you believe. It is about receiving what the Creator is communicating. If you do not believe there is a Creator, you cannot believe He is communicating to you. If you do not believe there is a communication from the Creator, you will not be listening for it. If you are not listening, you cannot be empowered by what He is telling you. Without the empowerment, you cannot change. Without change, you continue to live a destructive lifestyle.

You may feel your life style is not destructive. This comes from listening to the wrong message. There are two categories of messages taught in the world today. One says that if you study and learn, you can become a better person. It instructs that guidance is available from spiritual leaders, but it is your responsibility to overcome the evil in your heart. The other message says that no one is capable of overcoming evil; only the work God personally exercises in an individual's life can overcome their inherent evil. This is the message I give to you.

All religions, including Christianity, put the responsibility on the shoulders of the person and claim a method for success. They allow people to create their own belief systems and standards of right and wrong. These religions are lies and everlasting failure is unavoidable, for they walk the pathway of man's thinking. Those who discover the communication given by the Creator of the Universe will walk the path He laid out. It leads to everlasting life. The abundance of knowledge is not the right path. Friendship with the God of the Universe is. Which path do you walk?

May the Light of Love, which is found in the Message from Yahweh; be a Tree of Life to you.

Tree of Life

Chapter 2

What Would You Exchange for Your Soul?

Choosing Jesus Christ is choosing Life

Then Jesus said to His disciples, "If anyone wishes to come after Me, let him deny himself, and take up his cross, and follow Me. For whoever wishes to save his life shall lose it; but whoever loses his life for My sake shall find it. <u>For what will a man be profited, if he gains the whole world, and forfeits his soul? Or what will a man give in exchange for his soul?</u> For the Son of Man is going to come in the glory of His Father with His angels; and will then recompense every man according to his deeds" (Matt. 16:21-27).

<u>"For whoever is ashamed of Me and My words in this adulterous and sinful generation, the Son of Man will also be ashamed of him when He comes</u> in the glory of His Father with the holy angels" (Mark 8:38).

During His public ministry, Jesus Christ made the most amazing statements. There would be a stir today, if someone were to say the words that Jesus Christ said in these verses. There is no wiggle room in what He says. He places the choice right in front, where we cannot miss it. He is either the Son of the Living God or a false prophet who leads people astray! Jesus Christ is either the Way, the Truth, and the Life (John 14:6) sent by the Creator of the Universe - or He is lying and in opposition to the Creator of the Universe!

In Matt. 16, Jesus made one of these amazing statements. He said that following Him is life and not following Him is death. He claimed that one could succeed in this world while failing in the spiritual realm by losing his soul. He said that hanging on to one's life is losing it. Jesus limits everyone to two groups: those who believe Him and respond to His leadership and those who reject Him by going their own way. We are either with Him or against Him.

In Mark 8, Jesus claimed there will be those who are ashamed of Him. He uses the Greek word **ἐπαισχύνομαι epaischunomai**; (Strong's number 1870) translated "ashamed." It comes from two other Greek words that, put together, mean, "To look on with

A Choice between Two Trees

dishonor." People dishonor the person of Jesus Christ by lightly esteeming (ashamed of) what He stands for (Rom. 1:18-22). Refusing to honor Him is rejecting Him and results in rejection by Him. The rejection comes on the day He returns to take His people, living and dead, to be with Him (Matt. 25:32-46). How does one face such a mighty God after loathing Him to His face? (Rev. 6:12-17).

Jesus Christ is either making a bold statement that will fail because He is not coming again or is representing the statement Yahweh God made that tells us the method that we use to achieve acceptance into His presence. Those who accept His Message receive the teachings that lead to Life. He is the Message of Reconciliation and the source of Life itself. No one will enter the presence of the Creator except through Him.

What would you give in exchange for your soul?

Take time now to think about my next question. What do you value the most in your life? Really stop and ask yourself the question. What is your answer? I hope you didn't think of a car. Hey! Many people would answer with some material possession like a car, a house, or a job. I hope you would answer such a question by naming people you love. I hope material objects with a dollar value are not what you think of. What people value can control them: gold, silver, diamonds, or other objects. They work all their lives to gain power and control, and do not have time for other lesser, uninteresting stuff, like flowers, sunsets, or family. Men have wasted their lives chasing the ownership of stuff, trying to gain recognition and fame, or striving for constant entertainment. I say they wasted their time - for how long can they last? How long will they be able to hold onto them?

Jesus Christ said that we can hang onto stuff in our lives to the point of losing our souls. He said that we are proud of worthless stuff and ashamed of the gift He is offering. He claimed that rejection of what is valuable results in everlasting death. If we accept what Christ said, we will need to reject obstacles that block us from the narrow pathway. What value do things have if we lose your soul?

Men have feared and hated other men who threaten their lives or threaten the life of someone they love or threaten the quality of their lives. Men have done incredible acts to save their physical lives

Tree of Life

on this earth. Others have done some horrific acts to save their physical lives on this earth. People put much value on physical life. The value we place on our physical life affects how we reason out the message Jesus gave. We can measure how much we value something or someone by what we are willing to do or not do with our physical lives. For the earthly things of this physical life are fleeting and pass through our fingers. What physical objects will we have 100 years from today? How will choices we make now affect what we have in 100 years?

For some of you, when Jesus speaks of losing life in the previous scripture from Matthew, you think He is talking about losing a physical life only. But He spoke of denying one's self in the same text as losing life. We can think of dying in a spiritual sense. Jesus Christ asks us to lay down the quality of our life for someone else. Perhaps He will ask us to deny ourselves for an aged parent or terminally ill spouse. We may be asked to deny ourselves in smaller ways, like attending the kids' ball game, helping a neighbor with a project, or just being kind to those around us. Maybe we can't be as prosperous as we want. Maybe we can't have all the things others have. Are there things in your life that you are unwilling to give up that interfere with how you accept Jesus? Are there things you are afraid He will ask you to do that prevent you from obeying Jesus?

I ask you, "What is your soul worth?" What would be of equal value? What has worth enough that you would exchange it for your soul? The idea of losing your soul is scary. We can handle thinking about what it would be like to lose a physical life. People die every day and we know we shall die also. We do not like to think about dying, but we are somewhat comfortable with the prospect that dying will happen. We feel bad for those whose lives ended early and who did not get to experience all life has to offer. Still, we think when we die we will still possess our souls! To lose our souls would be to die an everlasting death! Is there anything that prevents you from accepting Jesus?

"And <u>do not fear</u> those who kill the body, but are unable to kill the soul; but rather <u>fear Him</u> who is able to <u>destroy both soul and body in hell</u>" (Matt. 10:28). "For what will a man be profited, if he gains the whole world, and forfeits his soul? Or <u>what will a man give in exchange for his soul</u>?" (Matt. 16:26).

A Choice between Two Trees

For the <u>Word of God is living and active and sharper than any two-edged sword, and piercing as far as the division of soul and spirit, of both joints and marrow, and able to judge the thoughts and intentions of the heart.</u> And there is no creature hidden from His sight, but all things are open and laid bare to the eyes of Him with whom we have to do (Hebrews 4:12-13).

In these verses, Jesus Christ warns us there is one who can destroy both body and soul! Hebrews says the Word of God is active and sharp, able to distinguish between the thoughts you have no plan of acting on and the purpose of your heart, which motivates your actions. When the Word of God looks so deeply into your soul, where can you hide? (John 1:1-3). The Word of God is not looking deeply into your soul to find fault, but rather to evaluate it as a doctor would a patient. He searches to find the aliment and recommend the cure. Those who refuse to come to Him as patients will die and stand before Him as one stands before a Judge. When Jesus said "not to fear," it was because we do fear the one we do not need to fear. We fear others and what they might think or what they might do. Things that are out of our control cause us to fear, because of what might happen. We should not fear anyone who rules on this physical plain, but fear the One who rules both the physical and the spiritual.

Jesus points to two contending views of Life. The world's view is the most widely held viewpoint and may be the only one you have exposed yourself to. It comes in many flavors but is recognizable by its emphasis on man's progress and ascension to a higher plane. People always want to be the conquering hero. The other less-known view of Life comes from the Creator of the Universe. He claims to be the originator of man's purpose for existing. He says that man has no other purpose than the one He appointed for him. He claims that His teachings bring True Life.

The Tree of the Knowledge of Good and Evil represents all thinking that opposes His teachings. Now when I say that something opposes the teachings of Yahweh, I am not referring to any denominational system of belief. I mean the Tree of Life is what the Creator of the Universe is telling you through His Son, Jesus Christ. Anything that I or anyone else believes that contradicts the Word of God and the purposes of His heart is from the Tree of Death. It is our

Tree of Life

responsibility to search out the heart of God and know the difference between the teaching that is His and that which claims to be His but is just the lies and imaginations of men. Then we must abandon the false to accept what is His.

Jesus Christ is telling us that the men of this world can only have an effect on us while we live on this physical plane. No matter how men threaten us, they can only do so for a short time, say 70–100 years. But there is one who can influence our worldly lives and our everlasting lives in the spiritual world. Ignoring the Creator and the Message of His heart has everlasting results. Who are we listening to while we face the everyday situations? The answer will impact our everlasting spiritual lives as well as our temporal physical lives.

In Matthew when He said, "fear Him," it was because He holds us accountable to the one who can destroy both body and soul in hell. No man, angel, or demon can deliver us from His hand when He chooses to bring us to account for what we have done! If He chooses to bring us into fellowship with Him, who can steal us out of His hand? (Rom. 8:26-38). There is none as powerful as He. Do not let what other people think influence you when it comes to answering the most important questions. The God who created you is watching you as you read this. The answer you give in your heart interests Him. Who are you going to listen to? Which tree will you eat from? What choice will you make regarding eternity with Him?

He knows your innermost thoughts and feelings. You cannot hide your soul from Him! He intimately knows your deepest feelings, the ones you cannot put into words (Psalms 139). He knows what is good about you, for He made you. He also knows what is wrong about you and where you need healing and fixing. He sees the sin in your life, yet He still puts much value in knowing you. He knows the worth He has placed on your soul and He sent His Son, Jesus Christ, to communicate to you the worth He has placed on your soul (John 3:14-21, Rom. 8:25-27). What does God hear you saying about the relationship He is offering you? What value do you put on sharing God's soul?

Is there someone in your life who is more valuable to you than your own soul? Jesus Christ claims that you are more valuable than His. He exchanged His soul for yours. His physical death on the

A Choice between Two Trees

cross is symbolic of the spiritual death He died for you. He values you more than He values His own well-being. Jesus Christ paid for your soul by what He suffered in your place. We do not fully understand the true cost, but we do know the price He paid declares the worth He finds in us. We therefore do not see the cross as an instrument of death, but an instrument of life, the Tree of Life. The more we understand the personal cost to Jesus Christ, the more we understand the communication. To better understand the truth about the cost, we must first understand the truth about our sinful selves.

What about the quality of your everlasting life? If you spent eternity in hell, would that be the same as losing your soul? Considering life is so short, is there anything so important that having it is worth everlasting damnation? (Gen. 6:3, Psalms 90:10). Remember, we are talking about God the Creator of the Universe who wants to bring good things into your life, but who is also able to destroy both body and soul in hell. Sending someone to hell is not the choice He wishes to make. It is a choice He needs to make. He must make a choice regarding your spiritual life and spiritual death because He loves those around you (2 Peter 3:9). Love for those who follow Him demands that He do something about the destructive nature of those who do not. Do you want to be among those He must deal with?

You are making the most important choice of your life every day

Life here on earth can get bad, but we always have the hope it will get better. What happens if we know it will not get better? Jesus said we are to strive to enter by a narrow gate (Luke 13:23-28, Matt. 7:13-14). He said the path is hard to find and many will not find it. We cannot go through life hoping it will turn out all right in the end. We cannot go through life paying little attention to Jesus Christ without it having a negative effect.

Think about a time when you were lost. Maybe when you were little, you were in a department store and did not know where your parents were. Think about how that felt. Did you feel frightened and alone? Imagine feeling lost and without hope, with no chance of redemption, forever. Now think about how it will feel, knowing you had all the opportunities to prevent such an outcome. Are the offerings of this world worth the risk of living through eternity with

Tree of Life

that feeling? Imagine spending an eternity being angry or hurt or rejected! Yet most who have lived on this earth, head for such an eternity. Hell is worse than any horror film ever made and it is real, with no end!

You can get a glimpse of the glories and the horror of spiritual everlasting life by the experiences you have in this earthly life. Where would you like to spend eternity? What feelings would you like to experience forever? Maybe you do not often think about these questions. But you answer them daily with what you do, think, and say! The fact you never think about eternity is no excuse for throwing your opportunity away. With every minute of this earthly life, you choose the quality of life that you will live for eternity. What you hold as the most valuable today dictates the way you will spend your life and the way you will spend your life is likely the way you will spend eternity. What lifestyle are you choosing? Where is Jesus Christ on your list of what is valuable? Not the list you make with your mind but the one you make with your actions? He has communicated the value He has placed on you. He is looking for you to be thinking about how important He is to you.

Perhaps there is someone telling you that a loving God would not put people in hell. I say their opinions do not count. They are not the one who must decide who and why someone goes to hell! It is the Godhead of the Universe that you need to concern yourself with! He is the Judge and final authority of all who have ever lived on this planet. What is it that He has said? Look at the last book in the Bible and you will see the following.

And He said to me, "It is done. I am the Alpha and the Omega, the beginning and the end. <u>I will give to the one who thirsts from the spring of the water of life without cost.</u> He who overcomes shall inherit these things, and I will be his God and he will be My son. <u>But for the cowardly and unbelieving</u> and abominable and murderers and immoral persons and sorcerers and idolaters and all liars, <u>their part will be in the lake that burns with fire and brimstone</u>, which is the second death" (Rev. 21:6-8) (Matt. 8:10-12, 22:2-14, 25:13-46).

I want you to take time and think about the following questions. Is the God of Creation claiming that those who make the

A Choice between Two Trees

wrong decision concerning His Son will have the Lake of Fire? How can Yahweh be a loving God and put people in the Lake of Fire? <u>Wrong</u> question! We need to ask, "How can Yahweh's Love be true, if He does not stop sin and He allows nonstop hurt for the ones He created?" If you saw someone beating your beloved child, would you stop it? The violence and hatred on earth today cannot go unchecked forever and He will not allow it in heaven, He must separate the good from the evil. And He will do just that (Matt. 25:31-46). He offers springs of living water to those who hear the Message, but they must first face the truth about their sin.

What we do with our lives is not as valuable as what Jesus Christ can do with our lives. He is ever-working, mending us, and creating in us the same beauty that we find in Him. He is the Refiner and Purifier of our souls. His is the Potter, a skilled worker molding those who are His, for we are like clay in His hands.

But now, O Lord, Thou art our Father, We are the clay, and Thou our potter; and all of us are the work of Thy hand (Isaiah 64:8).

We are His workmanship (Eph. 2:10). We are proud and thankful that He has the skill and the patience to work with such stubborn people. We are proud and thankful that He is willing to take the time to do the job right. Many would rather go to hell than believe that they need God's work in them. Their pride is more important to them and they value themselves too much. They accept so little for such a small amount of time. In exchange, they lose their souls. Therefore, they gain an eternity of sheer agony for the right to do what they want for a short time. Choose better than that!

May the value Yahweh puts on your soul be a Tree of Life to you.

Tree of Life

Chapter 3

Jesus is True Life

There is only one who has the complete Truth

There is only one who has the complete Truth. There are many manmade religions on earth today. Within each, there are many sects or denominations, with subgroups and sub-subgroups. Each has what they believe is truth and each teaches what they believe to the disciples of their faith.

The English meaning of "religion" is "one's faith in God; a habit that defines them." Religious beliefs consist of certain principles that define what actions are good and what actions are bad. They then leave it to the disciple to overcome the bad and gain favor with God. Religions are, by nature, man-centered. They expect God to respond favorably to their efforts. Man-made religion always sees humanity as the initiator and refuses to respond to the efforts of Yahweh to interact with them. Such religious thinking comes from the teachings of the Tree of the Knowledge of Good and Evil and opposes God the Creator.

It is possible to identify some of these religious faiths by their outward appearance and lifestyle as their followers attempt to obey their doctrines. Eating from the Tree of Life is not about joining a religious denomination, wearing the proper clothes, or religiously performing the same rituals each day. The Tree of Life is much more than a religion because it involves interacting with the person of God. All of man's efforts fall pathetically short of impressing Yahweh (Rom. 3:10-24). The Tree of Life is about knowing the heart of God and being impressed by Him. Eating from the Tree of Life is about joining ourselves to the person of God. Some may teach that joining a religious faction is also joining the person of God but they are not the same. Some believe they are the only group that stands righteous in the sight of God.

This may be hard to understand, but knowing the person of Jesus Christ is more important than having our souls rescued from hell. He is Life and the source of all life. Without Him there is no life, for He made all (John 1:1-4, Col. 1:15-21). He created the physical elements of creation for reasons known to Him and for a

A Choice between Two Trees

purpose He intended. He also created the spiritual elements of heaven that we cannot see.

We must lose one life to gain another

"For whoever wishes to save his life shall lose it, but whoever loses his life for My sake, he is the one who will save it" (Luke 9:24).

{NOTE: In the NAS Bible the Greek word translated life in this verse, elsewhere translated "life" 36 times and "soul" 33 times.}

Many have trouble understanding this concept, giving up one life to gain another. Why should they want to? We know that man has only one life to live. We know that we can only be one entity. Some may say they have lived many physical lives, but even they admit to recycling the same soul. We believe men live one physical life and the choices they make last an eternity (Heb. 9:24-28).

We have a privilege beyond words, because we fellowship with Jesus Christ. So valuable is the person of Jesus Christ that we eagerly exchange our imperfect life for His perfect Life. This is a one-sided exchange. For we give up a painful life, not worth having, for a life full of joy, peace, and love. The lives we live have no value when we compare them to being in the presence of Jesus Christ (Philip. 1:20-21 and 3:7-11). We are more than willing to suffer loss now for the gain He has promised, which is knowing Him in greater detail. We have also gained in this present life. By standing in the presence of a Holy God, He transforms us into His likeness (2 Cor. 3:18). He is an awesome God who comforts us and we can feel the peace that passes all understanding, even in the times of great distress (Philip. 4:7).

He is also willing to discipline us like a parent would discipline his child because He loves us (Heb. 12:1-11). The Lord our God knows what life is about and how He designed us. Therefore, we must be willing to yield our lives to the One who can teach us how to live. We cannot continue to do our own thing. We yield to the One who can lead us the right way. The cost is great and the reward is much greater.

And He said to them, "Truly I say to you, there is no one who has left house or wife or brothers or parents or children, for the sake of the kingdom of God, who shall not receive many times as much at this time and in the age to come, eternal life" (Luke 18:29-30) (Matt. 19:27-30, Mark 10:28-30).

Jesus Christ is worth many times more than whatever we might give up for Him. There is nothing so valuable that we would choose it and abandon the chance to follow the True Life. There may be others telling you that you can have True Life and all the world has to offer at the same time. They are the ones who ask," Since there is no God, why give up the life you have now?" Others say, "God is a god of love and He will never send you to a hell like that." They are telling you lies. The one instructing them is the father of all liars, Satan (John 8:44).

Who should you believe?
Let's return to these verses. For the question before us is important to understand. We need to meditate on the charge the Bible lays out.

"And do not fear those who kill the body, but are unable to kill the soul; but rather fear Him who is able to destroy both soul and body in hell (Matt. 10:28).

For what will a man be profited, if he gains the whole world, and forfeits his soul? Or what will a man give in exchange for his soul?" (Matt. 16:26).

There is only one you should listen to, Jesus Christ, the Word of God, who is active and sharper than a two-edged sword. He is the one who can look deep inside to your innermost parts and give healing and True Life (Heb. 4:12-13, Psalms 139).

If we receive the witness of men, the witness of God is greater; for the witness of God is this, that He has borne witness concerning His Son. The one who believes in the Son of God has the witness in himself; the one who does not believe God has made Him a liar, because he has not believed in the witness that God has borne concerning His Son. And the witness is this, that God has given us eternal life, and this life is in His Son. He who has the Son has the life; he who does not have the Son of God does not have the life. These things I have written to you who believe in the name of the Son of God, in order that you may know that you have eternal life (1 John 5:9-13).

A Choice between Two Trees

Yahweh has testified concerning the Son of God, Jesus Christ. Those who do not believe His testimony call Him a liar. We have the Witness dwelling in us and we also testify to you the same testimony He has made to us. Those who reject our testimony do not call us a liar, for we only repeat His testimony (John 15:1-15). Yahweh Himself is the one testifying. Yahweh testifies that eternal Life is in those who have Jesus Christ. Those who are in Him have eternal Life and need nothing else to qualify for everlasting life.

There was a time when our sin separated us from our God. Jesus Christ removed the issue of our sin for all-time. Jesus Christ proclaimed forgiveness while nailed to the cross (Luke 23:34). Never again will the issue of our sin divide us from Him. Now the only question before us is, "Do we believe Him when He tells us the provision He made is enough?" Do we believe Him so much our lives change because of that belief? It is testimony about the person of God becoming a man and proving His Love. If we believe in Yahweh's testimony then we believe in His love. We have trust in His love for us. We know He will not leave us or give up on us. We believe that our eternity is safe when placed in His hands.

<u>If we believe in His testimony, then the responsibility for cleansing us from our sin is no longer ours.</u> Yahweh placed all responsibility for sin on His Son's shoulders. We must agree with the testimony He has made. Who can argue with the Creator? If it is His will to give everlasting life to those who have His Son, who can stop Him?

I must ask, "Are you arguing with Yahweh now or are you agreeing with Him?" For what do those who argue with the Giver of Life gain by their arguments? Do you think they can win the argument? It is His way or no way. Everyone must choose. Which way you will go? Which tree will you eat from? The testimony of Jesus Christ is not the words of men and does not come from the thinking of men (Isaiah 55:6-11). It was not a man who put the plan together before the foundation of the earth (Isaiah 40:21-29). It was the great, mighty, and awesome Eternal God. His desire is for all to understand what He is saying in the message of Jesus Christ's Life.

We need to agree with the God of Eternity and not men

To reach agreement with the One who can destroy us, body and soul, (Matt. 10:28) we must first face certain facts of life. If we are unwilling to face these facts, we are choosing to agree with men and argue with Yahweh. Do not listen to someone because they have written a book. I am not anyone you should listen to just because I wrote a book. My purpose is to point you to the Source of Life, Jesus Christ. He is the Vine and we are only helpless branches (John 15:1-17). A fact to face is that

Tree of Life

having the knowledge that Jesus is the Tree of Life will not help if you never go and eat. Until you admit you need the food on that tree, you will not go to it and eat. No one else can help you. Only Jesus Christ through the Holy Spirit can help you.

Pride often obstructs the path of those looking for True Life. Men come as seekers, looking for wisdom and understanding. They want to understand the mysteries of life and apply them to improve the inner person. They find out that they cannot improve the inner person on their own, so they turn away from the truth. When men find the true answer to the mystery of life, it tells them the Creator must make them anew into the image of God (John 3:5-8). They do not like the answer, so they reject it!

And He was also telling them a parable: "No one tears a piece from a new garment and puts it on an old garment; otherwise he will both tear the new, and the piece from the new will not match the old. And no one puts new wine into old wineskins; otherwise the new wine will burst the skins, and it will be spilled out, and the skins will be ruined. But new wine must be put into fresh wineskins. And no one, after drinking old wine wishes for new; for he says, 'The old is good enough'" (Luke 5:36-39).

Jesus taught that we cannot mix and match the thing of life with the things of death. We cannot have our cake and eat it too. If we follow the Shepherd of Life, we cannot walk as we see fit. To follow another is to give up the right to make the decisions. If you do not follow the directions of the leader, you are not following. For if the one you follow turns left and you turn right, you are on your own. You just happen to be on the same road together. Therefore, the pride of life hinders many who want to control the direction of their lives. They go as they see fit, but cannot find the right path. They have lost their way.

There is a path that leads to destruction and men find themselves on that path without trying (Proverbs 14:12, 10:29). There is an old saying in the Roman Empire. "All roads lead to Rome." You see that is how the Roman Empire built the roads. The conquerors did not build roads for the people whose countries they conquered, but for their own use so they may get around from one country to the next. So it is with this world, all roads lead to destruction unless you find the narrow gate (Matt. 7:12-23).

You hear men say, "There are many paths to heaven. You are on one of them and I am on another." We must ask, "How will the Creator respond when you try to explain this theory to Him?" Imagine trying to explain to God Almighty why you did not believe He existed. Or why you did not hear Him, when He told you of His plan. What value will such an argument have before a God who knows your inner thoughts? What value

A Choice between Two Trees

will pride have if it ends in misery? Do you exchange your soul for your pride and therefore your misery?

Are you ready to call God a liar - to His face? Or are you ready to agree with the Father about the statement He made? Are you ready to accept what He says about your sin? Are you ready to accept Jesus Christ as your pathway?

May the testimony of Yahweh be a Tree of Life to you.

Tree of Life

Chapter 4

Adam's Legacy

Adam did not bring evil in to the world

Remember the Garden of Eden (Genesis 3:1-24)? That is where Adam ate the fruit. Please note the Bible does not call it the Tree of Good and Evil. It's called the Tree of the **Knowledge** of Good and Evil. Some have taught that evil entered the world the day Adam ate the fruit. Evil could not have begun the day that Adam sinned. The Serpent represented evil when he accused God of lying. You see, either the Serpent was sinning in accusing the Creator of lying or the Creator lied and the Serpent told the truth. Therefore evil must have previously existed since someone is guilty of lying before Adam ate of its fruit.

When the knowledge of evil entered Adam's mind, sin entered his heart. When sin entered Adam's heart, his soul died a spiritual death. Knowledge of evil made sin and death the legacy Adam would pass down to his children. Adam could have accessed the Tree of Life and that could have been his legacy. The legacy Adam passed down to his children led Cain to kill Abel. Why did Cain kill Abel? *"Because his* (Cain's) *deeds were evil, and his brother's* (Abel's) *were righteous" (1 John 3:12).*

The first Adam earned a legacy of death that he passed to all. God the Father sent God the Son as the Second Adam (Rom. 5:10-18, 1 Cor. 15:19-28). The Second Adam earned a spiritual legacy of Life that He passed to those who believe. He has given them the power to become children of God (John 1:12). They are no longer partakers of a heritage of death, but now inherit Life. He passes to them His thoughts leading to joy, peace, understanding, and grace.

Fallen man cannot properly judge right from wrong

After Adam gained knowledge of evil, he had a major problem: sorting out the good from the evil. His new knowledge left him unequipped to do that. What was the first decision Adam made after he ate? He decided that his nakedness was wrong and he could not meet with his Creator, as was his habit. He tried to come up with his own remedy to cover himself. His attempt was inadequate and he

A Choice between Two Trees

felt exposed and ashamed. Adam hid from the only one who could help him. That was his next best solution! It did not work well (Psalms 139:7-12, Gen. 3:6-19).

Adam started making mistakes with his new knowledge. His first was to declare something a sin that God did not say was a sin. His second mistake was that He did not counsel with his Maker. Based on his own knowledge, Adam decided something that was formerly acceptable to the Creator was now unacceptable. I say he was mistaken because if a naked Adam were sinful in the sight of the Creator, He would have clothed him. After creating Eve, He would have presented Eve to Adam clothed as well.

His third mistake was that he hid from the only one who could help him. He was afraid to face his God, the same God who often visited him in the cool of the day. Mankind has been spiritually hiding from the Creator ever since. Hiding from God did not improve Adam's situation and it does not improve ours. Adam's attempt to cover himself was inadequate and it was not until he came before God that he became properly covered. Adam began rejecting God in his life and this caused Him to die spiritually.

With all of this new knowledge, Adam became guilty in his own eyes and did not know how to solve his problem. He could detect something was wrong but he could not fix it and make it right. He became aware of the existence of evil, but he could not judge good from evil and he did not ask his Father for advice (Isaiah 20:1-5, 1 Sam. 19:18-24) (Job 1:21, Ecc. 5:13-16). Adam knew he had sinned but the true nature of sin confused him. He did not realize that his real sin was not his nakedness. It was eating of the fruit and disobeying God! He did not assess his problem correctly and therefore did not come up with the real sin or the real solution. Adam decided what is right and what is wrong, becoming like God (Gen. 3:22-24). He did not become completely like God because he judged poorly. God the Father had to identify the real sin by asking, *"Who told you that you were naked? Have you eaten from the tree of which I commanded you not to eat?" (Gen. 3:11).*

His Father was the only one who had the answer to his problem, and he ran away to hide from Him (Gen. 3:9-11). Mankind is following Adam's example by making the same mistakes. Man

Tree of Life

compounds the mistakes made by Adam by telling God, "You are wrong and we know better." Man is now telling God, "What you said was good and it worked back then, but times have changed and we need a new way of thinking." Mankind's legacy is his rebellion. He refuses to acknowledge the existence of a Creator, wishing instead to believe an accident brought him into existence!

Times have not changed and we repeat the mistakes of Adam and Eve with the same results. Adam's descendants would later kill the answer to their problems. If men understood right from wrong, how could they have crucified God in the flesh? (John 1:14). They had no idea what they were doing (Luke 23:34). Jesus Christ could have led them to the spiritual promised land. Their pride and arrogance stopped them from hearing Him and they rejected the Author of Life. Today's leaders are rewriting right and wrong. They will tell you that God's ideas are old-fashioned, that you need to be "enlightened with the universal truth found in all religions." They continue to reject Him as the Savior of Mankind. However, those who have come to know Him have fallen in love with Him. They know the beauty of His character and wish all could know Him, as they know Him.

Back in the beginning, before there was anything except for the Godhead, Yahweh knew He would create man resembling Himself (Genesis 3:22). He created Adam so He could communicate with him and share about Himself. He knew humanity would gain the knowledge of good and evil and that they would not be able to understand or control it. Yahweh understood that when they became "like unto Himself," they would need His help to understand and overcome evil. He would give the Law of Right and Wrong and then later send His only begotten Son as part of His design for correcting their situation. He knows the right way to live. He knows what will work and what will not work. He knows that creation needs to follow Him because He is the only one who knows the correct answers. He provided the way and a Helper so men might learn the truth He is teaching (John 14:16-26).

Man has become like God, knowing good and evil. Because man could not handle such knowledge, Yahweh needed to prevent man from accessing the Tree of Life and live forever (Genesis 3:22-24). The Godhead is the architect and builder of everything and

A Choice between Two Trees

knows how He created His creation. The citizens of Heaven know that the evil unleashed by Satan here on earth is unacceptable and Yahweh will not tolerate it. Such a legacy of evil will never be acceptable in Heavenly Places.

The world today is full of fighting, hating, and war
    The world we live in is a wreck and we must take responsibility for the shape it is in. We have helped make the world the way it is. Yes, I know, we join causes in an attempt to undo the results of people's sin, but we are not willing to stop the sin or stop sinning ourselves. We can make a difference by calling the sin in our lives for what it is. We cannot control the world and stop it from sinning. We can get our own lives straightened out by going to the only One who can teach us how we ought to live.
    Here are the words to a song named "In the World Today." Take time to hear the meaning behind the words.

Verse 1
In the world today there is fighting;
In the world today there is war;
In the world today there is hating;
On the path we walk there be more.

In the world today people suffer;
But the world today doesn't care;
Living in the world's getting rougher;
All the pain we cause we must bear.

Verse 2
O the world today is a jungle;
People being killed every day;
And the children's caught in the struggles;
Moral values fall in decay

O the world can only get darker;
As the truth of sin is blocked out;
And the crimes will only get blacker;
Cause that's what the lie is about.

Tree of Life

The world today is like a jungle, a dog-eat-dog world where people kill one another every day. They block out the truth of sin, so why are we surprised when the crimes get more violent and sinister? This pattern is what the lie is about. There are shootings, raping, drug dealing, murders, sex, and thefts every day. And that is just in the schools we send our children to! What do you think it is like on the streets?

In the world today there is war. On the path of godless living that we are walking there will be more war. Think about what is happening in the world today. People fight wars because they hate each other, or to stop those who hate each other from destroying the rest of us. They are unreasonable in their thinking toward one another and try to turn others against their opponents using any means possible. They find something wrong with the other side, at all cost, so they refuse to work out their differences. They hang on to their prejudice no matter what.

Because of hate, we live in a world where mothers must fear that their children will find an unexploded land mine or cluster bomb. There are children in this world whose playground is a war zone. These children know what funerals are, for they attend them far too often. People starve because armies fight just outside the doors. Relief agencies cannot help because the armies steal the food. The weather does not cause all famines. Man's hate causes many. How long can this go on?

There are wars going on between individuals also. The anger between two people is the same attitude that reveals itself in war. No global conflict could exist if individuals did not participate. The problems we see on the nightly news are the natural outcome of sin. The way we treat one another is an important place to begin. Road rage is not a global conflict. It is one person with anger and hate building up inside, boiling until an explosion occurs. Road rage represents the results of unconfessed sin. We make all kinds of excuses for hanging on to a sinful lifestyle. Some even sound reasonable.

I know what I am saying is true, for I had to come face-to-face with anger and hate myself. You also must come face-to-face with the truth, - that you are a part of the problem. No matter how wrong the other person is, it is never OK to allow yourself to hate.

A Choice between Two Trees

You have not lived your life so well that you have not hurt another. You have encouraged wrongdoing by looking the other way and offering no word of protest. You allow this planet to become a dangerous place to live in. You do not speak out against the hateful or hurtful actions by calling them as they are: sin.

Some of you will reply that you did speak out against some wrongdoing or another. You might speak out against war or prejudice while demanding legal protection for abortion. You call for woman's rights while protecting pornography and prostitution. To speak out against one type of sin while defending another is following the wrong tree. People's confusion about sin has caused sin to go unchecked in the world today.

The Lord our God knows how to remove the results of sin. He can overcome the legacy of hate in our hearts. God did not create the Earth with evil in mind. He created the Earth to be a beautiful place to live. We need to look beyond our own lives and see the tragedy taking place every day. If you do not see the darkness of the world, then you are a part of it, even if it is not now harming you.

What is Good and what is Evil?

The original Hebrew word translated as evil is, ר **ra** (Strong's numbering 7451) It means "distress, misery, injury, and calamity." It is the inability to measure up to a standard. The word translated as Good בוט **tob** (Strong's numbering 2896) means "pleasant, agreeable, a benefit, and welfare."

Everyone knows good from evil, right? If we hear of a young strong man knocking down an elderly woman and taking her purse, we know that is wrong. If we hear of another man chasing down the evildoer and getting the purse back, we know that is good. What about abortion, pornography, homosexuality, fornication, adultery, divorce, prostitution, witchcraft, drugs, greed, robbery, violence on TV, racial hatred, begging for money to support your ministry, or driving too fast? *There is a way which seems right to a man, But its end is the way of death. (Prov. 14:12)* (Prov. 12:15, 21:12).

Is it good that we must lock our doors and stay in at night for fear of what happens in the streets? Must mothers worry that their children will find a land mine while playing? What thinking would say that child molestation is evil but child pornography is good, since one leads to the other? What thinking says child pornography is wrong and adult pornography is protected? Yet this thinking is common among world leaders. This thinking comes from eating fruit from the wrong tree.

Mankind feeds on thinking that says, "Violence is good to watch on TV." Shows and movies make heroes out of those whose lawless behavior takes the law into their own hands. Their stories honor the lawbreakers while other characters do not notice the destruction the law-breaking heroes do. They kill people and damage property and show no regret at all, and everyone accepts it as normal. The TV teaches a philosophy that says, "Do what you think is right!" (Judges 21:25). The end justifies the means. In real life, we arrest those who follow this teaching; who use violence to get their way.

Man does not have any more capacity to figure out his sin than Adam did. We miss the real sin behind what is causing all these problems. When will people stop making the same mistake that Adam made? Mankind has turned its collective back to God and does not repent evil deeds.

There is an answer

The song I shared earlier has a chorus. It goes like this.

> But a Light still shines in the pages;
> Of a book that is centuries old;
> To right the wrong that rages;
> The answer's more valued than gold.
>
> O read the words of the Bible;
> It tells of a Savior from sin;
> And Love is the key to survival;
> Now is the time to begin.

The Lord our God gave us the answers in the Bible, which tells us about Jesus Christ and that He is the one who can lead us to the spiritual Promised Land. It also tells us about sin and the cost it took to undo Adam's mistakes. We must face the truth: we are a part of mankind and are also a part of what makes this world such an

A Choice between Two Trees

awful place to live. There is only one place that has the answers. We must go to the One who wrote the Bible. We must take the time to listen to Him as He explains what He wrote. We are lost without Him and unable to set our lives onto the correct course. The Bible is our compass and our map. The Holy Spirit is the one who teaches us how to use it.

You might say, "Life isn't so bad." Hey, that is why you are still a part of the problem - because you don't care about sin and its result on others. Jesus Christ is the answer, but He is not a benefit to us if we say, "I don't need Him!" He is the answer for all who see the hate and the sufferings caused by sin and want someone to do something about it.

Then He cried out in my hearing with a loud voice saying, "Draw near, O executioners of the city, each with his destroying weapon in his hand." And behold, six men came from the direction of the upper gate which faces north, each with his shattering weapon in his hand; <u>*and among them was a certain man clothed in linen with a writing case at his loins*</u>. *And they went in and stood beside the bronze altar.*

Then the glory of the God of Israel went up from the cherub on which it had been, to the threshold of the temple. And He called to the man clothed in linen at whose loins was the writing case. And the Lord said to him, <u>*"Go through the midst of the city, even through the midst of Jerusalem, and put a mark on the foreheads of the men who sigh and groan over all the abominations which are being committed in its midst."*</u>

But to the others He said in my hearing, "Go through the city after him and strike; do not let your eye have pity, and do not spare. Utterly slay old men, young men, maidens, little children, and women, but do not touch any man on whom is the mark; and you shall start from My sanctuary." <u>*So they started with the elders who were before the temple*</u> (Eze. 9:1-6).

These verses are only part of a much larger section of Ezekiel that concerns a vision he received from Yahweh. What struck me is the reason Yahweh gave for placing a mark on some, sparing them from the execution. It was not that they refrained from taking part in the abominations, or that they were righteous and sinless, or that they were vocal about the sin around them. It was because they felt grief about the sin they saw around them.

The Lord is upset by the lack of concern mankind has about sin. He is even more upset with His people when the sin around them does not cause concern in them, or more importantly the sin that is in them. There is a hardening of the heart that deadens our feelings. We want to treat the results of our sins as if we can make them go away.

We cannot make the results of sin go away until sin goes away. Sin is like a dandelion on your lawn. You can cut the plant off, level with the surface, but it will come back because the root still lives. The problem remains until you remove all the root. We keep treating the leaves and leaving the roots so sin can come back strong, healthy, and thriving. We complain about the problem instead of facing the facts. See the sin in you for what it is and you have taken a big step in overcoming it.

What are you getting in exchange for your soul?

And do not fear those who kill the body, but are unable to kill the soul; but rather fear Him who is able to destroy both soul and body in hell (Matt. 10:28). For what will a man be profited, if he gains the whole world, and forfeits his soul? Or what will a man give in exchange for his soul? (Matt. 16:26).

The question is still before you and it will never go away. You can choose to ignore the question and then the answer you give is, "I exchanged my soul for the privilege of not thinking about sin, death, or eternity." If that is your answer, it will haunt you forever.

As for me, I wish to exchange a worthless possession for the greatest gift known to man. It means I must give up a legacy of lies and hate for a legacy of truth and love. I need to give up a life of no lasting value for friendship with the Author of Life. It means I must give up my way of thinking for the thinking of God. I no longer wish to eat from the tree of the Knowledge of Good and Evil, but wish to eat from the Tree of Life.

Satan hates to see anyone taught by the Holy Spirit and will send his followers to discourage them. He wishes to take our eyes from Jesus Christ and onto our failed attempts at virtue. Our thoughts

A Choice between Two Trees

should focus on the cross of Christ and what he is doing in us. Then we can resist the attacks of the enemy.

All must agree with the Creator about who we are from His viewpoint. He, who forms the hearts of all men, knows all men's hearts. He knows us better than we know ourselves. We must agree that human beings cannot build a better world and we must agree that we have personally helped to make the world a terrible place to live.

<u>Not ready to make that statement</u>? Let's look at what the Bible says about sin and sinners. Admitting that we are sinners is not something that should shame us. Instead, we must understand that it is the reality of our life after Adam ate form the wrong tree. This will continue to be our legacy until our eating from the Tree of Life changes us.

May the legacy of Jesus Christ be a Tree of Life to you.

Tree of Life

Chapter 5

We Must Agree with God

God says, "All men sin and are in need of salvation from that sin."

<u>If we say that we have no sin, we are deceiving ourselves, and the truth is not in us</u>. <u>If we confess our sins, He is faithful and righteous to forgive us our sins and to cleanse us from all unrighteousness</u>. If we say that we have not sinned, we make Him a liar, and His word is not in us (1 John 1:8-10).

As it is written, <u>There is none righteous, not even one; There is none who understands</u>, There is none who seeks for God; All have turned aside, together they have become useless; There is none who does good, There is not even one. Their throat is an open grave, With their tongues they keep deceiving, The poison of asps is under their lips; Whose mouth is full of cursing and bitterness; Their feet are swift to shed blood, Destruction and misery are in their paths, And the path of peace have they not known. <u>There is no fear of God before their eyes</u>. (Romans 3:10-18) for all have sinned and fall short of the glory of God (Romans 3:23).

What a true description of civilization down through history! The King of the Universe sees us as sinners, whose evil deeds far outweigh our good. As I write this book, I think of things and picture them in my mind. Right now, I am picturing that I am having a conversation with a reader about Yahweh's opinion of humanity. The subject is new to the reader. I picture this reader working overtime to figure it out. During the conversation, I ask, "Are you perfect?" I hear the reader answer something like, "Hey, nobody is perfect." Then I hear myself asking, "Are you a sinner?" Then I hear the answer, "No! Not really. Hey I'm not that bad. I haven't done any harm to anyone." These would be common answers, even for those who have heard all of this before.

You see, none of us wants to think that we have an inheritance of sin. If someone thinks of us as less than perfect, that's O.K. I mean 99% correct is less than perfect, but it is an A+. Coming real close to the goal, but not making it, is something we will admit.

A Choice between Two Trees

You know, we want to be able to say in the end, "We gave it the good-ol' college try," and "We almost made it." We can take pride in our failure if we are working hard to succeed. "If you have never failed, then you have never tried." (I used that one myself!) We want to prove that we can do better next time. If we change a few things, success will soon be in hand. We can feel good about ourselves, if we fought the good fight and ended one point short. We want to believe that we could have won. We want to feel that failure is not a sign of who we are. People want to earn credit for the way they live their lives. Therefore being less than perfect is a good place to be, for we are within reach of perfection.

For some, being a sinner is like staying back a grade after getting an F. People equate being a sinner to being a complete failure. Nobody wants others to think they are a failure. Failing miserably in life by being a disaster is the last thing anyone wants to admit. If we admit we have made a total mess of life, it would devastate the ego. We treasure what other people think of us and do not want them thinking less of us, even just a little. Failure is tragic and we avoid it at all cost. We want to be acceptable and being a sinner is unacceptable.

False teachings work against us by drawing attention to our goodness and our ability to live by the laws of right and wrong. Many debates between believers, which only divide and confuse us, center on man's opinion of right and wrong. Such debates polarize; each side possesses detailed measuring sticks to tell who lives life correctly and who does not. When they decide someone is failing, they declare that person unacceptable.

The ones who do the debating are no more able to judge right from wrong than Adam was. One side judges one way and the other side judges another way - and they all believe they are the only ones who are right. The people caught in the middle feel judged by the self-righteous on both sides. It is no wonder they do not want to think about the issue of sin. If the experts in religion and politics cannot agree, how are we supposed to figure it out? These men fail to live out what they claim, and their failure adds to the confusion. They cannot even hold themselves accountable to their own teachings.

The debates give people negative feelings and they associate those negative feelings with God as if He were the one causing the

Tree of Life

confusion. They wonder, "Since I can never measure up, why even try?" Doubting Yahweh, they do not turn to Him for help. Their lives are so messed up that nothing matters anymore. Their circumstances force them to admit that they are failing. They only accept the truth about themselves when there is nowhere else to go.

There is no shame in admitting we are sinners!

The teaching from the Tree of Life is not like the teaching from the Tree of the Knowledge of Good and Evil. God's thinking sets us free to admit the truth about ourselves and helps us accept the solution to our failed lives. When God calls us sinners, He means that we are less than pure. Although 99.996 percent is good for soap, it is not pure enough when it comes to Heaven.

You see, it "only takes a spark of sin to get a fire of destruction going" and "where there is the smoke of sin, there is the fire of judgment." The seed of sin must not prosper in the presence of God or His Elect. One act of disobedience in the Garden of Eden became our legacy of pain and destruction, which led to the horrible actions taken by man throughout the ages. The Lord allows sinful acts to continue here on earth, for a time; so to educate the angels in Heaven. He will not allow sin to prosper in Heaven itself.

Coming to a point where we can admit we are sinners does not condemn us in God's eyes or His people's eyes. It only puts us into position to receive the solution. The Tree of the Knowledge of Good and Evil shows the need to deal with sin. The solution that it suggests never works for long and always ends in failure. It suggests that we study hard and find out what is right and do what is right by overcoming sin through the power of our will. People sin against one another without even realizing it. We all fail. Living life without failing is not an option for us. We live in Adam's legacy of sin.

There is another legacy. The Tree of Life teaches about a narrow path that leads us through Calvary and the Cross of Agreement. The minimum expectation is 100% correct. *Therefore you are to be perfect, as your heavenly Father is perfect (Matt. 5:48).* The original Greek word translated "perfect" is τέλειος **teleios** (Strong's numbering 5046), which means "complete, having reached its end." When a person goes out into the garden looking for a tomato to put into his salad, he looks for a ripe one ready for harvest. This is

A Choice between Two Trees

the meaning of this word, "TELEIOS." It means mature, grown up, come to the end. Or you could think of it as "a finished work."

When we admit we are sinners, we agree with God that He has unfinished work. The key is to admit we cannot do the work. We must rely on someone else to finish us and make us ready for everlasting life, holy and sinless in the presence of God.

The Tree of Life teaches forgiveness through repentance. Even Jesus yielded to John's baptism, a baptism of repentance. He said to John that He had to fulfill all righteousness (Matt. 3:13-15). The one who knew no sin became sin for us and proved His friendship with sinful men by fellowshipping in the baptism of repentance (Mark 1:1-11, Acts 19:14). He showed acceptance of us while we were sinful, not after we fixed everything.

The Holy Spirit said in 1 John 1:8-10 that if we do not admit we have sin, we are deceiving ourselves. He also said that we need to confess our sin before cleansing from sin can occur. Everyone helped by the Holy Spirit has first had to come to Him as one who needs help (Mark 2:16-17). This is true of every human being who has ever lived.

Sin is not a bad idea to agree with Yahweh. So since all men are sinners, those who admit that they are sinners are free to accept their failures and accept others just as they are, with their failures. There is no need to make them acceptable because all are sinners and Jesus Christ makes all equally acceptable. If we are all equally acceptable, what are we trying to prove? To reject one is to reject all and to accept one is to accept all, for we are all sinners.

We do not have to make excuses or cover up what makes us feel inadequate because we are all in the same boat. We can feel good about ourselves. We do not need to put grand expectations on anyone. Since all fall short, we expect to fall short and we expect others to fall short. We do this without condemnation. In fact, agreement with God about sin is a matter of everlasting life. Men cannot be cleansed of the sin they say they do not have.

If it is not shameful to admit that all are sinners, what holds men back from admitting the truth? They do not want to admit they cannot control themselves and are unable to stop sinning. They want to be in control of their lives. They fool themselves into believing that they are in the lifestyle of their choosing and the acts they commit are by design according to the will of their spirits. The truth is, no one is fully in control of their lives.

Therefore, to one who knows the right thing to do, and does not do it, to him it is sin (James 4:17).

Every time we do something we know is wrong, we have sinned. When we do what we agree is wrong, we show that we do not have what it takes to do right. If we do not act on what we believe is right and we do what we believe we should not do then we are not in control of our lives (Romans 7:14-25). *But if I do the very thing I do not want to do, I agree with the Law, confessing the Law is good. So now, no longer am I the one doing it, but sin which dwells in me* (Rom. 7:16-17).

Take the first step!
The first step in overcoming any addiction is to admit you have an addiction. We all have an addiction to sin and will feed that addiction even to death, just like a chain-smoker who keeps smoking after learning he has cancer or heart disease. Mankind will keep sinning until the "Last Day," even if it produces an everlasting spiritual death for them. Without the help of the Holy Spirit, no one can overcome sin in their lives.

Try putting your name in the blank. "I, _____, have directly helped to make this world a harder place to live in and have contributed to the condition we now find on this earth."

Agreeing that all men inherit a legacy of sin and are individually responsible for their actions is a first, but not the only, step. Confessing our sin opens us to receiving forgiveness and then cleansing from our sin. If you have taken the first step, the journey has just begun. We will talk more about giving our lives over to Yahweh, who has already completed the work that makes our lives sinless.

Perhaps you are not ready to put your name in the blank and do not believe that you contribute to this earth's hateful attitude. We will look further at why we say, "All men are guilty before God." For right now, we will say, "It is necessary to admit the truth before the truth can set you free" (John 8:31-32).

A Choice between Two Trees

Many of you are Christian and go to church every week. Christians who do not face the truth are even guiltier before God than unbelievers, for they should be shining as bright lights in a dark world. Many people who attend church skip through the part where they face their sin and go straight to the "I am saved" part of the "You must repent" sermon. There are those of you in the "Ministry" who care more about success and look to save people from sin for selfish reasons, but do not care if they receive the legacy that cleanses them from sin.

Those who have heard the Message of the Tree of Life, which is Jesus Christ, understand the truth of sin (1 John 1:1-2:11). They embrace the truth of who they are and gain an understanding of Love.

Why seeing the truth about sin is important to salvation

What we believe about our sin will change our view of Yahweh's Love. Agreeing with Him about our sin gives us a proper perspective by which to understand the testimony He makes about Himself. By aligning ourselves with Him, we better understand who He is and what He is thinking. If we believe we are good, it is easy to believe He can love us and He would die for us. "Why wouldn't a loving God show love to good loving people?" But when we see how great our sinfulness is, His Love takes on a new meaning (Matt. 5:38-48, Mark 6:27-38). "Why would an all-powerful God love those who are destroying His works, attacking and hurting those He loves, insulting Him to His face, and teaching others to ignore what He tells them?"

If we understand how great our sinfulness is, we can better understand how great His Love is. It is important to come to a right understanding, for there is much difference between Yahweh and the ones He is making holy. When we understand the difference between the Creator and His creation, we begin to appreciate Him in an honest and true way. When we gain a true appreciation of God, we fall in love with Him. The love we have for Him spills over to those who are around us and we are no longer a part of the problem. Our attitude changes in ways we could not understand before we began the journey.

Tree of Life

If I shut up the heavens so that there is no rain, or if I command the locust to devour the land, or if I send pestilence among My people, and <u>My people who are called by My name humble themselves and pray, and seek My face</u> and turn from their wicked ways, then I will hear from heaven, will forgive their sin, <u>and will heal their land</u> (2 Chronicles 7:13-14).

These verses are a promise from God to those who called by His name, those Yahweh sees as belonging to Him. Technically, they talk about the descendants of Israel. They also include all those who have joined themselves to the person of Jesus Christ because He is a descendent of Israel through Mary (Matt. 1:1-17). If someone humbles himself, praying while seeking to be in God's presence, and is willing to leave the old nature to embrace the new, our God is faithful and true to cleanse him from all unrighteousness (1 John 1:9).

If we do not humble ourselves before God, we cannot come to Him on His terms. The Lord our God is not being stubborn by wanting it His way. There is a reason He looks for us to be humble before He heals the land. Pride is the problem and healing the land will not benefit us when our pride persistently destroys the land. The destructive attitudes and behaviors must stop before there can be healing. We must confess our legacy of sin, first to God, then to ourselves, and then to others. We must confess that people cannot change the course of this world and that this world races toward destruction unless God intervenes (Matt. 24:21-22, Luke 18:1-8). Next we must change our direction. We must put our fate into the hands of a faithful God and follow the Good Shepherd of our souls, who gave His life for us, His sheep.

Satan wishes to make God out to be a liar

As early as the Garden of Eden the Serpent has been battling with the Creator over the minds of men. Satan told Eve that she would not die and that the Tree of the Knowledge of Good and Evil would make her wise (Genesis 2:16-17, 3:1-5). Today, science believes it has great knowledge. Scientists try to explain away creation and therefore the Creator. They say that He did not create Heaven and Earth. They come up with all kinds of theories they call

A Choice between Two Trees

facts. It takes much faith to believe the beginning started as an accident - more faith than it takes to believe there is a God who designed and created the universe?

The issue of Evolutionism vs. Creationism is not about how the universe came into being. The controversy is about a simple question, "Is there an Intelligent Being who designed, created, and now controls the universe?" Before we die, we must answer: "Is there a God and will I stand in judgment before Him?" If we answer yes, we must ask, "Did He tell me what He expects from me?" Satan used the Tree of the Knowledge of Good and Evil to confuse the real issues. He continues to use worldly knowledge to keep men's eyes off from the only faithful and true witness of the Truth.

In the name of science, men follow Satan down the path of damnation. They argue about how old the earth is, tell of big bangs that no one can repeat, and search for "missing links" of creatures evolving from one form to another. One day, they will have to face the truth. Since the truth includes Yahweh, how will they give an answer to Him for the position they have taken, which says, "God does not exist!" Will they continue to argue with Him about His existence or will the truth force them to admit they were wrong? If they admit they were wrong, will they wish they had come to this conclusion before it was too late? (Philip. 2:9-11).

<u>If we receive the witness of men, the witness of God is greater; for the witness of God is this, that He has borne witness concerning His Son.</u> <u>The one who believes in the Son of God has the witness in himself; the one who does not believe God has made Him a liar</u>, because he has not believed in the witness that God has borne concerning His Son. <u>And the witness is this, that God has given us eternal life, and this life is in His Son</u>. He who has the Son has the life; he who does not have the Son of God does not have the life. These things I have written to you who believe in the name of the Son of God, in order that you may know that you have eternal life (1 John 5:9-13).

The Lord our God has testified that there is eternal Life in His Son, Jesus Christ. He has made a statement that people of the world are trying to prove wrong daily. To the worldly, faith is all about enlightenment, having knowledge of some mystery that is unknown to others. To them, faith is about making themselves better people, as they try to achieve a higher spiritual level. Even some so-called "Christian Churches" teaching a gospel different from the one Yahweh spoke of (Gal. 1:6-12).

Satan can lie as much as he wants and in as many variations as he wants to give men what they want to hear. He offers them systems of belief that convince them they can have control over sin. Satan helps them believe they are independent of a "higher authority." He tells them that God only responds to actions they take and does not initiate on His own. Therefore the foundation of their faith is a work performed by man and not by God. Worldly men want to believe Satan's lies, because they want to tell the Master when to come and when to leave them alone. They do not want Yahweh to be the Master, setting standards of right and wrong. What they want is an idol they can manipulate for their own benefit. They treat the God of Creation as if He were an idol! They treat Him as if He were a myth!

Stop! Think about this for a moment. "What is Yahweh thinking right now, about the way you are treating Him and the people He loves?" Be careful. He hears ever word you think. He searches the hearts of men and knows the deeper motives for their actions (1 Chr. 28:9, Rev. 2:23). Would you turn your back on the One who loves you, to follow the one who hates you and purposely misleads you? Would you turn your back on the One who wants to heal you through Love without condemnation?

Mankind is wagering their souls on a bet that God does not exist

Mankind risks eternity on a bet that God does not exist. This is logically not a good bet. They are betting the acts they do will not have an impact on eternity because there is no Judge to judge them. They bet there is no Eternal God, that no one created man and no one is communicating the terms by which men can enter the presence of the Supreme Being. It is the highest and riskiest bet placed by human beings and they place it every day.

If there is no God, then there is no Judge and no judgment and they win the bet, but they die physically and do not know they won the bet, for they no longer exist. If there is an Eternal God and He has communicated the terms by which He will allow men to enter

A Choice between Two Trees

His presence, they would have not met His conditions and would lose the bet. They will spend eternity in the worst possible state of affairs and will be sad to know they were wrong. If those who believe there is a Creator are wrong, they will not know it, for life was an accident. However, if they are correct, they will live eternally in the best possible state of affairs a being could imagine.

The conditions of the bet have no real winners when they bet against a Creator and no real losers who put their trust in a Creator. We do know there is a Creator, for we already have fellowship with Him. We bear witness that He lives and is the source of Life. He is the Author and the Finisher of our faith and into His hands we have placed our destiny. We have already gained by placing our trust in Him. We believe He is holding us accountable for our actions. We also believe that, because His nature is loving and kind, He will help us meet His expectations. We have come to Him as those who cannot live perfect lives and need His help to meet His expectations.

Summary

What we have discussed so far in the book is a question of everlasting life. What value does our present-day life have compared with the life we will live forever? We state there is nothing on this planet worth risking our eternal well-being for. It is prudent for us to evaluate the eternal long-term results of decisions we make today about our view of God. He is ready to judge the living and the dead based on their deeds or to judge them based on His loving kindness.

We claim that God communicated to us His expectations and He will hold us accountable for knowing them. Jesus Christ is the communication and is eternal Life.

We claim that Jesus Christ is more important than the lives we would live on our own. We are willing to separate ourselves from the lives we could have lived and He joins us to His Life.

We claim there are those who tell you the opposite. They say there is no God and that you will waste time looking for Him. Others tell of the many pathways to heaven and that you can chose the one you want to travel. They tell you that no one knows what God thinks and the Bible is not God speaking, that it is only a work of men.

We claim that such men wish to lead you away from the person of God and lead you into a discussion about them. They also

Tree of Life

work to convince you that you must earn your way to heaven. They are lying and, in doing so, make the Master of Creation out to be a liar. Their fate is on shaky ground.

May God's truth about your part in sin be a Tree of Life for you.

A Choice between Two Trees

Chapter 6

Eat From the Wrong Tree and Believe the Lie

There is more than one path, but only one path is right

And the Father who sent Me, He has testified of me. You have neither heard His voice at any time nor seen His form. You do not have His word abiding in you, for you do not believe Him whom He sent. <u>You search the Scriptures because you think that in them you have eternal life; it is these that testify about Me</u>; and you are unwilling to come to Me so that you may have life. I do not receive glory from men; but I know you, that you do not have the love of God in yourselves (John 5:37-42).

When I was young, there was a saying that went like this. "A boy chases a girl until she catches him." I think of that when I hear men say they seek God, as if He is hiding. He is not hiding and they are not seeking Him where He is working - in their lives. Yahweh works in every person's life, yet they do not honor Him. Men seek God until He causes their spiritual eyes to open and they can see that He was there all along.

We do not find Yahweh when we do not look for Him. We are man-focused because we depend on our own way of thinking or because we depend on another man's guidance. Yahweh is ever-present in our midst. We miss seeing Him because we do not take the time to be aware of His hand in our lives. We do not believe we can depend on Him because we cannot see Him with physical eyes. To realize His presence, we must see the effect He has on our lives (John 3:1-12). We see Yahweh by honoring Him as God and giving Him credit for the action He takes. Yahweh may send one of His disciples to be His physical representative. We are not to honor the representative. We are to honor the one who sent the representative (2 Cor. 5:20).

When we strive to take charge of our lives, we fail to do so because we put all of our efforts into the wrong place. Without the Holy Spirit to guide us, failure is our only possibility. Adam made the mistake of trying to cover his nakedness and failed. He no longer wanted to meet with God, as was his habit, because he did not want

Tree of Life

His maker to see him in the state he was in (Gen. 3:1-11). We must come to the Lord our God as we are, so He can expose us, so we may receive proper spiritual garments. Exposing our sin is embarrassing. Jesus Christ personally washes those who have come to him and they feel clean inside (John 13:1-10, 1 John 1:9).

You cannot eat of the Tree of Life if you do not believe you need to. You may believe you have True Life already or that you can get it another way. Jesus Christ tells us that those who seek will find, those who hunger will eat, and those who need get help (Matt. 7:7-11, Luke 11:4-13). If you do not admit that you are hungry and thirsty, you will not wish to eat or drink what He has to offer. If you do not admit you mourn, you have no need for comfort. If you do not admit you are lacking, you have no need for Yahweh to help you. If you do not look to see His work within, you cannot find Yahweh.

We live in a world that is needy. Many do not admit their needs. Do you believe that people are innately good? I do not! Do you believe we live according to His design? I do not! The Truth will set us free (John 8:32) but it cannot set us free unless we can come face-to-face with the Truth. In general, the world does not want to know where the Tree of Life is or how to get its fruit. The world wants a tree that is easy to find and leaves them feeling that they are in control of their destiny. They want the fruit from the wrong tree and are willing to believe a lie to get what they want.

How about you? Do you feel like you are in control or out of control of your life? The only way to maintain control is to give control over to the One who can guarantee the results: Jesus Christ, the Savior. Those who know the danger will give up their rights to be in charge so He can save them. Those who have no clue of the danger will argue over who should be in control until it is too late (Matt. 16:24-26).

Where in the world do you get the ideas that feed your thinking?

What influences our thinking is important. The battle between good and evil is for the mind. It is the tree of the Knowledge of Good and Evil vs. the Tree of Life. If you are not diligent, you will nourish your thinking from the tree of the Knowledge of Good and Evil. It is everywhere you go. Those who continually eat from this tree are spiritually dead. Spiritually dead men share their thinking in

A Choice between Two Trees

newspapers, on the evening news, on the radio, in magazine articles, in books, in subjects taught in our schools, in business seminars, and by preaching from the pulpits of our churches. Such men indoctrinate others to think that God does not exist or to minimize Him to the point of nonexistence. They repeat over and over, "There is no Creator." Therefore, mankind believes there is no one to give an account to. Others lecture the Creator is a hands-off God who leaves men to their own devices. Other times, they picture the Supreme Being as so loving that He will allow anything or so hateful that He is waiting for us to slip up so He can pour His judgment on us. In many ways, false teachers propagate the lie that Yahweh does not deal properly with sin and He is powerless to cleanse us from our sin.

    The thinking that comes from the wrong tree teaches that you must take care of yourself first, that you have a right to your anger, and that expressing your anger through hateful acts is good. Men teach that the things they do are right because they benefit from them personally. They do not account for the destruction done to another person's life. They only care if it is right for them. They teach men that it is weakness to put their wives before their own wants and desires. They teach women that it is a male-dominated world and that they must defend themselves against men, even their own husbands. Children hear that their parents are old-fashioned and out-of-date, so they should not respect them. Adults hear that children are a burden and they should avoid them. They encourage parents to not let children get in the way of their own dreams, pleasures, or fulfillment in life. These teachings destroy families by focusing our thinking on the wrong spiritual path.

    The result is a generation that despises authority with a passion (Romans 13:1-8, 1 Tim. 2:1-3). The indoctrinations of spiritually dead men encourage abandonment of all moral boundaries laid down by their forefathers, for a newer, worldly set of morals. Television uses pornography in commercials to sell goods and services, then air those questionable commercials during times when children are most likely to see them. Worst of all are the Christian men and women who watch this stuff without reservation. It is unsurprising that man today is anti-God. Mankind has taken references to God from the history books, schools, and government. Then we wonder, "Why is the world such a deadly place to live?"

Tree of Life

Man searches for answers to complex questions but will never find them for he looks in the wrong places.

We can easily recognize the teachings of man. They put man first and allow him to do what is right in his own eyes (Judges 17:6, 21:25). The hardness of a man's heart leads him to do much evil that he will excuse with meaningless words of personal freedom. The world encourages choices that lead to pregnancies and then demands the right to kill the innocent lives that result from such choices. Not only do they wish to kill the unborn to erase their problem, but also they want to us to consider them righteous before God while doing it! They fight God by proclaiming their rights while ignoring the Laws of Life and Love. They confuse and pervert the teachings of the Creator. In doing so, they sear over their consciences. They forget the Creator already knew and loved the innocent child they so willingly destroyed in the mother's protective womb (Matt. 1:16-18, Psalms 139).

Teachings of your church or church leaders may also be the teachings of death

The error in the thinking of man is also found in the churches. The false teachings coming from pulpits are akin to the teachings unbelievers give in their lectures. New Age teachings are strongly entrenched. They reword their teachings using Christian slang to make it sound like Christian teachings. Members of the church think, "Because a preacher said it, in front of the congregation, it must be true." False teachers in the churches slander Yahweh the same way the world does. Those who sit in the pews do not know what is happening, because they have never studied the Word of God. They will never think about the deeper meaning of the message given, for they are too busy feeding on worldly trash. You can discern the followers of men, for they will quote their pastor, or other teachers, as their source instead of the Bible, but cannot support the position they have taken. They do not know if what they are saying is even in the Bible, and they do not care. They like the false teachers because they tickle their ears with words that confirm their goodness before men.

For the time will come when they will not endure sound doctrine; but wanting to have their ears tickled, they will accumulate

A Choice between Two Trees

for themselves teachers in accordance to their own desires, and will turn away their ears from the truth and will turn aside to myths (2 Tim. 4:3-4).

False teachers will tell us that God's Word is not for us and not for our world today. (They are right in what they say, for God would never command any one to kill an unborn baby.) They teach that the Bible contains only the words and thoughts of men and was not inspired by the Holy Spirit. They also supply their own meanings to the words Yahweh has written into the Bible, meanings the Author did not intend. False teachers of the New Age teach messages that they received from other men and from Satan. They do not consult the Holy Spirit. Therefore, they do not even know that they are opposing the God of Life.

This is the spirit of the Anti-Christ foretold to us in the Scriptures (1 John 2:15-25, 4:1-6) and who is even now working and fighting for the souls of men. Satan wishes to rob God of a prize and he is looking at you. Satan indoctrinates us with his thinking when we eat from the wrong tree. It teaches a righteousness found in keeping the Law. They enslave their followers to a pattern of:

1. Living out the natural result of sin by committing sinful acts.
2. Getting a feeling of unworthiness because of the power of sin in their lives.
3. A confession of the act of sin they committed, but not the sin.
4. Feeling a false righteousness because of their confession.
5. Temptation to act out the fruit of their sin again.
6. Failure to maintain their righteousness.
7. Committing the act of sin or a likeness of that sin again.
8. Getting another and stronger feeling of unworthiness.
9. Repeating the process until they cannot feel anguish over sin.

Tree of Life

Such religions leave their followers feeling that they are in a hopeless cycle that will never overcome the sin in their life (Romans 7) or they become so self-righteous that they are blind to their own need for cleansing. False teachers only search the Scriptures to prove their point, so they never find the One who can overcome all unrighteousness. They disguise their teachings of "righteousness by works" with the words of "faith by grace."

Nevertheless, they think that they are in charge of their fate and see no need for yielding to the Holy Spirit. The result is a confused world acting like a drunkard on the brink of destruction who proclaims that he has the answers. In truth, human beings are the problem and never will have the complete answer. Man is not able to discern correctly right from wrong without the Holy Spirit to guide. Any teaching from the heart of a man is dangerous and full of evil thinking (Jer. 17:7-10).

God foreknew those who are His and He will miss none of His own (Romans 8:26-31, Eph. 1:1-14). He is willing for all to be with Him, but He knew, from the beginning, those who are willing to hear His voice and follow Him to everlasting life. The tree you feed from makes a difference. It affects what you think of yourself and those around you. If you feed on the material given to you by a decaying world, you eat from a Tree of Death. It is easy to get this food, for it is all around you. If you wish to eat from the tree of the Knowledge of Good and Evil, you need not be aware of what you spiritually eat. You need not work at getting good food for your thoughts, for the evil of the world's teachings comes to you naturally (1 Cor. 2:14).

The way to destruction is broad and can handle the many who travel it. The path of Life leads through the life that Jesus Christ lives and few there are who find it (Matt. 7:13-14). For those who do find it, Jesus Christ will give them the right to become the children of God (John 1:11-13).

As I end this chapter, I wonder: What is it that you spend your time thinking about? What value will those thoughts be to you in 100 years, 1,000 years, or even 10,000 years from now? There are thoughts that have value for a few days, and thoughts that have everlasting value. The ways of the world are Satan's ways and are of limited value. The question that is most important right now is, "Are

A Choice between Two Trees

you ready to die and face eternity?" Is your life full of the thinking that has everlasting value? If Jesus Christ is in your life, you have the Tree of Life and He is making you ready with the right kinds of thoughts.

May the narrow path of Jesus Christ be a Tree of Life for you.

Tree of Life

Chapter 7

Entangled in a Spider's Web

Why we should not judge

<u>Do not judge lest you be judged. For in the way you judge, you will be judged; and by your standard of measure, it will be measured to you.</u> *And why do you look at the speck that is in your brother's eye, but do not notice the log that is in your own eye? Or how can you say to your brother, 'Let me take the speck out of your eye,' and behold, the log is in your own eye? You hypocrite, first take the log out of your own eye, and then you will see clearly to take the speck out of your brother's eye (Matt. 7:1-5).*

When Yahweh looks on the people of His creation, the anger they display toward one another grieves Him deeply. He feels their anger and hate personally, which is fueled by their sense of being wronged. Each believes they are right and the other is wrong, so they are unwilling to forgive. They expect that they will eventually be proven right and that the other side is wrong. Stubbornly, they accept no other outcome. Being right becomes more important than anything else. They do not see their own sin, but are quick to point it out in others. They follow unwritten laws of right and wrong by which they judge others. They do not keep these laws themselves, but expect other to do so. They use the teachings from the tree of the Knowledge of Good and Evil to establish standards they have no intention of living up to.

A tenderhearted God is grieved by men's critical judgments of one another because they place men into a spider's web of deception. They weave a trap that ensnares them with the strands of their own judgments. Those judgments prove they know what the right action is and they leave no excuse when men fail to follow through on their knowledge. When people show mercy toward one another, it untangles the web and sets them free.

Jesus uses a parable about a speck in one person's eye and a log in another's (Luke 6:41-45) to explain the most common mistake people make. When Cain killed Abel, it was because God accepted Abel's sacrifice and not Cain's. Cain needed to face the truth and

A Choice between Two Trees

make necessary changes (take the log out). Instead, it was easier to kill his brother. The thinking that leads us to judging one another is the same thinking that tempted Cain to kill Abel (Gen. 4:1-16). It is easier to drag someone else down to our level than it is to rise to theirs.

We are unable to live our own lives properly according to our thoughts of right and wrong, yet we are more than willing to judge our neighbor's ability to live according to his. Jesus Christ's teachings emphasize the opposite. He died on the cross to forgive others. The Holy Spirit trains us to love our brethren, even at great cost, and to think of others as better than ourselves (Phil. 2:1-11, Rom. 12:3 and 14:1-13, Gal. 5:25-6:5).

I know we hear it all the time: Christians are to be fruit inspectors. Remember the Bible tell us to be fruit inspectors for the purpose of finding false teachers. When Jesus tells us that we will know them by their fruits, He is telling us to be aware of the false doctrines that they teach (Matt. 16:5-12 and 7:15-29). We look for the enemy who wants to destroy the work of the Holy Spirit. We are not looking to pass judgment, for that is not our place (John 12:44-50). True followers of the Lamb want people restored to their Heavenly Father. We are not looking for justice or revenge. We know that Yahweh passionately desires reconciliation with all, by His Demonstration of Love on the Cross. The process may be painful and feel like punishment. <u>He allows unpleasant events to happen to His people because it helps achieve the reconciliation.</u>

Only those in positions of authority should judge and they have permission to judge only those who are under their leadership (1 Cor. 6:1-8, Matt. 18:12-20). Even our Father in Heaven does not discipline those who do not belong to Him. That is how we know we are His children, if He disciplines us for His namesake (1 Cor. 5:9-13). He will not allow us to travel where it is dangerous. But those who are not His go where they will and appear to get away with it (Jer. 12:1-5). But they will not get away with anything for everyone must stand before the true Judge (James 5:1-10 and 4:10-12).

When you judge another, you appoint yourself to a position of authority. One receives authority from a higher authority; no one places themselves into authority. If you do, you put yourself into God's place for He is the only proper Judge (James 4:12). He is the

Tree of Life

one who said, "Vengeance is mine, I will repay" (Heb. 10:30.12:19, Deut. 32:35).

In becoming a judge, you prove that you understand the intent of the Law. If you know the right thing to do, under every circumstance, why don't you do it? When you do not complete the Law, you become guilty of the same Law, by which you judge (Rom. 2:1, James 4:11). How well you keep the Law is never to your credit, for fulfilling the Law 100 percent is the minimum expectation. If keeping the Law completely is not your expectation, why do you judge others? If you make such a judgment, you make known your expectation of perfection. If you expect others to fall short, why be so harsh when they meet your expectations?

The only one qualified to have such high expectations is the one who fulfilled such high expectations, Jesus Christ. If you judge another, you claim that you also have achieved a perfect life. Let's face it: you and I both know that we have already failed. The more willing we are to be a judge of the law, the more accurately we need to keep the law. We should be doing the same we expect others to do. For in the way we judge, we receive judgment, according to our own standards (Matt: 7–1-6). When we set the standards and do not keep them, we are without excuse, for we set the standards.

The world judges one another and is therefore condemned

Like a spider's web, the Law is a trap that catches people and holds them secure in a condemnation of their own making. The Law expects 100 percent compliance. There is no room for error: it is either compliance or noncompliance. Any violation of the Law is unacceptable. The Law expects purity and any violation removes the purity. This is not only true of the Law in the Bible but also of any laws by which men live or hold others to.

Remember, it is not Yahweh's judgment of others that is the focus of our discussion. We are talking about a time when each of us will stand before Him and He is an exacting Judge. How we treat people while living this temporal life is the measuring stick He will use to judge us.

Applying standards of right and wrong to others is a spider's web men get caught in. The more we judge others as acceptable or unacceptable, the more entrapped we get. The more we prove we

A Choice between Two Trees

understand the principle of Law, the more condemned we are when we break those principles.

And just as they did not see fit to acknowledge God any longer, God gave them over to a depraved mind, to do those things which are not proper, being filled with all unrighteousness, wickedness, greed, evil; full of envy, murder, strife, deceit, malice; they are gossips, slanderers, haters of God, insolent, arrogant, boastful, inventors of evil, disobedient to parents, without understanding, untrustworthy, unloving, unmerciful; and, although they know the ordinance of God, that those who practice such things are worthy of death, they not only do the same, but also give hearty approval to those who practice them.

Therefore you are without excuse, every man of you who passes judgment, for in that you judge another, you condemn yourself; for you who judge practice the same things. And we know that the judgment of God rightly falls upon those who practice such things. *And do you suppose this, O man, when you pass judgment upon those who practice such things and do the same yourself, that you will escape the judgment of God?* Or do you think lightly of the riches of His kindness and forbearance and patience, not knowing that the kindness of God leads you to repentance?

But because of your stubbornness and unrepentant heart you are storing up wrath for yourself in the day of wrath and revelation of the righteous judgment of God, *who will render to every man according to his deeds*: to those who by perseverance in doing good seek for glory and honor and immortality, eternal life; but to those who are selfishly ambitious and do not obey the truth, but obey unrighteousness, wrath and indignation. There will be tribulation and distress for every soul of man who does evil, of the Jew first and also of the Greek, but glory and honor and peace to every man who does good, to the Jew first and also to the Greek *(Romans 1:28-2:10)* (read in context).

Such is the web-like trap that mankind has put himself in. Man has created a society that both approves of those who are living according to a "depraved mind" (that is, mankind's approval of doing that which is not proper) and one that passes judgment on those who do act according to a "depraved mind." Human beings, in one way or another, have agreed with God on what is wrong. Then they make excuses for doing what they agreed with God was wrong. The fact they see the wrong done by others leaves them without excuse when they do the same. They are blind to what they are doing and are storing up wrath for themselves by judging one another.

Read again the Scripture passage above. Represented here is everyone who passes judgment on another. Condemned are all men by their own thoughts and actions. They prove daily that they know what is right and are unable to do it. The Lord God has proclaimed the results for such, first to those who claim to know Him, and then to all else who claim to live without Him. He will consider how we treated others when judging us. He forgives those who forgave the transgressions of others and He will deliver judgment on those judging others, a plain, simple, and deadly truth (Matt. 6:14-15 and 18:14-35). Those who live by the Law will die by the Law, but those who are not under the Law will die without the Law (Rom. 2:12-13). Where there is no Law, there is no condemnation from the Law (Romans 4:15, 5:12-15, Gal. 5:22-23).

Love and Forgiveness are the Keys to Heaven, without judging
But love your enemies, and do good, and lend, expecting nothing in return; and your reward will be great, and you will be sons of the Most High; for He Himself is kind to ungrateful and evil men. Be merciful, just as your Father is merciful. And do not judge and you will not be judged; and do not condemn, and you will not be condemned; pardon, and you will be pardoned. <u>Give, and it will be given to you; good measure, pressed down, shaken together, running over, they will pour into your lap. For by your standard of measure it will be measured to you in return</u> (Luke 6:27-38. (Read also Romans chapter 14.)

How will we stand before this Holy God? Remember the words of the Master Himself, for in them is the key to how we should live. Condemn others and you stand condemned. Pardon those who sin against you, you shall be pardoned. By the measure that you give, it shall return pressed down and overflowing.

Any teaching that encourages judging is from the Tree of the Knowledge of Good and Evil. Knowing good from evil is the basis

A Choice between Two Trees

for judging. To judge, you must acquaint yourself with what makes something right or wrong. But, as we have seen from pervious chapters, man does not have the skill to properly judge what is good and what is evil.

Love, mercy, forgiveness, and understanding are from the Tree of Life. It is easier for us to forgive those who trespass against us then it is to never trespass against another. We all need forgiveness. Everybody is shut up in his sin and needs the grace and forgiveness we find in Jesus Christ (Romans 11:32, Gal. 3:22). If we are not willing to forgive others, then He is not willing to forgive us (Matt. 6:14-15). Love builds up those who are in contact with it. Hate tears down what it touches.

Man entraps himself by his *ability* to know when someone else is in violation and his *inability* to stay out of violation himself. It puts him into an impossible situation, like being in the spider's web. The more he moves, the more ensnared he becomes. Whether he moves or not, the spider will come and suck the life out of him. Mankind is not going to admit his impossible situation and will not ask for help. Those who recognize their predicament can call for help and the Redeemer of their souls is able to help them and He will save their souls from complete destruction. He takes our hard, unforgiving hearts and makes them soft, full of mercy. In the world of His reign, the lion will lie down with the lamb (Isa. 11:1-10).

Let me ask you again: What is more important to you than your eternal soul? Will you live out your life knowing the spider of your own judgments is coming for you? Will you ignore your impending doom? The answer is simple. **The cost of following Jesus is nothing, compared with the cost of not taking His offer**. Turn now to the Savior and He will show you the path to the Tree of Life. He will teach you to forgive, which will change your thinking of others and of yourself. The lessons are hard at times, but they are for your everlasting welfare and for peace in your inner soul.

Do not speak against one another, He who speaks against a brother, or judges his brother, speaks against the law, and judges the law; but if you judge the law, you are not a doer of the law, but a judge of it. <u>*There is only one Lawgiver and Judge, the One who is able to save and to destroy; but who are you who judge your neighbor?*</u> *(James 4:11-12).*

Tree of Life

As James 4:1-7 tells us, the source of our quarrels is our selfish pleasure. We long for more of what the world has to offer. We lust for what we don't have and oppose God because of it. The only answer is to draw nearer to God and begin to walk the walk that will save us from us. We must become sober in our estimation of ourselves and of our situation, putting Yahweh in His proper place. We must turn to the one who can both destroy our body and our soul. He is the Tree of Life and everyone who comes to Him, He will in no way turn away (Isaiah 55, John 6:35-40, Matt. 11:28-30). This is a promise we can bet our life on.

May forgiveness from Yahweh enable you to forgive and be a Tree of Life to you.

A Choice between Two Trees

Chapter 8

Righteousness, by what Law?

The Law of the Spirit of Life in Christ Jesus
Therefore there is now no condemnation for those who are in Christ Jesus. <u>For the law of the Spirit of life in Christ Jesus has set you free from the law of sin and of death</u>. For what the Law could not do, weak as it was through the flesh, God did: sending His own Son in the likeness of sinful flesh and as an offering for sin, <u>He condemned sin in the flesh, so that the requirement of the Law might be fulfilled in us, who do not walk according to the flesh but according to the Spirit</u> (Roman 8:1-4).

The first eight chapters of Romans deal with principles found in the Jewish Law. It explains the Law's inability to help us overcome sin. Paul contrasts the principles of the "law of sin and death" with the principles of the "law of the Spirit of Life in Christ Jesus" (Romans 8:2). When we think about the meaning behind the Law as defined by the Spirit of the Law, we eat from the Tree of Life. Jesus Christ revealed a better way of achieving the intent of the Law. He fulfilled the letter of the Law by living according to the Law of Love. Jesus Christ is God (Col. 1:15), God is Love (1 John 4:6-11), and the Two Greatest Commandments sum up the Law (Matt. 22:35-40). Jesus Christ personifies the Law.

Love is not a legislative law by which you follow a set of rules. The law of the Spirit of Life is like the law of gravity or the laws of physics. Love is the principle by which Yahweh built the universe. Jesus Christ embodies the Law of Love, a reflection of the character of Yahweh. Jesus Christ is the Blueprint on which Yahweh designed the Law of the Universe. If we stay within the design, there are no negative results for they only come from straying from Love's principles.

For many, the first eight chapters of Romans are difficult to grasp. If you are unfamiliar with them, please take the time now to read them before trying to follow this portion of the book. Please also read the verses quoted in their context in the Bible. Do not limit

Tree of Life

yourself to only the ones reproduced here. There are just too many verses and I strongly encouraged you to read them first.

The Holy Spirit makes important points in these verses about which tree we are feeding on. He speaks through Paul about obeying the flesh or obeying the Spirit. The flesh feeds from the wrong tree and the spirit feeds from the Tree of Life.

<u>*For the mind set on the flesh is death, but the mind set on the Spirit is life and peace*</u>, *because the mind set on the flesh is hostile toward God; for it does not subject itself to the law of God, for it is not even able to do so;* <u>*and those who are in the flesh cannot please God*</u> *(Romans 8:6-8).*

When the Holy Spirit says, "the mind is set," He is talking about what the mind is focused on. In other words, He is talking about what we mull over in our heads and set our hearts on. If something is important to a person, he spends much time thinking about it. He examines a subject from many different angles. He repeatedly researches every facet and possibility. Many men will do this for a favorite sports team, learning statistics of each position and player and some know all the stats for every team.

If something gets more attention people say, "It is on the front burner." And if it isn't getting much attention, they say, "It is on the back burner." Human beings have an enormous capacity to think, but too often they put on the front burner things that did not go their way. They can linger over the incident that caused them pain until it infests them with all sorts of evil thinking. Often they believe the issue is about love, but the selfish thinking is about selfish love. They make it an issue of fairness, of making it right, of getting revenge, and feeding the flesh instead of the soul. Hate and anger can increase the hurt until it burns a hole through their soul. Often, the real problem is that our self-centeredness was hurt. A person motivated by True Love would not enter a situation with an agenda. He would accept the incident the way it comes and not take the wrong into account (1 Cor. 13). He would put God's interests – and not their own - on the front burner.

What is on your front burner? Do you think about the physical objects of this short life or do you think about the Spirit of Life? Yahweh looks at your heart and He knows what thoughts have

A Choice between Two Trees

left their imprints there. A mind focused on spiritual matters of God eats from the Tree of Life and a mind focused on this world is eating from the Tree of Death.

We need to be good stewards, providing for the physical needs of those around us - like eating, working, maintaining the house, or paying the bills. Our purposes for doing so will differ when feeding from one tree instead of the other. The treasures of this world are minor and lose their brilliance when put into perspective before the matchless beauty found in Christ Jesus.

We are sinners, but we are not to sin

The Holy Spirit has not granted permission to continue in sin. In Romans 6:15, Paul asks, "Shall we sin because we are not under law but under grace?" He answers the question with this good point.

Do you not know that when you present yourselves to someone as slaves for obedience, you are slaves of the one whom you obey, either of sin resulting in death, or of obedience resulting in righteousness? (Romans 6:16).

Contrary to what some teach, Paul is not giving the O.K. to sin. He believes obedience to sin is death (Rom. 6:16). Some claim that Paul teaches, "People do not need to concern themselves with sin, because we sin and cannot help it." See Romans 6:1-7. When you hear someone teach that, know they agree with Yahweh that men cannot control their sinful beings. They enslave themselves to their sin. This thinking should not stop there, though, for it is those without the Holy Spirit who are slaves to sin. According to His Word, those yielding to the Holy Spirit become free from the power of sin (Roman 8:2). Any teaching that reduces the seriousness of continuing in sin is not of God and comes from a mind focused on a "Law of Righteousness," not the "Law of the Spirit." The world gives the O.K. to sin by telling men that they will never overcome sin anyway, so why try?

Yet Paul, the one they quote, says that obeying sin results in death. So following their logic, if all men cannot stop sinning and sin results in death, then all men must die in their sin. Not true! Paul is not making the claim that Holy Spirit is going to leave us in our sin! Paul is not teaching that God expects us to sin continually! Paul teaches that those who are without Christ are slaves to sin and those who walk according to the Spirit are slaves to righteousness.

My little children, I write these things to you that you may not sin…(1 John 2:1).

The Holy Spirit's instruction helps us stop sinning. People love to jump to the next part of that verse and never take time to understand what the Holy Spirit meant when He said, "that you may not sin" (Rom. 4:15). The intent of the Holy Spirit is to conquer sin and cleanse us from all unrighteousness. (1 John 1:9). Jesus Christ died on the cross to conquer sin. If the Godhead intends to conquer sin, it would be wrong to say that we have permission to continue in sin.

And if anyone sins, we have an Advocate with the Father, Jesus Christ the righteous. (1 John 2:1).

Although our goal is not to sin and the Holy Spirit leads us in that direction, we do not become lost forever if we stumble and fall. We do have a voice before the throne pleading our case. Remember that Paul tells us not to use our liberty as an excuse to sin (Gal. 5:13-25). Accidents happen because of our weaknesses. Planned events of sinful actions are rebellious and His discipline is forthcoming.

In Romans 6:21, Paul asks, *"Of what benefit were you deriving from the sin of which you are now ashamed?"* Good question isn't it? What benefit are we getting from our bondage to sin? Trying to live righteously does not free us from damaging our lives and of those around us. The Law of the Spirit of Life conquers sin by freeing us from the need to be righteous. Instead of focusing our thinking on doing right or wrong, we are free to act in Love by following the One who loves us to the end. The Law of Righteousness can only tell us what is wrong. The Law of the Spirit of Life shows us why it is wrong and how to do it right.

With the Knowledge of Good and Evil, there is need for the Law

Remember, the fruit Adam ate was from the tree of the **Knowledge** of Good and Evil. Evil did not enter the garden when Adam ate the fruit. It was already present in the Serpent. Gaining such knowledge caused evil to occupy us. It was the knowledge of

A Choice between Two Trees

evil and our inability to control such knowledge that caused Adam to fall. Eating the fruit added the ability to think evil thoughts. Adam had enough knowledge to think good thoughts already, for He knew God (Rom. 1:18-21). Adam already had the knowledge he needed to build others up. Eating from the wrong tree added thinking that destroys. When Adam ate of the wrong tree his thinking changed and he died, first spiritually and later physically.

    The Law became necessary as a guide to help man manage the thoughts that came with such knowledge. Man now has good and evil thoughts but cannot distinguish the difference correctly. He needs guidelines to help him apply the knowledge. Therefore, God gave the Law and the Law is good, but it cannot help man become righteous. Instead the Law reveals what is right and not right. It makes each of us guilty when we do not follow its teachings and act according to wrong thinking (See Romans 7). Jesus Christ is a much better Guide to help us manage the knowledge. He navigates us through this life and makes us righteous by doing the will of the Father. (John 14:10 and 16:13).

    Before Adam ate from the tree, there was no need for law. With no law there was no violation (Rom. 4:15, 5:13). You cannot be guilty of breaking something that does not exist. After Adam ate, he became a sinner and failed to judge the situation correctly. Adam needed the Law to help define right and wrong through rules and guidelines. The Law, however, could not empower him to understand why something is wrong. Understanding what motivates someone to do right, makes it possible to do right. Righteousness based on the Law is impossible to earn, for the more knowledge of the Law you have, the more you are in violation (James 4:17). Motivation from the knowledge of right and wrong is not powerful enough.

    On the other hand, Jesus Christ has no evil thoughts. When He shares His Life with us, through the Holy Spirit, He shares with us the same pure thoughts that He thinks. He becomes an integral part of our beings and empowers us to live according to His thinking and not ours. His nature never violates the law of the Spirit of Life. His nature converts us into the image of His thinking and we begin to think as He thinks and live as He lives (Romans 12:1-3 and 8:26-39, 1 Cor.15: 45-49, 2 Cor. 3:18-4:7, Col. 1: 13-23 and 2:23-3:17). Our nature will be like His and His nature never violates the law of the

Tree of Life

Spirit of Life. The thinking of Love for one another is a powerful motivation.

The condition of the world today is so sad. Not only are we not keeping the Law God gave us, we have written our own set of laws. We have made obeying a set of spiritual laws as easy as we can make it and we still do not keep it.

We cannot discount even one law

I was in the grocery store today while I wrote this piece. I picked up three items and went to the express checkout lane. The sign said there was a limit of 10 items for this lane. Several people in line had many more than 10 items in their carts. I did not need to count to know there were more than 10, maybe as many as 25. We cannot even do the checkout lanes right! It is for everyone's benefit that stores reserve checkouts for those with a few items. The ones who misuse these checkouts are likely the same ones who get mad if someone else does the same. If they are in a hurry, they want everyone using the fast checkout to have 10 items or fewer.

I mention this small matter about checkout counters, but it works the same for other areas of life as well. If we think it is O.K. for us to bend the checkout rules for our own purpose, but do not tolerate others doing the same, we likely have the same behavior in other areas of our lives also.

The same thinking can result in road rage. Today people consider it foolish to obey the speed limit. Some drivers, who get behind another driver driving at the speed limit, get upset at the driver who is complying with the law. I have heard of people who get caught behind another driver and erupt into fits of rage that can lead to fighting and death.

Me-centered thinking is wrong behind the wheel of a car and is the just as wrong in line at the checkout. When we overlook the slighting of one law, it suggests that we should ignore all laws. Therefore, when we justify breaking simple traffic laws, we also justify a company breaking environmental laws by polluting a river. It is the same thinking. We lament the results of the uncontrolled destruction of our society and pass laws to prevent it. But then we teach others to dishonor the laws we passed. The result is more lamenting of our society's destruction and passing more laws we do

A Choice between Two Trees

not expect people to honor. When will we see the hopelessness of such a lifestyle?

The thinking taught by the world, which I saw in the checkout lines, also produce child abuse, spousal abuse, school shootings, abortion clinic bombings, and all other unreasonable acts. Some people feel they must take it into their own hands to make it right. Someone must pay! The one who is not fulfilling the intent of the Law now will later be a most severe judge of others according to the Law. They are willing to judge someone else and, in doing so, judge themselves also. We will stand before a Holy God. He will not let us blame another for the same thing we are doing. Instead He will quickly bring our own condemnation on our head (Matt. 18:21-35).

The Law cannot make one person less guilty for the same offense as another. The standards we apply to others will be the standards applied to us. The judgments we apply to others will automatically apply to us. Considering the truth of that statement, it would be advisable to show mercy, for Yahweh shows us the mercy we show to others. (James 2:10-13). If, according to the Law, mercy can apply to one, then it is possible to apply mercy to others as well, including us. Which do you want applied to you, mercy or judgment? It is your choice. You decide by how you treat others (Luke 6:37-45, Mark 11:25-26, Matt. 8:5-13).

Whose life is this anyway?

Look closely at what Paul is saying in Romans chapters 6, 7, and 8. In chapter 6, Paul is most surely telling us that we are free from sin and we ought to act like it (Rom. 6:11-23). There is nothing in the Scriptures that gives us the right to continue our sin once we have received the Holy Spirit. The key to understanding this is in Rom. 6:1-11, which deals with Christ's death on the cross and our joining Him in the likeness of His death.

If the old sinful nature is dead and buried, it can no longer be a slave to anyone or anything. If the old nature is dead, it cannot respond to any temptation. If the old nature is dead, and we are still sinning, then we are allowing the new nature to become enslaved to sin. If we enslave the new nature, what act will release it from bondage? (Heb. 6:1-6, Rom. 8:1-2). We cannot crucify the Son of God a second time, which was the only solution for our first problem.

Tree of Life

If we enter back into slavery, our second problem is far worse than the first (Matt. 12:43-45). It is not possible for the new nature to become enslaved to sin, because that would enslave the Spirit of Holiness that dwells within us as well. If we continue enslaved to sin, then the old man is not dead and we do not have a new nature.

You have heard some explain Chapter 7 of Romans to say the old nature is warring against the new nature. Let me explain why I say it is not. Paul is talking about his hopeless condition **before** Christ entered his life. Sin was at war with his old nature (Rom 7:23). Paul's old nature agreed with the Law but sin warred against his spirit and caused him to do what he did not want to do. Sin enslaved him and the Law was helpless to free him. Paul describes the goodness of the Law as a trap for him because it made him aware of sin and how powerless he was to conquer it.

In Romans Chapter 8, Paul shows his excitement by praising God, because he is free from the old Law to serve the new law of the Spirit of Life. Jesus Christ assimilates us spiritually into His death on the cross, so we can become assimilated spiritually into His resurrection (Rom. 6:1-10). The old nature dies a spiritual death with Jesus Christ on the Cross and at the same time dies to the Law of Righteousness. Because we no longer try to earn righteousness by overcoming sin, we are free to serve according to the new nature of Jesus Christ. We cannot walk in the Spirit of Life while serving as slaves to sin. We either battle sin in our old nature according to Chapter 7 or walk in the newness of Life according to Chapter 8. We cannot do both.

Men, who want to continue in their sin, will say that they cannot help themselves, that they will lose the battle over sin, that it is unavoidable. What they say is true, for they fight the wrong battle empowered by the wrong nature. There is a way to overcome this weakness by confronting sin through the Love of Jesus Christ. He prepared the way of the cross that conquers sin by His Demonstration of Love. He has made available a new way of thinking for those who believe. We now have the mind of Christ and the nature of Christ. He is not a slave to sin. So if we walk in the power of His resurrection, how can we be enslaved to sin? If He cannot sin and we become one in Him and walk as He walks, how is it possible for us to sin? The letter of James tells us that being a hearer or a judge of the Law is of

A Choice between Two Trees

no benefit to us. We must be doers of the Law before it is a benefit to us (James 1:22-26 and 4:7-12).

In the days of Noah, Yahweh's judgment swept away those not in the Ark and saved those in the Ark (Gen. 6:1-8:22). Jesus Christ is our Ark and the same holds true for us. Those who join Him in the likeness of His death can share in the likeness of His resurrection (Romans 6:1-11). It will not do if we only talk. We must literally be in Him. The only ones safe from Yahweh's judgment are those in the Ark of Jesus Christ's life. Those left outside perished in the flood of judgment. There is no benefit for us to claim to be in Christ if we are spiritually separate from Him. He is the Head of the Body. To be one with Christ we must be one of His literal members. We must be one in His death, one in His resurrection, and one in His perfect Life. We must be born again (John 3:1-8). If we continue to sin in the likeness of Adam, how can we live in the likeness of Christ, the Second Adam? This is the narrow gate we are looking for and few are they who find it!

Look at Chapter 6-7 and at what the Holy Spirit is saying about slavery to sin. In 7:1-4, He is telling us the Law only applies to us while we live. If we are dead in Christ, we are no longer alive. It is Christ who lives in us (Gal. 2:17-3:3). It is not our life to live, but Christ's life to live as He sees fit. In Rom. 6:11-23 and Gal. 2:15-3:3 and 4:1-10, the Lord expects us to live according to the Spirit. Paul asks in Rom. 6:1-11, *"Shall we continue in sin because we are not under the Law?"* And he also asks, *"What is the benefit that you are receiving from the sin you are ashamed of, seeing that it ends in death?"* And in Gal. 4:9, *"How is it that you turn back to be enslaved all over again?"* How can we yield ourselves again as slaves to sin? The Scriptures do not give the right to continue as slaves to our sin, once we have received the Holy Spirit and the power to overcome sin. We can find much in the scriptures about yielding to the authority of Yahweh. We must turn our lives over to Him.

It takes a new way of thinking to conquer sin

In the following verses of chapter 7, Paul brings forth some interesting comments about sin and our slavery to sin. Listen to what he is saying. If Paul is not the one committing the wrongdoing

Tree of Life

because he has chosen to act according to the law, then sin is acting out the wrongdoing against Paul's will. Since sin can control Paul's actions against his will, sin has mastery over him and Paul is a slave to sin.

For what I am doing, I do not understand; for I am not practicing what I would like to do, <u>but I am doing the very thing I hate</u>. But if I do the very thing I do not want to do, I agree with the Law, confessing that the Law is good. <u>So now, no longer am I the one doing it, but sin which dwells in me</u>.

For I know that nothing good dwells in me, that is, in my flesh; for the willing is present in me, but the doing of the good is not. For the good that I want, I do not do, but I practice the very evil that I do not want. <u>But if I am doing the very thing I do not want, I am no longer the one doing it, but sin which dwells in me</u>.

I find then the principle that evil is present in me, the one who wants to do good. For I joyfully concur with the law of God in the inner man, but I see a different law in the members of my body, <u>waging war against the law of my mind and making me a prisoner of the law of sin which is in my members</u>. Wretched man that I am! Who will set me free from the body of this death? (Romans 7:15-24) (Read in context.).

Paul tells us that he agrees with God about what he should do, but he does not always do what he has agreed with God to do. He decides the following: since his spirit is willing to do right but his flesh does not comply, he is not in control of his flesh. Sin fights with his spirit and commits the evil that he does not want to do.

Paul then reasons that it is no longer he who commits the evil, but sin within him that is committing the evil. It would be reasonable for us to conclude that under these circumstances, Paul is enslaved to the sin that forced his nature to do evil against his will. Paul never asserts that his nature can master the sin that wars against him. Instead he pleads for rescue from the contradiction he sees in his body.

If Paul's nature could not be master over the Law of Sin in his body, do you feel your nature can do better? If your nature could master sin, why do you still choose to do evil? If you do evil and it is not your choice, it shows that you are a slave to sin and not master

A Choice between Two Trees

over it. Paul does not stop where I stopped quoting, for if he did you would be in a no-win situation. Paul continues with these verses.

Thanks be to God through Jesus Christ our Lord! So then, on the one hand I myself with my mind am serving the law of God, but on the other, with my flesh the law of sin.

Therefore there is now no condemnation for those who are in Christ Jesus. For the law of the Spirit of life in Christ Jesus has set you free from the law of sin and of death (Romans 7:25 - 8:2).

Back in chapter 4 of Romans, so far back we can forget he said it, Paul tells us in verse 15, *"the Law brings about wrath, but where there is no law, there also is no violation."* With everything said in this chapter, we must remember the principle in this verse. To conquer sin, we must have a different law than the Law of Righteousness. Overcoming evil by controlling sin with the knowledge of good and evil will never cleanse us of sin. We will remain slaves to sin as long as we battle sin on this battleground.

Jesus Christ is the Master over sin, for He lived a perfect life as a man by the power of Love and did not sin. He meets the requirements of the Law of Righteousness. Since Jesus Christ offers to share the Life that overcame sin, those who take part in His Life live as He lives. Since He is the Master over sin through Love, we must admit that He would also be Master over sin in our lives. He cannot allow sin to continue in us, since He shares His Life with us; for He would be joining in the evil with us. If Jesus Christ was to join us in sin, how could He continue as judge over others who sin?

If He allowed sin to continue in us, He would be choosing to engage in our evil, He would no longer be without sin, and no longer Master over sin. How could He then judge the evil of sin if He is not Master over sin? The slave does not have authority over the master, but is under authority to the master. If He is to remain sinless, it is impossible for Him to take part in evil by allowing us to continue in our sin. We are unable to exercise authority over sin, for we are slaves to sin. Therefore, Jesus Christ, who is the Master over our sin, must be the responsible one in our lives by exercising His mastery over our sin. By doing so, He cleanses us of all sin. He has promised to exercise His authority over sin as our advocate, allowing us to live sinless lives through His workmanship.

Tree of Life

Therefore it is not our responsibility to become masters over our sin. Pursuing our own mastery over sin shows unfaith in His mastery over sin. We would be calling Him a liar since we would be expressing our belief that He is unable to stop us from sinning. We would be rejecting His offer to be master over our sin and trying to carry out the work of obtaining mastery over sin.

Since we cannot gain mastery over sin, we remain in our sin. Since Jesus Christ is responsible for obtaining mastery over sin and is the only one who can, why do we fight to keep the responsibility? If we do not have the ability to gain mastery over sin and Jesus Christ has already gained mastery over sin, it's logical to yield responsibility to Jesus Christ for overcoming our sin. He is the only one who can clean us from our sin and He has promised to create His goodness in us. We should trust Him to keep His promise and show faith by placing our welfare into His hands.

If Jesus Christ has the responsibility to conquer sin in our lives, it is no longer we who triumph over sin. Christ Jesus, who lives in us, will overcome sin in us. Since Jesus Christ has the responsibility and competence to overcome sin, any virtue that is in us is not ours but Jesus Christ's who is overcoming sin and has already begun to overcome sin in our lives. It is no longer us, but Jesus Christ who is in us (Gal. 2:15-20).

We should no longer encourage people to work on their own to overcome sin, as if they have the power to overcome it. We must encourage people to allow the Spirit of God to exercise His authority over sin. Those who have Jesus Christ in them were once slaves to sin but are no longer slaves to sin. Instead, they are a part of the new way and are slaves to righteousness in Christ Jesus. Since all of us are like Paul, unable to conquer, we must point them to the one who is able; Jesus Christ.

If we point them to the one who can overcome sin, we must also point them to the method by which He overcame sin. Jesus Christ's death and resurrection is the only way to overcome sin! All must come to Him, admitting their need for cleansing from sin and He is faithful to cleanse them from all their unrighteousness (1 John 1:5-2:2). Remember that Paul did not claim to obtain the goal. Rather, he pressed on toward the goal (Philip. 3:8-15). We do not look at it as achieving the goal. Instead we recognize that it is Jesus

A Choice between Two Trees

Christ who achieves the goal by the Life He lives in us. His life, lived in us, is the narrow gate and the Tree of Life. No one comes to the Father except through Him.

Jesus gave us a parable in Mark 2:21-22 and Luke 5:36-39. New wine in an old wineskin doesn't work because the old wineskin is stretched out. As the wine ferments and expands, the old skin would burst. A new piece of cloth on an old garment would tear as the new cloth shrinks and the old cloth does not. Grace cannot be completed using the thinking found in the Law. All things are new and we cannot apply the thinking of salvation by grace as if it was a new set of laws. The old way could not save us and applying the old way to the new Life will not help either. He fulfills grace using the thinking found in Love.

Men twist what Paul said in Romans when he explained that we are not to be slaves to sin through the Law any more (Romans 3:8, 6:15). They claim that He expected sin to continue because we could not stop ourselves from sinning. Some say that if we accept Jesus, then sin is O.K. as long as we confess our sin. I say the Holy Spirit is not teaching that through Paul. Instead He is teaching that Jesus Christ provided a new way in the Law of the Spirit. To understand the new way, we must change our way of thinking. We need to come into agreement with Yahweh. Nobody can help another to know what Yahweh is thinking; only the Holy Spirit can do that.

May the Law of the Spirit found in Jesus Christ,
                        be a Tree of Life to you.

Tree of Life

Chapter 9

Righteousness by Obeying the Law of Love

Where there is no law, neither is there a violation of the Law
Then Jesus said to His disciples, <u>"If anyone wishes to come after Me, let him deny himself, and take up his cross, and follow Me. For whoever wishes to save his life shall lose it; but whoever loses his life for My sake shall find it.</u> For what will a man be profited, if he gains the whole world, and forfeits his soul? Or what will a man give in exchange for his soul? For the Son of Man is going to come in the glory of His Father with His angels; and will then recompense every man according to his deeds" (Matt. 16:24-27).

This chapter is about removing the clothing of the old way of thinking, leaving it behind, and putting on garments of a new way of thinking. It is about refocusing our thinking on the excellence of the Person of Jesus Christ and the work He is doing in our lives through the Holy Spirit. This new focus of our thinking aligns us with Yahweh's thoughts. The Holy Spirit exposes the Godhead's thoughts to us that we might know them (Isaiah 55:6-11, Psalms 40:5).
The mouth of the righteous is a fountain of life, but the mouth of the wicked conceals violence. Hatred stirs up strife, <u>But love covers all transgressions</u> (Proverbs 10:11-12) (Prov. 17:9, 1 Cor. 13:4–7, James 5:20, 1 Peter 4:8).

The battle of Good vs. Evil is a battle of Love vs. hate. Changing the way we think will require us to lay down our old lives that are full of all kinds of hateful thinking. When we do, we may feel like we are giving up our identity and taking on someone else's. If we yield to God, we have the privilege of sharing Life with the most fantastic Being who has ever existed.

Read all of Proverbs 10. In there, Yahweh contrasts the people of Love and the people of violence. We must give up the lies the world gives us and embrace the truth, which is that Jesus Christ lived His life free from any wrongdoing. Because he lived His life free from wrongdoing and we share His life free from wrongdoing. We may enter the throne room of God through the passageway He

A Choice between Two Trees

created by His righteousness life. <u>The Life He laid down on the Cross makes visible the path that we must take.</u> We must study and analyze this Demonstration of Love. We must allow it to take over our lives so we can become members of His body and thus join Him as He performs His Demonstration of Love. Our God nailed our sinful nature to the cross as a certificate of debt with the words "Paid in Full" stamped on it in blood (Col. 2:13-17). Because we replace the old garments of our thinking with the new garments of the cross, we can trust that His love will save us. Love becomes a part of us and we become one with the Person of Love. We now live according to the Spirit of the Law by living out the principles of Love.

<u>*Now to the one who works, his wage is not reckoned as a favor, but as what is due.*</u> *But to the one who does not work, but believes in Him who justifies the ungodly, his faith is reckoned as righteousness, for the Law brings about wrath,* <u>*but where there is no law, neither is there violation*</u> *(Romans 4:4-5 and 15).* (What a verse!)

This is a hard concept for most people to understand and a difficult idea to explain. How can there be order in the universe if there is no Law? There must be something to guide us in knowing right from wrong. Men want something that will declare that they have the right answer to the question, "How should I live my life?" This is why men keep returning to the tree of the Knowledge of Good and Evil. Men want to point to something that says, "Look at what I have done. This makes me acceptable." People spend much of their time striving for acceptance. Maybe it includes being with the in-crowd, a church group, a street gang, or at the nightclub. Whatever the standard of acceptability is, people try to do it. The problem is that a standard of acceptability is also a standard of unacceptability. Enforcing unacceptability requires a judge to pass judgment.

We have no excuse because we know two points that were made in the last two chapters. We know that judging can be a spider's web of condemnation, and the Law is unable to cleanse us from sin. As the title of this chapter says, we believe in the Law of Love. You might point out that it is still a Law. Love is much more than a legalistic law. It is the complete definition of the intent of the legalistic Law and Yahweh framed the universe with it as the foundation. The Law could never do what His Love does! Those who try to keep the letter of the Law will continue to fail, for the Law is only able to show what is wrong. It cannot help to do what is right. Those who follow the Spirit of Love keep the Law of Righteousness instinctively, without thinking about mastering the complexities of the Law. They keep the Law and may be unaware that they are fulfilling the law because their purpose is Love. Thinking that comes from the Law can tell us that an act is good or evil. True Love reveals why an act is good or evil. The Law is two-dimensional while Love is three-dimensional. Those who act according to Love understand the depth of the Law and grasp its full meaning. Since good is beneficial and evil is destructive, living according to the Law of Love benefits all, not just a limited few. This is a true statement: "We can be right according to the Law without acting right according to Love." We cannot perform an act motivated by Love that is contrary to the intent of the Law!

Owe nothing to anyone except to love one another; for he who loves his neighbor has fulfilled the law. For this, "You shall not commit adultery, You shall not murder, You shall not steal, You shall not covet," and if there is any other commandment, it is summed up in this saying, "You shall love your neighbor as yourself." <u>Love does no wrong to a neighbor; love therefore is the fulfillment of the law</u> (Romans 13:8-10).

True Love changes the focus of men's thinking to the knowledge of Yahweh and His Message of Love. Under this new thinking, we no longer strive to become experts in the discernment between the Lie and the Truth. We strive to become experts in noticing the effect our actions have on Yahweh's people and look to benefit others in Love. The Law is good and God gave it to us so we could see how poorly we are able to adhere to a concept of right and wrong. The condition of our world proves, without a doubt, that man cannot grasp the complexities of his life. Love, on the other hand, does not wrong another human being. If we strove to understand the principles of Love and acted according to the morality of Love, we would not harm one another.

A Choice between Two Trees

Let us look at one difficult question

Difficult questions become easier to answer when evaluated through Love and not through right and wrong. Is abortion an act of Love (seeking for another person's well-being) or is it an action committed by one who judges right and wrong selfishly? According to the teachings of men, we should balance our judgment between the rights of the woman over her body and the unborn child's right to live. We should debate what lifestyle the baby will have. We question which is crueler: death now or a lifetime of sorrow. Moral arguments can go on for days with no resolution, with each side claiming to have the more correct position. They may even debate which position is more loving.

Following the thinking from the Tree of Life, we should realize abortion is just one choice at the end of a series of choices. We must ask, "Is the act of conception an act of Love (seeking for another person's well-being)?" If the act of conception ends by destroying the baby, can it be a true act of Love? Or is it a selfish act of pleasure? If each choice we make is from the viewpoint of Love, would we need to ask, "Is abortion right?" Could a path of Love lead us to such a state of affairs? The thinking of Love is an evaluation of our actions both past and future. The past opens our eyes to what the Spirit must change or has changed. The decisions we make today carve out our future. The thinking of Love looks for the path that is best for all concerned, so we must ask about the lifestyle of the baby before conception and not after.

The worldly thinking in the case of rape is not Love. Rape is an outpouring of hate. It is a destructive act that forever changes the victim. Society's best interest is to create an environment that prevents and discourages such acts. Instead, it could be argued that society encourages it. There is moral failure that deteriorates the rights of all human beings. So we must ask, "After one human being has her rights violated, is it Love to violate another human being to right the wrong committed? Should one act of destructive selfishness lead to two destroyed lives? Or can the situation be put into the hands of Love?

The difficult question remains: "After conception, is abortion an act of Love?" The thinking of Love would ask, "Is giving the child up for adoption instead of killing it a better act, an act of Love?

Tree of Life

Is the suffering someone faces to carry the pregnancy to full term a measure of the Love given to the innocent baby involved?"

Destruction is never an act of Love, so destroying the unborn child is an act outside Love. Satan sold the lie that the unborn child is not a human being and encourages men to argue about when life begins. What does man know about life, its origin, or what it takes to make life?

Talk to the children of mothers who decided not to have an abortion. How many would say they wish their mothers had aborted them, regardless of their lifestyle now? Would killing them now be an act of Love? If killing them now is not an act of love, how is killing them before birth an act of love? Do you not understand that life is passed on from the parent to the child? When God created Adam, He breathed life into Him, which He did not do for any of the animals. He did not create life in Adam - He passed it on from Himself. The life Adam received had its beginning in Yahweh. When He created Eve, He did not breathe life into her; He passed the life He gave Adam to Eve through the rib. From that point, the mother and father pass Yahweh's life to their children.

If, in Yahweh's eyes, the unborn is His child and the unborn is a part of His being, is killing the unborn an act of Love in His eyes? His opinion is the only one that remains, throughout eternity, and, in truth, is the only one that counts now (Read Psalm 139). There is no way that killing an unborn child can be an act of Love.

In the same way that Eve received Yahweh's life through Adam's rib, we receive our new birth through Jesus Christ. He passed new Life to us by joining our souls to Jesus Christ's death on the cross, which allowed us to take part in His resurrection. The Holy Spirit is ours as a seal of acceptance forever (Romans 5:1-6:11). Hate and anger shown to an unbeliever, who has yet to receive the Holy Spirit, is like killing the unborn child in Yahweh's eyes.

Stop reading and think about this for a short time. The God of Creation shows the depths of Love by accepting us, while we adopted thinking that destroyed what is precious to Him. How much more will He accept us and show Love when our thinking establishes and builds them up? (Romans 5:8-11). If He died for us while we were His enemies and now shares His Life with us, what does He think about the unborn believer whom we mistreat?

A Choice between Two Trees

If we base our decisions on Love, we make better choices than if we decide based on the knowledge of right and wrong. When answering the question of the unborn, if we use a perception based on who is right or based on preserving someone's rights, the battle will rage on. If all acts committed by humans were true acts of Love, the question of killing the unborn child would never come to mind!

Those who know God know Love, for God is Love
For you were called to freedom, brethren; only do not turn your freedom into an opportunity for the flesh, but through love serve one another. For the whole Law is fulfilled in one word, in the statement, *"You shall love your neighbor as yourself."*

But if you bite and devour one another, take care lest you be consumed by one another. *But I say, walk by the Spirit, and you will not carry out the desire of the flesh.* For the flesh sets its desire against the Spirit, and the Spirit against the flesh; for these are in opposition to one another, so that you may not do the things that you please. *But if you are led by the Spirit, you are not under the Law.*

Now the deeds of the flesh are evident, which are: immorality, impurity, sensuality, idolatry, sorcery, enmities, strife, jealousy, outbursts of anger, disputes, dissensions, factions, envying, drunkenness, carousing, and things like these, of which I forewarn you just as I have forewarned you that those who practice such things shall not inherit the kingdom of God.

But the fruit of the Spirit is love, joy, peace, patience, kindness, goodness, faithfulness, gentleness, self-control; against such things there is no law. Now those who belong to Christ Jesus have crucified the flesh with its passions and desires. If we live by the Spirit, let us also walk by the Spirit (Gal. 5:13-25).

I love these verses. There is so much in them. We have a freedom to love each other. Love is the key to set our spirits free. Love is what the Law guides us to do. Even in the first century AD, Love fulfilled the Law. Why isn't our planet characterized by its love for one another? Why do we allow selfishness to remain the most widely accepted worldview? Hate and the deeds of hate are of the flesh. Love is of the Spirit. The Kingdom of God goes to those led by the Spirit. If we followed the Spirit more, Love would be our way of

Tree of Life

life. Which list, in the verses above, would you like your corner of the world to be known by? Which list describes the way it is now? Which list describes you? The Spirit will lead you in the path of Love. Go follow!

When someone responds to God's Love by loving others, he is changed. The spider web trap of keeping the Law does not exist when Love motivates. The person acting according to the thinking of Love finds True Life. This is true even if the person offered Love does not receive it or does not return it.

There is a freedom that comes with Love. When we live and walk in Love, there is no longer a fear of rejection by Yahweh, for we know that Jesus Christ died for us to restore us to the Father. If He was willing to die for us, then He must love us enough to accept us. Perfect Love cast out fear. Love casts out our fear of death and punishment (1 John 4:16-19). Living and walking with the Holy Spirit is a walk along Love's pathway. Our love for others casts out the fear they have of our rejecting them. Unity in the Spirit is a unity of Love. If the fruit of the Spirit guided all of humanity, what a wonderful world this would be.

We are from God; he who knows God listens to us; he who is not from God does not listen to us. By this we know the spirit of truth and the spirit of error. <u>*Beloved, let us love one another, for love is from God; and everyone who loves is born of God and knows God. The one who does not love does not know God, for God is love.*</u> *By this the love of God was manifested in us, that God has sent His only begotten Son into the world so that we might live through Him. In this is love, not that we loved God, but that He loved us and sent His Son to be the propitiation for our sins. Beloved, if God so loved us, we also ought to love one another.* <u>*No one has beheld God at any time; if we love one another, God abides in us, and His love is perfected in us.*</u> *By this we know that we abide in Him and He in us, because He has given us of His Spirit (1 John 4:6-13).*

The message is clear. Those who know God know love, for God is Love. Those who know Him hear this Message because the Message is Love. Yahweh has manifested His Love in us through His Son that we might live through His Love. We reveal our love for Him by the list we live by. Immorality, jealousy, outbursts of anger,

A Choice between Two Trees

disputes, envying, drunkenness, carousing, and the like are the ways of the world. Would you want to be treated this way? It is time to change our thinking to Yahweh's.

We cannot behold God physically, so we cannot personally return Love to Him. Even if we could, our love would fall well short of what it should be. He is willing to credit us with loving Him when we love one another. Recall the parable that Jesus gave in Matt. 25:32-46. In that parable, the King separates the sheep from the goats, based on the way they related to one another. He told them that their actions toward the least of His sheep are actions toward Him also.

Since we want to return His act of Love, we must do so by acts of Love shown to fellow human beings who share the same trials and agitations as we do. Our actions toward the least of these speak volumes about our love for their Creator. In the same way that we now freely walk with our God, our fellow travelers should be able to walk freely in our midst. They should be equally confident in our acceptance of them as we are of our acceptance before Yahweh and His Son.

Life by the Law of the Spirit does not need to earn a reward
<u>Now to the one who works, his wage is not reckoned as a favor, but as what is due</u>. But to the one who does not work, but believes in Him who justifies the ungodly, <u>his faith is reckoned as righteousness</u>, for the Law brings about wrath, but where there is no law, neither is there violation (Romans 4:4-5 and 15).

When we come before our God, we do not look for a reward or a wage. For rewards are recognition of an act performed and a wage is given to settle an account by paying off a debt. Now, I do not know about you, but I could never earn enough to settle my sin account or pay what I owe. I have been spiritually in the red my whole life and will be for the rest of my life.

In truth, I know what condition your spiritual account is in. It is every bit as hopeless as mine. You may not think so. You may believe you repair every wrong and have confessed every sin and that you pleased God the Father with your life. But you make a sad mistake. You do not come near to satisfying the full judgment for

Tree of Life

your sins. You are not now nor ever will be ready to bear the penalty for your sin.

Those of us, who have accepted Jesus Christ know the Creator nailed our debt to the Cross of Calvary in the person of Jesus Christ. He settled our accounts by an unselfish act of Love. It is all found in what Jesus Christ did for us (Col. 2:9-3:4). Anything a man may do to improve his standing with God, or with other men, is a work of the flesh and is in conflict with the Spirit of Love. The works of a man are filthy rags and will never be anything else (Isaiah 64:6, Romans 3:10-20). As long as we try to prove our self-worth, we will continue to live under a law of condemnation. Where there is a law to adhere to, there will be violations of that law.

We cannot break a law that does not exist
For the Law brings about wrath, but where there is no law, neither is there a violation (Romans 4:15).

If we no longer live to fulfill the Law of Righteousness, but trust the Lord Jesus Christ to do that for us, we shall live our lives for another purpose. We, therefore, understand that we obey the "Law of the Spirit of Life in Christ Jesus" by following His example of Love. Love fulfills the Law and those who feed on the Tree of Life trust in Love. They get the strength to trust that they have salvation, from the trust they have that God loves them. The more they trust in His love for them, the more they believe He has given them salvation.

Where there is no law, neither is there a violation of the law. Our approach to other people is different, if we do not hold them accountable to our vision of the Law. Our expectations become reasonable and we are not so offended when people do not meet our expectations. Our response to their failure is like the one we received from Jesus Christ (1 John 2:1). He treated us with Love when we least deserved it. Remove the expectations of the Law and we can love others when they least deserve it.

To break the cycle of sinning, repentance, fulfillment by righteous deeds, and failure to do those righteous deeds, we must focus on the desirable qualities of Jesus Christ and not on our own goodness. We need to listen to the Holy Spirit, who bears witness with our spirit that we are the children of God (Romans 8:16). We

A Choice between Two Trees

must believe that we are free from the Law and are now subject to the Spirit of God. Those who are slaves of Love fulfill the Spirit of the Law of Righteousness.

Therefore, we can now do the acts that we previously couldn't. We can live in Romans 8 and not stay trapped in Romans 7. In truth, it is not something we do, but rather Jesus Christ is performing the work in us. If Jesus Christ is living in us and is working through us, who is going to commit a charge against us? (Romans 8:31-39). For if they commit a charge against us, they also charge Jesus Christ with sin before the Judge. Jesus Christ stands innocent of such charges, but the one making the charge will also be examined and will not withstand his own accusations. Yahweh will use their standard of measure to judge them and to the extent the accuser showed mercy, He will show mercy. The accuser will find himself in a spider's web of judgments that he has created.

Those who eat from the Tree of Life live in freedom from the Law of Right and Wrong. Our focus is not on how holy our lives are, for our lives no longer exist. If the selfish nature is dead, it makes no sense to accuse the dead man of wrongdoing or give him credit for anything done right! Therefore, it is not about us, it is about Jesus Christ. He is the one who will receive condemnation or praise as the result of what He does in our lives. He is Love and His actions are never against the Law, for Love fulfills the Law (Romans 13:10). Every action we take, while being led by the Holy Spirit, will comply with the Law, because God cannot sin. The power of the Holy Spirit enables us to overcome the sin that had enslaved us.

Love is the answer. Living according to a lifestyle of Love is the narrow gate we are seeking. Few will find it because they look selfishly for their benefit. When they see the gate, they reject it because traveling that path does not fulfill their goal. They see no reward and have no wish to give something for nothing. Those looking beyond their own benefit find the gate. The path draws them for it promises the chance to benefit others. They are not looking for a reward and are not repulsed by the sacrifice they must make.

Which road are you on?

May the freedom in the Law of Love be a Tree of Life to you.

Tree of Life

Chapter 10

We Can Trust the God of Love

God the Father loved us from the beginning
For whom He foreknew, He also predestined to become conformed to the image of His Son, that He might be the first-born among many brethren; and whom He predestined, these He also called; and whom He called, these He also justified; and whom He justified, these He also glorified. What then shall we say to these things? *If God be for us, who is against us? (Romans 8:29-31).*

We are forever secure in our knowledge that we will never again face separation from the Love of God, for it is God who is working to bring us to Him. Who is it that can undo the work He has done by condemnations they may speak? Will they change the mind of God and turn Him against us? After He paid the extremely high price of personal suffering to His soul, will He now fail to include us into His companionship? Can Satan stand before God and convince Him to desert us because we are not worthy of His suffering? What, in all of creation, can change the testimony God the Father has made about His Son and Life found in Him? After such a great price was paid for our redemption, will Yahweh now abandons us? The answer is that nothing can separate us from the Love of God (Romans 8:31-39).

As those who trust Yahweh, we do not talk about our steadfast love. We talk about the steadfastness of His Love. His Love is more powerful than our failures, our weaknesses, our limitations, and our sins. Love from God withstands anything we shall face during our time on earth. We have a Representative (1 John 2:1) who knows the frailty of the human race and a High Priest who understands the temptations that challenge us every day, for He met temptation but He did not sin (Heb. 4:12-16).

Many people think of Yahweh as someone watching from a distance in a place called Heaven and that He is looking to see if we make a mistake so He may deal out punishment. Nothing could be further from the truth. We have a God who takes an intimate interest in us for our good. Psalm 139 was written more than 3,000 years ago

A Choice between Two Trees

and it proclaims the interest Yahweh has for His people. Jesus said the Father knows the number of hairs on each person's head (Matt. 10:20-31). We don't even know that, for that number changes every day (at least on my head). In the passage above, Paul says that Yahweh foreknew us from the foundations of the earth He planned for our arrival. Then, He predestined us to become justified by Christ's death on the cross. Next, He calls those He predestines to conform to the likeness of Jesus Christ. And finally, He glorifies those whom He foreknew by conforming them to the image of His Son, Jesus Christ (Rom. 8:29-30).

The Father loved us from the beginning, He has a plan for us

Yahweh has a Blueprint, a designed plan that He is working out in His called ones. Before He laid the foundation of the universe, He already knew all there was to know about everything and everyone there was to know about. His plan is perfect because He considers everything there is to consider. What these verses say is that our God does not react to what happens in our lives. He planned His actions before we even existed. Are we ready to trust this statement? Can we place what is important into the hands of Yahweh and trust He knows what He is doing? Or will we take matters into our own hands and try to deliver them ourselves. I believe those who take matters into their own hands lose the most and those who trust Him, no matter how bad it looks, gain the most.

Is this not an amazing thought? "Our God prepared Himself fully to handle every issue that is going to arise in our lives?" He already knows the outcome of every decision ever made by every person who breathes. He knew what we needed and He knew what He would do about it. The answer is in His Son, Jesus Christ, the Word of God (John 1:1-3). The fall of Adam and Eve was not a mistake. He did not need to find a solution. He already knew what to do. He allowed Adam's fall because of the plan He predestined from the beginning. He knew what your reaction to these thoughts would be before I wrote them in this book. He knew before the beginning of time those who would join Him in friendship. Those who receive Him also receive the power to become the Sons of God (John 1:11-13) by conforming them into the image of Jesus Christ (Col. 3:10, 2 Cor. 3:12-18) who is Himself the Image of God the Father (Col.

Tree of Life

1:13-20, 2 Cor. 4:4). The birth of Yahweh's children does not come about because of wisdom or because of the abilities of man, but by the will and power of Yahweh alone.

On our own, we cannot know the plan or find the way. Unless the Shepherd of our souls leads us in the Way of Life, we remain lost and without hope. Those who eat from the wrong tree are dead as we also were once dead (Eph. 2:1-5). True Life has made us alive, if our fellowship is with Jesus Christ. Our fellowship is not with teachings that tell us about God. It is with the Person of the Godhead. If He planned from the beginning to conform us into His image, will He not finish the work He has begun? (Philip. 2:1-13). Yes, He is faithful and true. He will carry out everything He has purposed in His heart.

Yahweh's love causes us to go beyond the Law of Righteousness

And not only this, but also we ourselves, <u>having the firstfruits of the Spirit</u>, even we ourselves groan within ourselves, waiting eagerly for our adoption as sons, the redemption of our body. <u>For in hope we have been saved</u>, but hope that is seen is not hope; for why does one also hope for what he sees? But if we hope for what we do not see, with perseverance we wait eagerly for it.

<u>And in the same way the Spirit also helps our weakness; for we do not know how to pray as we should, but the Spirit Himself intercedes for us with groanings too deep for words</u>; and He who searches the hearts knows what the mind of the Spirit is, because He intercedes for the saints according to the will of God. <u>And we know that God causes all things to work together for good to those who love God, to those who are called according to His purpose</u> (Romans 8:23-28).

What then shall we say to these things? <u>If God is for us, who is against us? He who did not spare His own Son, but delivered Him up for us all, how will He not also with Him freely give us all things? Who will bring a charge against God's elect? God is the one who justifies; who is the one who condemns? Christ Jesus is He who died, yes, rather who was raised, who is at the right hand of God, who also intercedes for us.</u>

<u>Who shall separate us from the love of Christ?</u> Shall tribulation, or distress, or persecution, or famine, or nakedness, or

A Choice between Two Trees

peril, or sword? Just as it is written, "For Thy sake we are being put to death all day long; We were considered as sheep to be slaughtered." But in all these things we overwhelmingly conquer through Him who loved us.

For I am convinced that neither death, nor life, nor angels, nor principalities, nor things present, nor things to come, nor powers, nor height, nor depth, nor any other created thing, <u>shall be able to separate us from the love of God, which is in Christ Jesus our Lord</u> (Romans 8:31-39).

This great set of verses is worth reading again. Think about what the Holy Spirit is saying here. There is too much for me to bring out. These verses should change our approach to life if we only listen. Jesus Christ, through the Holy Spirit, is now interceding on our behalf before God the Father. With the certainty of Yahweh's Love and with the knowledge that God is making such intercessions on our behalf, we can have faith to go beyond the Law of Righteousness. We do not continue to evaluate ourselves to see if we are pleasing to God, for we know that God displayed Love for us and works to make us pleasing in His sight. We are free to fulfill the will of the Father based on acts of Love.

We no longer judge one another to see if they measure up, for God proved His love toward them also (1 John 4:6-12). We are free to fellowship with one another based on acts of Love. If Yahweh has such positive thoughts about our fellow travelers, will He listen to our complaints and accusations against them? Should we be the accusers of the Brethren? (Rev. 12:7-10). No. Instead, Yahweh preordained us to follow His lead and treat one another as He has treated us. As He loved us so we ought to love one another (1 John 4:11). Everything in our lives changes and any truth based on those changeable things can become untrue. But God never changes and therefore the truth of this statement made by the Holy Spirit through Paul in Romans will always remain true. Nothing can separate us from God's love for us!

Yahweh does not base His love on our character and therefore we do not need to earn it. He loves us because Love defines His character. Since He bases His love on His character and His character never changes, there is nothing in the spirit world or the physical

Tree of Life

world that can change His mind and stop Him from loving us. As we fellowship with the God of Love, we begin to take on His nature, which, in turn, changes the basis of our love for one another. The love we have is based on who we are becoming in the Lord. It is not based on the goodness of the person we are called to love. If we give love because it is our nature to love, then nothing will be able to separate us from each other's love.

This portion of Romans clearly makes this statement: "Since Yahweh is for us, there is none who have the power to stand against us." Those who accuse us will fail. Our mistakes, our sins, and our bad decision-making are no longer hindrances to our fellowship with God. We know that God is Love, those who are His children love also (1 John 4). We are free to feed on the Knowledge of Love found in the Life of Jesus Christ. What we find in Him empowers us to do well. We can trust Him to do that which needs doing to keep us with Him, for He is faithful and true.

Notice that, in Romans 8:1-2, the Spirit of Life is in Christ Jesus. We are to be in Christ Jesus and the law of the Spirit of Life is in Christ Jesus. The Spirit of Life is not in the minds of man, or in the teachings of right and wrong, or in our attempts at being better people. It is in the Person of Jesus Christ and we share His Spirit when we share His Life. If God the Father would not spare His own Son, but gave Him up for us, He will finish the work He began in us. Yes, God the Father will honor the Son's work by bring those who believe into the family of God (John 17:1-16).

Exchanging our thoughts for His thoughts

Knowledge based on the Law of Righteousness brings only spiritual death. Knowledge of the person of Jesus Christ brings spiritual Life. In Isaiah 55, the Lord asks why we spend our resources on what cannot satisfy. He tells us we should give up our ways and our thoughts for His ways and His thoughts. His Word, His thoughts, do not fail to carry out all He intends to do and they supply seed to the sower and bread to the eater.

Why are we still searching for the knowledge that will destroy us by feeding on destructive thoughts of hate? We have available to us, in the Bible, the thinking of Yahweh and the example set forth by Jesus Christ. We have available to us the Holy Spirit of

A Choice between Two Trees

God to explain His intent. We have available to us the work of redemption and the expressed will of the Creator that we be redeemed. Why do we still choose death over Life by rejecting the Blueprint Yahweh designed for us from the beginning? We should embrace the lifestyle of Love and reject me-first lifestyle that the world teaches.

"Ho! Every one who thirsts, come to the waters; And you who have no money come, buy and eat. Come, buy wine and milk <u>Without money and without cost</u>. Why do you spend money for what is not bread, And your wages for what does not satisfy? <u>Listen carefully to Me, and eat what is good, And delight yourself in abundance.</u>

<u>*Incline your ear and come to Me. Listen, that you may live; And I will make an everlasting covenant with you,*</u> *According to the faithful mercies shown to David. Behold, I have made him a witness to the peoples, A leader and commander for the peoples. Behold, you will call a nation you do not know, And a nation which knows you not will run to you, Because of the Lord your God, even the Holy One of Israel; For He has glorified you.* <u>*Seek the Lord while He may be found; Call upon Him while He is near.*</u>

<u>*Let the wicked forsake his way, And the unrighteous man his thoughts;*</u> *And let him return to the Lord, And He will have compassion on him; And to our God, For He will abundantly pardon.* <u>*For My thoughts are not your thoughts, Neither are your ways My ways,*</u> *"declares the Lord. For as the heavens are higher than the earth, So are My ways higher than your ways, And My thoughts than your thoughts. For as the rain and the snow come down from heaven, And do not return there without watering the earth, And making it bear and sprout, And furnishing seed to the sower and bread to the eater; So shall* <u>*My word be which goes forth from My mouth; It shall not return to Me empty,*</u> *Without accomplishing what I desire, And without succeeding in the matter for which I sent it" (Isa. 55:1-11).*

He plans what is beneficial for His People (1 Cor. 2:9). Jesus Christ, the Word (thoughts) of God, will not return empty-handed. He calls those who recognize they cannot help themselves. We do not need to bring anything to pay for the spiritual food. He gives good things to us freely, based on His good nature and not our worthiness. Yahweh tells us to listen to Him. He claims that He will

Tree of Life

give us Life and we will delight in His abundance. Our God has much to give us and we need not earn it. He has made an everlasting covenant with us through the death of Jesus Christ (Heb. 10:15-22, 2 Cor. 3:4-9).

He can change the hearts of men and therefore make our thinking like His. Our thinking right now is not like His thinking. He has provided a way for our thinking to change to be like His. To a soul who thirsts to know the Truth, the thinking of our Lord is like the rain of Living Water falling down on the hardness of our hearts, which softens the soil, causing the Tree of Life to flourish. No living creature on earth can live without water and we cannot spiritually live without the thoughts of Yahweh nourishing our souls. He promises that He will generously pardon because He is not like us. How glad we should be that He is not like us!

The Word of God is powerful and able to achieve all He sent Him to do. What He desires to bring about is excellent. He wants to get rid of the thorn bushes and replace them with seed for the sower. He wishes to provide for His children, if we will only turn from our wicked ways, give up our selfish thoughts, and take on the good thoughts He has for us.

Those who have tasted of the Tree of Life find that living in the presence of Jesus Christ is worth more than anything else. We are no longer concerned with our salvation, for we have put that into the hands of a most capable God. We are now free to think about His goodness. As we focus our thinking on Him, Love replaces the hate and destruction the world offers. He is the Father of our spirits, a stronghold in our darkest hour, a God of all comfort, attentive to our needs like the Good Shepherd of the flock, and the complete fulfillment of everything good.

<u>For the love of Christ controls us</u>, having concluded this, that one died for all, therefore all died; and He died for all, that they who live should no longer live for themselves, but for Him who died and rose again on their behalf.

Therefore from now on we recognize no man according to the flesh; even though we have known Christ according to the flesh, yet now we know Him thus no longer. Therefore if any man is in Christ, he is a new creature; the old things passed away; behold, new things have come.

A Choice between Two Trees

Now all these things are from God, who reconciled us to Himself through Christ, and gave us the ministry of reconciliation, namely, that God was in Christ reconciling the world to Himself, not counting their trespasses against them, and He has committed to us the word of reconciliation. Therefore, we are ambassadors for Christ, as though God were making an appeal through us; we beg you on behalf of Christ, be reconciled to God. He made Him who knew no sin to be sin on our behalf, that we might become the righteousness of God in Him.

And working together with Him, we also urge you not to receive the grace of God in vain for He says, "At the acceptable time I listened to you, And on the day of salvation I helped you"; behold, now is "the acceptable time," behold, now is "the day of salvation"(2 Cor. 5:14-6:2).

    The Holy Spirit says the Love of Jesus Christ controls us. If anyone is in Him, he is a new creature. He says that one died for all so all died together. Yahweh gave us the Ministry of Reconciliation and we are working with Him to urge all to receive the fullness of the grace God has shown by the One who became sin for us.
    The thinking in Isaiah 55 and 2 Cor. 5 is all about reconciliation. He sends out those who have eaten of the Tree of Life as representatives. We give witness to His grace. We are available to assist Him in making known what He has made known. That is to say, Yahweh was in Jesus Christ, reconciling the world to Him (2 Cor. 5:19). We cannot buy restoration for our souls to God with money or by service rendered. It is a gift that Yahweh gives to those who receive the Spirit of Jesus Christ in their lives (Rom. 4:4-5 and 6:22-23). To receive Him, we must be willing to replace the life we live with His Life. We cannot live two lives and we cannot serve two masters (Luke 16:13). To gain the one, we must die to the other. What advantage do we have by gaining the whole world if we give up our souls? He who keeps his life will lose it but He who yields his old nature will gain a new nature in the likeness of Life, Jesus Christ (Matt. 16:24-26, 2 Cor. 5:17).
    The Lord God of our Salvation has done a great work *for* us, but He is not satisfied. He wishes to do work *inside* us also. It is not enough that Jesus Christ died for the penalty of our sins. His intent is

Tree of Life

to clean us from all unrighteousness, resulting in Love issued from a pure heart (1 John 2:1, 1 Tim. 1:5). He is the Author and Finisher of our Faith (Heb. 12:1-4). Therefore it is not enough that He begin a work in us. He must also finish the work. We are like clay. His are the hands that mold us (Isa. 64:8). We are His workmanship and He takes a great pleasure in the work He has performed so far (Eph. 2:10).

Reaching agreement with Yahweh

Take time right now to enter an agreement with God about who you are and what you are doing in your life. Think about this list in preparation for looking at the mind of our God in Part 2 of this book.

- We all must agree with Yahweh that we are sinners and we have all contributed to the lowly estate, that our world is in today.
- We must agree there is no amount of learning, we can do on our own, that will educate us enough to save ourselves from us - from our own selfishness and hate.
- We must agree our thoughts empower our lives and those thoughts must be the same type of thoughts God Himself has. The thoughts we have on our own are hateful and lead us to destruction and spiritual death, while His thoughts are loving and lead us to spiritual Life.
- We must all agree that we are powerless to find the Tree of Life on our own and need Him to lead the way. No man knows the path. There is only one who has gone on before and He alone knows the way. In truth, the Person of Jesus Christ is the Way, the Truth, and the Life. There is no other way. We must agree that knowing Jesus Christ exists will not save us. It is fellowshipping with the Person of Jesus Christ that creates the new man in us. He will perform the acts of salvation by cleaning us from sin.
- We must agree that knowledge of any kind, no matter how true, is inadequate for salvation. No man can achieve righteousness before God by keeping a standard that measures self-worth. We must be willing to be acceptable

A Choice between Two Trees

to Yahweh by His declared way, which we find in Jesus Christ's death on the cross.
- We must agree that we can trust in His love. We must agree that He is for us, not against us, that He is against sin and will not allow those who choose to continue in their sin to entangle the rest, therefore destroying His works. Trying to master sin by fleshy deeds is a spider's web of works that ensnares us. Unless He saves us from the trap we have created by our judgment and accusations, we doom ourselves by our own judgmental thoughts and have no access to the Tree of Life.
- We must agree to have our old nature of spiritual death replaced by the new nature of Jesus Christ. We must give up the old method of goodness based on our overcoming sin by the Law of Righteousness and take up the new Life given to us by the Spirit of Love.

Listen carefully to Me, and eat what is good, And delight yourself in abundance. Incline your ear and come to Me. Listen, that you may live; And I will make an everlasting covenant with you (Isa. 55:2-3).

Final thoughts from Part 1

If God took the time to communicate His own heart through the Life of Jesus Christ, would it not be a good idea to know what He intended to say? Do not listen to any man as a guide to the truth (and that includes me), for if we claim to hear God, you should be able to hear Him also. It is your eternal life that is on the line. Other men have already placed their bets on what they think is true and may be wrong. They remain forever wrong! As you look over and think about the list above, ask yourself this question: "What in this life is more important than knowing the God of Creation and His love?" The answer: Nothing!

If you are not joined to Jesus Christ, if you do not know Him personally, now is a good time to reach out to Him. He has always been close to you. He longs to hug you with great joy, if you are willing to turn around, stop rebelling, and put yourself in His capable hands (Luke 15:4-10).

Tree of Life

I permitted Myself to be sought by those who did not ask for Me; I permitted Myself to be found by those who did not seek Me. I said, 'Here am I, here am I,' To a nation which did not call on My name. I have spread out My hands all day long to a rebellious people, Who walk in the way which is not good, following their own thoughts, a people who continually provoke Me to My face... (Isaiah 65:1-3).

May your trust in the God of Love be a Tree of Life to you.

The LOGOS of God is the Tree of Life

A Journey to Discover the Heart of God

Part Two

In The Beginning was the LOGOS of God

A choice we must make, a question we must answer.

As a result, we are no longer to be children, tossed here and there by waves and carried about by every wind of doctrine, by the trickery of men, by craftiness in deceitful scheming; but speaking the truth in love, we are to grow up in all aspects into Him who is the head, even Christ, from whom the whole body, being fitted and held together by what every joint supplies, according to the proper working of each individual part, causes the growth of the body for the building up of itself in love (Ephesians 4:14-16).

Tree of Life

In The Beginning was the LOGOS of God

Chapter 11

The Meaning behind the Words

Yahweh uses real life events to give meaning to His Word

From that time Jesus Christ began to show His disciples that He must go to Jerusalem, and suffer many things from the elders and chief priests and scribes, and be killed, and be raised up on the third day. And Peter took Him aside and began to rebuke Him, saying, "God forbid it, Lord! This shall never happen to You." But He turned and said to Peter, "Get behind Me, Satan! You are a stumbling block to Me; <u>for you are not setting your mind on God's interests, but man's</u>" (Matt. 16:21-23).

For whoever wishes to save his life shall lose it; but whoever loses his life for My sake shall find it. <u>For what will a man be profited, if he gains the whole world, and forfeits his soul? Or what will a man give in exchange for his soul</u> (Mark 8:35-36).

You recognize these verses? You're sooo observant. You have noticed that we spoke about these in Part 1. Are you impressed that I could get many ideas from one set of scripture verses? I am not impressed, for there is sooo much meaning in God's words that we will spend a lifetime trying to understand them.

For example, take the smallest verse in the Bible, "Jesus wept" (John 11:35). The obvious meaning is that Jesus shed tears. Looking deeper, we see that Jesus cared for another person and their feelings moved Him. Reading the context of the chapter, we know that Jesus was about to raise Lazarus from the dead. Jesus was a friend of Lazarus and had stayed at Lazarus's house (Luke 10:38-42) where Mary later anointed His feet with a costly perfume (John 12:1-8).

We read that Martha and Mary sent for Jesus saying, "He whom you love is sick" (John 11:5). We learn that they thought of Jesus Christ as a friend of the family. Jesus Christ knew the Father was about to use Him to raise Lazarus. He trusted in the Father so much that He waited before leaving (John 11:6). He wanted everyone to know that Lazarus was physically dead and not just in a coma or something. Jesus knew the extra time Lazarus was in the tomb would

Tree of Life

magnify the miracle of Lazarus's bodily resurrection. They already believed that Jesus could keep someone from dying (Mark 5:22-43). He also wanted them to see that death, even after many days, was no match for Him (John 11:17). He wanted them to trust their eternity to Him (John 11:23-26).

Jesus also knew there would be much happiness and celebrating after Lazarus walked out of the tomb. People were going to be so amazed! If you were to receive a loved one back from the grave, wouldn't you celebrate? If I were in Jesus' place, I would have anticipated joyful reactions. It was going to be such a dramatic demonstration of God's power. If I knew God was about to use me in such a way and change the lives of people I love, then I would be thinking, "You cry now but wait just a moment, you're going to forget about all crying." Think about it. Don't you believe that this should have been a joyous occasion in the heart of Jesus Christ? Jesus knew that their tears would soon be turning to joy.

"Jesus wept." What was happening in the heart of Jesus Christ the Messiah that caused His tears to flow? What was He seeing and feeling? John 11:33 tells us. When He saw them weeping, He was greatly moved. How about that! We have a God that is GREATLY MOVED BY OUR TEARS! He knows the ending. He knows how good we are going to have it after He finishes His task. He knows the struggles we go through to get to the place He has prepared and the good we will find there. Yet when He sees us in the condition we are in, He feels for us and is GREATLY MOVED!

He saw the pain Lazarus's death had caused in the people He loved. He felt the same pain they felt and He knew the agony His waiting caused them. It was for everyone's good that Lazarus come back to life after a long period in the grave. The time in the grave was the exclamation point on the Father's power to overcome death. Nevertheless, Jesus knew that it hurt and there were many more whose loved ones would not come back to life in their lifetimes.

We have such an awesome God because He cares. He knows what He is allowing in our lives is good. He also knows that sometimes what we need the most hurts the most. He understands the pain He causes when He waits, but also knows the good that waiting does. So, He waits to act and He is "GREATLY MOVED" by our pain. It hurts Him when doing what is right hurts us. It does not need

In The Beginning was the LOGOS of God

to bother Him. He could just say, "That's the way it is, so learn to live with it. At the right time I will take care of it." Instead our God is an awesome God because He cares! He feels our pain!

You see there is much meaning behind God's words. Yahweh paints pictures using real life events like Lazarus's death and resurrection to communicate His thoughts to us. Anyone who has the Holy Spirit as a teacher can understand His meaning. He helps us apply the scriptures to our world and our lives. He helps us relate to one whose beloved brother died. He leads us to share their feelings and bring those feelings into the context of today's life. Their pain is for our enlightenment. We learn from their experiences.

The Holy Spirit helps us ask the questions that open the true meaning. Questions that we might ask are, "What if it was one of us who were about to bring someone back to life, how would we feel?" "What would the reactions of those watching be?" "What caused Jesus to weep in that circumstance?"

The phrase, "Jesus wept" tells us about an emotion belonging to the Son of God. We need to stop, ask the Holy Spirit questions, listen for His answers, and meditate on what is He is saying. We need to ask the Holy Spirit to help us know His Word and the meaning He puts behind His Word. We should not pass over His words in a flash of devotional time but must incorporate their meaning into the fabric of our lives. You could stop right now and think about what those two words are saying. Think about how He cares about you. Think about how He knows every detail of your life (Psalms 139). He loves you. He weeps and rejoices over you and with you.

Tuning in the mind of God

We need to go back to the verses that started this chapter. (I hope you enjoyed the thoughts about Jesus Christ caring as much as I did.) Did you realize that Peter received a compliment in the verses just before these in Matt. 16? Jesus told Peter the Holy Spirit had revealed something to him. Then, Peter turns right around and listens to Satan. Peter pulls Jesus aside and rebukes Him! It was not Jesus who needed correction. It was Peter. Jesus said Peter was setting his mind on man's interests and not on Yahweh's interests.

Tree of Life

Did you ever think of Yahweh as having "interests? The King James Version of the Bible puts it this way. "*Get Thee behind me, Satan: Thou art an offense to me: for Thou savourest not the things that be of God, but those of men*" *(Matt 16:23)*. Savourest the things of God, has a ring to it don't you think? The word "savourest" is **φρονέω phroneō** (Strong's 5426), which means, "To have understanding, to think." The NASB translates it as "setting your mind." Would you have ever have thought about the "the things of God" as being in His "interest?" Jesus wanted Peter to set His mind away from what *man* thinks about and place his mind (Savourest) on what *God* thinks. Have you ever thought that Yahweh has specific interests? Ever think that Yahweh wants you to think about what is important to Him? I mean, our issues move Him. Shouldn't His issues move us?

The Greek word used here for stumbling block is **σκάνδαλον skandalon** (Strong's numbering 4625). Its meaning is like baiting a trap or an object that causes one to stumble. The NASB translates **skandalon** in Romans 16:17 as "hindrances," used by Paul to describe teachings that are contrary to those of the Holy Spirit. Now pause a minute and think about what Jesus was saying to Peter, His chosen disciple, and apply it to your own life. Where are you in Jesus Christ's estimation? Are you an "offense" or a "stumbling block" to the Creator of the Universe? Peter thought according to the interests of men, according to his own viewpoint, and he became a stumbling block to his Lord.

If your thoughts promote the interest of men, they do not promote the interests of God. You are thinking contrary to God's thoughts and are in opposition to Him. When you open your mouth and tell people what you think, you argue against what God tells them. Do you want the Judge of all to find you in opposition to Him?

If you oppose His will by promoting the interests of men, you commit yourself to an attitude that works everything for evil to those who believe and are called to His purpose (Rom. 8:28). Isaiah 55 tells us that Yahweh will do all that He intended in His heart. Those who oppose Him will not like the results. You may say that you do not believe in Hell, but are you prepared to bet your eternal soul that it does not exist? (Rev. 19:19-20:15). Hey, you can have all the contrary thoughts you want when it comes to my thinking. You need

In The Beginning was the LOGOS of God

to be more careful when it comes to what Yahweh is thinking. You need to devote yourself to honest inquiry and study of the LOGOS (WORD) of God. You need to study the person of God! You need to know the One who stretched out the heavens and filled it with stars.

You need to be careful and know for certain that you are not spiritually traveling a pathway that takes its cue from the tree of death. He has not revealed all Truth. Finding all the truth on all subjects is not your quest. You cannot know the depths of God's heart by focusing on the works performed by men or by knowing the depth of secret knowledge. Jesus Christ is the heart of God's thinking. It is not that Jesus is thinking like God. He is exactly what God has been thinking from the beginning.

Peter received a compliment from Jesus and then a rebuke all in one standing. He was listening to the Holy Spirit one minute and Satan the next. This was because he did not constantly center his mind and intentions, on God's mind and intentions. Later, Peter made a stand for his Lord and he centered his mind on the issues of God. What about you? Do the interests of God interest you? He is the one who cries when you cry and rejoices when you rejoice. He has great joy when a lost one accepts His offer and becomes found (Luke 15:3-24). Remember, Jesus wept because He was greatly moved. The great religious acts people do to impress the Father are not what interest Him. It is His people themselves. He knows the number of hairs on your head (And how big the bald spot is getting) (Matt. 10:30 Luke 12:7).

What is in the Bible anyway?

The Bible is about Yahweh, the God of Creation. The Bible took place in real time and is not a make-believe tale in a storybook world. It is about real people living real lives and feeling real emotions before a real God. It's about a real God becoming a real man and living a real life with real feelings, like yours and mine. In doing so, He showed us that He understands what it is like to live a human life. He shows that He knows what it is like to lose someone He loved very much. He tells us things in the Bible that are important to Him. He wants to make them a part of our everyday real lives. He knows that He is the answer to the evil freely working in the lives of men. When men know and understand God, they love Him and begin

Tree of Life

to love those who travel with Him. The hardness of their hearts softens to the point where their actions toward others promote friendship and a fellowship like what Jesus Christ has with His Father.

The Bible is full of chapters like Matt. 11. We read about miracles, like Jesus raising Lazarus from the dead, helping blind men to see, and healing women from sickness. But we get so ingrained in earthly thinking that we miss thoughts like, "Jesus wept." It is a short verse, takes no time to read. It is easy to pass over such verses without much thought. We can miss the "message, Yahweh is communicating. We need to listen and change the way we think so we may take on the way our God thinks. Like in Isaiah 55:8-9, His thoughts are much greater than our thoughts. His thoughts are Life and the Light of men (John 1:4).

In Part 1, we spent time looking at the thinking of men. This thinking causes spiritual death. Mankind focuses on the Law of Right and Wrong, which, applied to their lives, makes them feel like they can never live holy lives, so they want to give up. (Or they are not honest about sin and become prideful in their goodness.) When they apply the Law of Right and Wrong to other people's lives, they begin to judge each other, which causes them to disrespect each other and they begin to hate.

Jesus gave us the Message almost 2,000 years ago and we have yet to learn the lesson. The truth of Love is in the verses of the Bible. God's Love is deep in the meaning of the words. The Message can change a person, starting inside where no one else can see. It turns a hurtful feeling into a grateful feeling. If we listen to the Message, there will be no more war. Fighting between two friends would not happen. Families would not break up because the parents could not get along. Jesus showed us what it would take to turn sinful lifestyles into loving caring lifestyles.

September 11, 2001, was a day that touched many people's lives. Many of us cried as we watched men and women look for their loved ones. Many of us were moved by the grief and fear in the eyes of those facing loss, causing us to relate to the victims and what they must have felt, causing us to cry with them. There is a God who looks over the face of the earth and sees victims of sin of hate and is GREATLY MOVED to tears every day. Grief and fear are present in

In The Beginning was the LOGOS of God

every part of the globe. We must want to know the heart of a God who cries and rejoices over His people.

I am sad to say not everyone cried September 11, 2001. They could not make the connection and didn't feel anyone's pain. I am sad to say there are people who read the Bible and do not want to think about what made Jesus weep. They do not know nor do they care, that God is GREATLY MOVED by what afflicts the people around them.

How about you?

Focusing on the thinking of this world causes our hearts to harden to the hardships others face. The Message from Yahweh can soften the stone of our hearts and replace it with a heart of caring, true caring (Eze. 11:15-20 and 36:21-29, Jer. 31:31-34).

May Yahweh's compassion be a Tree of Life to you.

Tree of Life

Chapter 12

In the Beginning was Jesus

In the Beginning was the Message

In the beginning was the Word, and the Word was with God, and the Word was God. He was in the beginning with God. All things came into being by Him, and apart from Him nothing came into being that has come into being. In Him was life, and the life was the light of men. And the light shines in the darkness, and the darkness did not comprehend it (John 1:1-5).

There was the true light which, coming into the world, enlightens every man. *He was in the world, and the world was made through Him, and the world did not know Him He came to His own, and those who were His own did not receive Him.*

But as many as received Him, to them He gave the right to become children of God, to those who believe in His name, who were born not of blood, nor of the will of the flesh, nor of the will of man, but of God. *And the Word became flesh, and dwelt among us,* and we beheld His glory, glory as of the only begotten from the Father, full of grace and truth (John 1:9-14).

No man has seen God at any time; *the only begotten God, who is in the bosom of the Father, He has explained* (John 1:18).

In the beginning, before there was anything else, there was I AM (הָיָה **hayah**), the Person of God (Exodus 3:14, John 1:1-3). In the beginning, before there was any creature, there was the Word that created all and for whom all was created. In the beginning, הָיָה (I AM) had something to communicate to those who would listen. The Message הָיָה (I AM) wished to communicate originated from the deepest part of His being and came forth as the Word of God. הָיָה (I AM) sent forth the Message to perform the desire of His heart. The Message reveals what makes "I AM" who HE IS (I AM Who I AM) (Ex. 3:14). The Message is the essence of His person, which He longs for us to know.

The Message is the Designer and Creator of the universe and therefore its owner. All that exist in the physical world belongs to

In The Beginning was the LOGOS of God

Him and He has the right to do with it as He pleases. He can tear apart this planet in a fiery blast by the awesome power of the word of His voice. There is no one who can stop Him. When we think of creative power, we must also realize the same power used to create can destroy. There is no one who can force Him to be compassionate toward those whom He has created. We are His to do with as He pleases; if He wishes to torture us, who in heaven or earth could stop Him? Instead He has sent the Message to declare His Love. The Message claims that, "We have a God that is GREATLY MOVED with compassion towards His creation. He was so moved by their condition that He became like them to guarantee their well-being (John 1:14, 3:16, Rom. 5).

In Exodus 3:14, when Moses asked about His name, He said "I Am Who I AM." The meaning of His name states the fact that He exists, and refers to how He exists, by pointing to His character. I AM (I Exist) is not enough of a description! I Am Who I Am (I Exist as I Exist) refer to the person inside who makes up the Being of God. The Message, sent from the heart of Yahweh, reveals what Yahweh considers to be His most important characteristics.

The LOGOS is the meaning behind the words

When the Holy Spirit said in John 1, "The Word became flesh," He tells us the Word became like one of us. John 1 declares the Person of God descended to our level and joined us in our limited human existence. He felt the same hunger we feel, the same weariness we feel, and the same sorrow we feel. He wept and understands why we weep. The Message declares that Yahweh wants to companion with us, here, now, and without reservation. Think about it: the Message (the Word) is the Creator of everything and everything was created through Him. He wants to companion with us by becoming like us. In doing so, He makes us like Him. The Message is Light and the Life of men. He becomes like us, so He might become one with us, so He may shine in us, and turn our lives of darkness into lives of Light.

In the beginning, before any creative work happened, before there was an earth or any other planet, before there were stars or angels or any created thing, there was the Word of God **λόγος logos**. The Message is the Light of the Word of God (LOGOS) and is all

Tree of Life

wisdom and the fullness of the Godhead bodily (Col. 1:13-20). He is all that we need to be "like God". That is, we need Him to recreate in us His image (Romans 8:29, Col. 3:1-14).

The Word is Life and the Light of men. In the beginning, before there was any created thing, our God had something He wished to communicate to us, and He works among us now to aid our understanding of His Message (Jer. 11:1-5, John 3:16, Romans 5:8 1 John 1:1-2:11 and 4:1-5:12).

The original Greek word used in John 1 is **λόγος logos** (Strong's numbering 3056), and translates as "Word." It comes from the Greek word **λέγω legō** (Strong's numbering 3004g). **legō** is not derived from another Greek word; it is a primary root word. The NAS Bible normally translates **legō** as "to say." In other translations, **legō** may be translated both "word" and "to say."

It is interesting to look at the differences in the two similar Greek words and their meanings. As I best understand the meaning of **legō**, it is an expression of an idea, articulated speech. The words used to get an idea or thought across. The meaning of **logos** is the intended meaning carried by a set of words and normally translated, "word." To write this chapter, I have already used many words assembled into sentences and paragraphs. That would be my **legō**. But to understand the purpose of my words, one would need to get the meaning I intended to convey, which would be my **logos**. With the Lord's help, I pray that I write the **legō** of this book well enough that you can understand my **logos**.

Someone could supply their own meaning (**logos**) to my words and claim my meaning is something different than what I intended. If someone supplies a meaning to my words that is different from the meaning I intended, it would no longer be my LOGOS for it would no longer be the thinking I thought while I wrote these words. If someone supplied a different meaning to my words than what I intended, it would be their **logos**. It would be a reflection of their thinking and not mine.

I cannot stop someone from reading their meaning into my words. If they do, it is because they want my words to say something they want to hear. The reader can twist the meaning of my words and get something far different than my way of thinking. I most likely will disagree with what they claim I said. They may then say, "You

In The Beginning was the LOGOS of God

said this and now you are changing your mind." The truth will be that I have, within me, what I intend to say. If they supply their own meaning, it is not any longer what I say. If someone wishes to know my heart, then he would have to divorce himself from his thinking to understand mine.

Such it is with the false teachers of this world. They supply their own meanings to the words God has written and changed them from the Word (thinking) of God into the words (thinking) of men. Like the Pharisees of the Jewish religion, (Matt. 23:1-39) false teachers in the Christian Churches are twisting the meaning of God's words. They supply their own meaning and fight those who live the true meaning of what God intended to say. They argue with Yahweh and call Him a liar (1 John 5:9-12). They are the darkness of this present age and they hate the Light (John 3:20, 1 John 2:9-11). They claim to teach according to the Gospel of the Bible, but they use the Gospel to disguise their lies. They feed on the teachings they received from the Tree of the Knowledge of Good and Evil. Their followers eat the same garbage they feed on and then spread the same darkness as if it were Light.

No doubt Jesus is the Word of God

When Jesus entered the course of human history, the people of Israel expected Yahweh to reveal His prophesied Messiah (Daniel 9:22-27). John the Baptist sparked the interest of the whole nation with his preaching, causing them to think to themselves that, "Now the time has come." When John the Baptist pointed out Jesus as the Messiah and then baptized Him (John 1:19-36), the people began debating whether Jesus could be the Messiah. It was the major topic of conversation (John 7:25-31, Luke 3:15).

Religious leaders did not like what Jesus (the LOGOS of God) was saying. They did not like the Message He gave and disliked that He did not seek their approval. They did not like that He was directing the crowd to the Father directly and not making them the intermediate to Yahweh. So, they killed Jesus instead of recognizing Him as their King. Imagine killing the Message of Life and the Word of Light, sent to enlighten all men, without whom they could not exist. They killed their own Breath of Life.

Tree of Life

If His thoughts were like the common thoughts of men, they would feel the full fury of God. But the Message, sent from the heart of Yahweh, spoke clearly that God is not like man, God is Love. The death of Jesus Christ was not a miscalculation. Instead it was essential to the plan from the beginning. Jesus died on the cross to explain the LOGOS (meaning) of His communication in the Bible. His death was a calculated act designed to benefit our well-being. Through this one act, God grants those who receive the gift a place in the Body of Christ to share His Life as a branch shares life with the vine (John 15:1-11).

Jesus Christ shined Light into the darkness of men's minds by correcting false teachings, thus angering the ruling Jewish religious authorities. (Matt. 5:17-20). They perceived Him to be a threat when He refocused men's minds away from their interpretations of the scriptures and applied the true meaning to what God wrote. (Matt. 5:21-48) The Pharisees and Sadducees worked against Jesus because He undermined their manmade place in the minds of men (John 7:31-32). Jesus' education was not from their religious schools and therefore they thought Him uneducated (John 7:14-17). His education came from the Holy Spirit. Therefore, He was not a teacher of their making and not a reflection on them or what they believed. Jesus taught men about a path to righteousness that was different from what they taught.

Men were listening to the Message instead of them and He became a threat to their position in life. They wanted Him removed. They tried to find fault with what He taught and tried to entrap Him in what He said. Instead, they entrapped themselves (John 8:1-11). Little did they understand the Scriptures they quoted. When entrapment did not work, they conspired to kill Him. The Pharisees opposed the Message from Yahweh because their teachings were of darkness. He brought the Light of understanding to the Scriptures. The Pharisees twisted the meaning of the Scriptures and added their own thinking to them. In doing so, they added to the confusion among those who longed to know the truth.

The Pharisees focused on the interest of men. They argued with God, and became an obstacle to His work. (They did not think of themselves as opposing God, but they were.) The Pharisees taught from an understanding they received from the Tree of the Knowledge

In The Beginning was the LOGOS of God

of Good and Evil. They were on the opposite side from the Giver of Life. Men looking on might have thought that they were just disagreeing on a religious belief. But the Light had come and the darkness refused the Light.

It is like that today also. The false teachings of so-called "Christian Leaders" oppose God's thinking by promoting man's thinking. It may look like a difference in opinions between two believers. Instead, it is God's thinking vs. man's thinking, which is Life vs. death. The Creator uses the wickedness of the Pharisees to carry out the greatest act known to civilization. In rebellion and hatred, they hung the Son of God from a cross for a crime He did not commit. But by dying on the cross, Jesus Christ made everlasting life available to all who believe. With a heart of Love, Jesus Christ forgave those who killed Him. He removed the sin that separated us from Him by joining His sinless being to ours. He did not wait until we were clean but took us into Him, while we were His enemies. He made our sin His own and then bore the penalty for those sins (2 Cor. 5:18-21). Jesus Christ changed an instrument of death and torment into a Tree of Life (Romans 5). He joined us to His death so He could join us to His Life (Romans 6).

Jesus Christ came as a Light to the hearts of men. Darkness does not overcome the Light but is overcome by the Light. You can buy a flashlight to create light in the darkness. You cannot buy anything that creates darkness where there is light. You can block out the light and create an absence of light, which we call darkness. The absence of Yahweh's thinking causes darkness in man. Shining His thoughts into the man's thinking drives the darkness out of that man, the same way the light of day replaces the darkness of night (Luke 11:33-36). Understanding Jesus Christ's teaching will enlighten the minds and hearts those who listen. We take the time to look more deeply into the words and find the meaning that is there. Knowing the person, Jesus Christ, is more important than knowing what He said and did, but you need to know what He said and did to know Him. Understanding who Jesus Christ is, and what makes Him what He is, brings Light into the darkened world of a man's heart.

Tree of Life

What to eat?

With all the conflicting claims from today's religious leaders, how can you know what is the "True Word of God?" Read the Bible yourself and rely on the Holy Spirit to guide you. Those lead by the Holy Spirit will find Jesus Christ. The Person of God is the "True Word of God." Knowledge of right and wrong is the by-product of knowing Him and not the destination. If what you find is knowledge, you are looking in the wrong places for the wrong stuff. Jesus Christ is the "True Life."

When we see the Bible through the Life of Jesus Christ, we have access to the Tree of Life. Those who do not believe will lessen what the cross teaches, calling it foolishness. But it is a symbol of Life and salvation to those who believe in the Message the LOGOS of God (1 Cor. 1:18). Take time now and think about the God who hung on the cross of sin and shame for our well-being. Think about the One who forgave all of our sins. Our God is now ready and willing to clean us of all unrighteousness (1 John 2:1). Think about what motivates God. What caused Him to become a man and die on a cross? Jesus Christ delivered the Message that describes the heart of the person that I AM is. We must look past the religious garbage that we hear every day and find the meaning the Author of the Bible intended to say, about Himself. The message He communicated comes from the deepest part of who HE IS. Be still and know I AM God (Psalms 46:10).

May LOGOS be a Tree of Life to you.

In The Beginning was the LOGOS of God

Chapter 13

Jesus Christ is the True Meaning

Jesus is what the Bible is talking about
    Many, O Lord my God, are the wonders which Thou hast done, And Thy thoughts toward us; There is none to compare with Thee; If I would declare and speak of them, They would be too numerous to count. Sacrifice and meal offering Thou hast not desired; My ears Thou hast opened; Burnt offering and sin offering Thou hast not required. <u>Then I said, "Behold, I come; In the scroll of the book it is written of me; I delight to do Thy will, O my God; Thy Law is within my heart." I have proclaimed glad tidings of righteousness in the great congregation;</u> Behold, I will not restrain my lips, O Lord, Thou knowest I have not hidden Thy righteousness within my heart; <u>I have spoken of Thy faithfulness and Thy salvation;</u> I have not concealed Thy lovingkindness and Thy truth from the great congregation (Psalms 40:5-10).

    Therefore, when He comes into the world, He says, "Sacrifice and offering Thou hast not desired, But a body Thou hast prepared for Me; In whole burnt offerings and sacrifices for sin Thou hast taken no pleasure." Then I said, 'Behold, I have come (In the roll of the book it is written of Me) To do Thy will, O God.'" After saying above, "Sacrifices and offerings and whole burnt offerings and sacrifices for sin Thou hast not desired, nor hast Thou taken pleasure in them" (which are offered according to the Law), then He said, "Behold, I have come to do Thy will." <u>He takes away the first in order to establish the second. By this will we have been sanctified through the offering of the body of Jesus Christ once for all</u> (Heb. 10:5-10).

    Read all of Psalms 40 and Hebrews 10, which speak of Jesus Christ as being our sin offering. Old Testament Law dealt with sin by instituting animal sacrifices. Psalms 40 tells us that animal sacrifices were not pleasing to God the Father. A sin offering was necessary but not gratifying, because it involves sin. Sacrifices and offerings are not what Yahweh wanted. Animals dying and bloodshed represented the seriousness of sin. The wages of sin is death (Romans

Tree of Life

6:19-23, 2 Tim. 1:3-9). The animal sacrifice did not stop men from sinning, for it did not cleanse anyone from their sinful nature. It only pointed to a need for atonement and looking ahead to a better solution. God the Father allowed men to substitute certain animals instead of requiring the death of the sinner. Look at sin from Yahweh's viewpoint. There would be no need to atone for sin if no one committed sin. He would rather we live in such a way that there was nothing to atone for. The death of the bulls, goats, sheep, and doves were not pleasing to the Creator.

Like a father, the Creator of the Universe would rather His children not sin. Parents want to see their children succeed and do well in life. Our God wants to see us succeed. His solution is deeper and much richer than just covering up the sin or justifying the sinner. He wants His people to win over sin and eliminate the need for any more sacrifices and bloodshed. This is why He sent Jesus Christ to be the LOGOS of God. He came with the Message of Love: to give those who receive Him the power to overcome their sinful natures and to become children of God (1 John 2:1, John 1:1-14).

Under animal sacrifices, the people continued in their sin. Thus the need for a better sacrifice. In Psalms 40:7-8, the prophecy of the Messiah said, *"Sacrifice and meal offering Thou hast not desired; My ears Thou hast opened; Burnt offering and sin offering Thou hast not required."* Then I said, "Behold, I come; in the scroll of the book it is written of me; *I delight to do Thy will, O my God; Thy Law is within my heart."* Jesus Christ fulfills this prophecy as explained in Heb. 10. He came to do the will of Him who sent Him. The Scripture tells us about Jesus Christ to explain who He is and the purpose He fulfilled by His visit on Earth.

To grasp the message that He came to communicate, you must first understand the truth about sin. Embedded into the story of Adam eating of the Tree of the Knowledge of Good and Evil is the predicament of sin, with the resulting legacy of sin and spiritual death. The Message involves sin but is not about sin. It is about Love overpowering sin and therefore being the answer to sin. The Holy Spirit wrote the scripture to tell of the LOGOS of God. The LOGOS had a body prepared for Him so He could do the will of Him who sent Him. Yahweh's will is this: "No longer should there be a need to cover sin." This can only be true if there is no sin to cover.

In The Beginning was the LOGOS of God

Thy Law is written within My Heart

Jesus Christ lived the will of the Father and did not sin. Finally on the stage of humanity, there is a human being who is without sin, who lives according to the intent of the Law, and does not need a sacrifice to atone for sin. The Life that Jesus Christ lived is pleasing to Yahweh because when there is no sin, there is no need for penalty. Because there is no sin there is no need for death. As a result, Jesus Christ's Life has the power to conquer death (Romans 6:1-14). Those who share in the sinless life that Jesus Christ lived also share in His power over death.

In Hebrews, the Holy Spirit gives a detailed analysis of how the sacrifices of the Law failed to cleanse men of their sin (Heb. 7:1-10:25). He tells how the High Priest had to give a sacrifice for himself first and then for the nation. The Holy Spirit points out that it was necessary to repeat the sacrifice annually because it failed to remove sin. In Hebrews 10, He uses the verses in Psalms to show that Jesus Christ fulfills the Law's provision. When it says in Psalms, "I come, I delight to do Thy will," it also says, "Thy Law is within my heart."

The Law and Jesus Christ are one and the same. The purpose of the Old Testament is to write about Jesus Christ and about the Law written on His heart. Jesus Christ fulfills the Law, because HE IS the Law. He fulfills the Law because He is God and the Law is a reflection of who God is. The Law is not a foreign idea that Jesus Christ molds Himself into. He is the mold the Law is cast from. The Law is a description of His character. He does not work to fulfill the Law. It is the natural outcome of His nature. Those who share His Life automatically have the Law written within their hearts and fulfilling the law is the natural outcome of His life in them.

Those who believe that Yahweh would lay aside the Law so He could accept them into His presence make a sad mistake, for that would mean laying aside His nature. Jesus proclaimed the Law would not be abolished until Heaven and Earth passes away (Matt. 5:17-22, Luke 16:14-17). Jesus did not come in bodily form to supersede the Law but to fulfill its True Meaning. Jesus Christ does not face judgment. He fulfilled the will of the Father and did not sin. All others who have lived on this earth have fallen short of the will of the Father and are not clean but are guilty before the Judge (Romans

Tree of Life

3:10-22). Men fail to keep the Law and need a substitute according to the Law or face judgment according to the Law.

Now I make known to you, brethren, the gospel which I preached to you, which also you received, in which also you stand, by which also you are saved, if you hold fast the word which I preached to you, unless you believed in vain. <u>*For I delivered to you as of first importance what I also received, that Christ died for our sins according to the Scriptures, and that He was buried, and that He was raised on the third day according to the Scriptures*</u> *(1Cor. 15:1-4).*

On the Cross at Calvary, a demonstration took place that revealed the full meaning of the Law. Yahweh openly displayed for all to see a human who lived under the same conditions as other men, but without committing sin. The creatures Jesus created rejected Him and crucified Him. He forgave them and died as a substitution for their sin. They buried Him in a tomb over the Sabbath rest, and He resurrected on the third day, according to previous writings in the Scriptures.

He did not need to pay a penalty for sin and did not need a substitute but rather became our substitute and the judgment for our sin was on Him (Isa. 53:4-8). All of us have sinned and need a substitute to atone for our sins. A death must take place for our sin because the penalty for sin is death (Romans 6:23). He grants us the right to share in the perfect life He lived. For us to share in the Life of Jesus Christ, we also must share in the Death of Jesus Christ. If we are in Jesus Christ as He died and it is for a man to live and die once, then we cannot die a second time and the second death does not have power over us (Rev. 20:6-14, 21:8, 2:11). Since Jesus Christ shares His Life with us, we share our life with Him. There is still a need for a death because of the sin in our life, but Jesus Christ has already died in our place and took the penalty for our sin. It is now no longer us who live according to the sinful ways of man, but Jesus Christ who lives in us according to the will of the Godhead (Gal. 2:20). Now we, too, have the same power over death that Jesus Christ has. This is a hard teaching to understand but it is Life everlasting. Sin is a serious matter and Jesus Christ represents the serious answer.

In The Beginning was the LOGOS of God

Romans 5 examines Christ's death on the cross and explains that God's Son died to atone for His enemies, because He loved them. He died for those who opposed and hated Him, because He loves those who hated Him (Matt. 5:38-48, Luke 6:20-46). In John 15:13, Jesus told us there is no greater love than the love that causes one to lay down his life for a friend. While we might do so for a friend, He willingly died for His enemies.

We have opposed Jesus Christ at some time or another. When it says that He died for His enemies, the Bible is talking about you and I being His enemies (Eph. 2:1-4). Love's Demonstration as found in His death is so important that we must spend time meditating on it. We need to understand the Message Yahweh has sent to us through it.

What is Jesus Christ communicating by atoning our sin?
"Teacher, which is the great commandment in the Law?" And He said to him, "'You shall love the Lord your God with all your heart, and with all your soul, and with all your mind.' This is the great and foremost commandment. The second is like it, 'You shall love your neighbor as yourself.' "<u>On these two commandments depend the whole Law and the Prophets</u> *(Matt. 22:36-40).*

I suggest to you that Love is the summary of the intent of the Law and written on Jesus Christ's Heart. The Message tells us about the Love Yahweh has for us and is the example we are to learn, so we may be able to love one another (John 15:9-17, 1 John 4:1-21). Love fulfills the Law, the Law describes who Jesus Christ is, and Jesus Christ reveals the great "I AM WHO I AM."

The Message is about holiness based on Love. The Message is about placing our faith in Yahweh's Love. It is about trusting that Love will change our approach to righteousness. We trust Jesus Christ to change our souls into His image, as we become like Him and love as He loves. His Love motivates us to live according to the will of the Father, the same way He lived according to the will of the Father. We become cleansed from our sin. His Love fills us and causes us to love not only those who love us but also our enemies. We are to love those who strongly oppose us - in the same way He loved and gave Himself for those who hated Him. He calls us to

Tree of Life

follow His teachings and live our lives in Love just as He lived His Life in Love. By living according to the Light of Love, we show we are His disciples (John 13:34-35).

If Love (Jesus) is the foundation of the Law, we must conclude that by abiding in Love and living according to Love, we also fulfill the Law as He fulfills the Law. If we fulfill the Law by the love we have for one another, there remains no condemnation (Romans 8:1-3). If by Love He fulfilled the Law, it follows that all those whom the Holy Spirit is changing into His image also love and fulfill the Law. His Spirit will guide those who set their minds on the interest of God (Romans 8:1-14). Where there is no Law, there is no violation of the Law (Romans 4:15). Where there is no sin, there is no need for atonement. There is no Law written against Love (Gal. 5:13-26). Therefore Love fulfills the Law (Rom. 13:8-10).

What good is the Word of God without the meaning of God?

In the beginning was the Word, and the Word was with God, and the Word was God. He was in the beginning with God. All came into being by Him, and apart from Him nothing came into being that has come into being. <u>*In Him was life, and the life was the light of men. And the light shines in the darkness, and the darkness did not comprehend it*</u> *(John 1:1-5).*

It is possible to study the Word (LEGO) of God and not be studying the Word (LOGOS) of God. It is possible to apply our own LOGOS to God's LEGO and miss the real message of what our God intended to make known. Those who wish to know the truth must ask, "Are we too focused on becoming righteous and not focused enough on receiving and giving Love, as envisioned by our Maker?" Are we focusing on how well we love others, while ignoring the times we are hateful? Are we so tuned into our benefit that we lose the opportunity to be a benefit? Yahweh communicated the foundation by which He created the universe. He educates us about the law which governs society.

We argue with Him if we teach the Bible as anything other than what Yahweh intended: love given based on the character of the one giving love. If we understand and believe what He intended to say, we are in agreement with Him. Our diet is what we meditate on.

In The Beginning was the LOGOS of God

Meditating on the Message of Love is like eating from spiritually healthy food. Not meditating on the true meaning of Love leaves us spiritually hungry. Think of it another way: When we misinterpret God's Word, we poison our spiritual food. Incorporating worldly thinking into our thinking fills our minds with thoughts that kill us.

I believe many teachers and preachers have used the Word (LEGO) of God to mislead the flock by applying to it their own selfish meanings. If we apply any meaning to the sayings of God other than His original intent, we become false teachers. When we misrepresent the meaning of God's communication, we take Life away. It is spiritual murder to misrepresent the Word of God.

We add to the problems of hate in this world (as we discussed in Part 1). The blood of the innocent is on our hands. We should be careful that we lift the truth up according to Jesus Christ when we stand to teach. Teachers are under a stricter judgment and become even guiltier before God (James 3:1). He takes these matters seriously and will be hard on those who mock Him (Gal. 6:7-10). He loves the people of this earth, therefore we must stand against those whose actions or teachings harm His people.

Look to Jesus Christ for the true meaning

Those who yield to the truth of this communication will learn to think and act as Jesus Christ does, which will conform them to His image (Rom. 8:29, Col. 3:10). Yahweh's communication became a man and remained with His people as a man, and He lived out the Message of Love as intended (John 1:9-14) (See Isa. 55: 7-11, Matt. 5:17, Luke 24:27 and 44, John 5:45, 1 Cor. 15:3 and 4, Heb. 10:7).

The thinking (LOGOS) of man attached to the sayings (LEGO) of God will only bring death to the soul of those who believe such foolishness. Why do we spend time on thoughts that do not have Life in them? To receive the wisdom of God we must have the thinking (LOGOS) of God. We must understand what the Godhead was thinking when He wrote the Bible. The life, death, and resurrection of Jesus Christ revealed what that thinking is. Jesus Christ is the complete fulfillment of the scriptures (1 Cor. 15:1-4, Luke 4:16-22 and 24:13-27, Heb. 10:7).

Tree of Life

The Holy Spirit teaches us about Jesus Christ's love, words, teachings, and actions, which in turn train us in the ways of righteousness. Jesus Christ is the way to the Father (John 14:6). He is the narrow gate that we must find (Matt. 7:12-15). He is the door by which we must enter (John 10:1-18). Anyone who enters without coming through the door is a false prophet and teacher (John 10, Matt. 7:13-23). Jesus Christ is the fullness of the Godhead bodily (Col. 1:19) and is Love (1 John 4:8).

Beware of the false teachers who draw attention to themselves. They will teach that you need them to understand the scriptures. You <u>do</u> need <u>them</u> to understand the Scriptures as <u>they</u> understand them. But you <u>need</u> the <u>Holy Spirit</u> to understand the Scriptures the way the <u>Holy Spirit</u> wrote them (1 Tim 6:3-5, 2 Tim. 3:1-9, James 3:1 and 2, 3:13-4:5, 1 Tim 1:1-6, Matt. 15:7-9 and 12-14). You do not need anyone except the Holy Spirit to understand the truth. If there is anyone telling you that you cannot know the path to the Father without their help, they are false teachers who want to take you captive to their way of thinking!

If someone reads this and wants to argue, I say, "The only way to the Father is through Jesus Christ not through an argument with me." Maybe you wish to argue with me because you want others to follow God by following you. If your need is to have others follow you the same way you follow others, you are in danger of being in opposition to our Creator. Repent such thinking for it is death. Jesus Christ is the only true path. You have nothing to offer others except the offer He is offering them. The Holy Spirit uses other people to help us understand, but does not use one man only and does not use the same man all the time. We are not to gather around one another or have others gather around us, as if we know the way. We are to gather around the Lord Jesus Christ. It is His Life, death, and resurrection that we conform to. He is the only way, for He is the only one who has fulfilled the Law.

May you share Jesus Christ's Life of Love
        and may that fellowship be a Tree of Life to you.

In The Beginning was the LOGOS of God

Chapter 14

The Holy Spirit is Our Teacher

Holy Spirit is the Author of the Scriptures

Yet we do speak wisdom among those who are mature; a wisdom, however, not of this age, nor of the rulers of this age, who are passing away; but we speak God's wisdom in a mystery, the hidden wisdom, which God predestined before the ages to our glory; <u>the wisdom which none of the rulers of this age has understood; for if they had understood it, they would not have crucified the Lord of glory</u>; but just as it is written, "Things which eye has not seen and ear has not heard, And which have not entered the heart of man, All that God has prepared for those who love Him." <u>For to us God revealed them through the Spirit; for the Spirit searches all things, even the depths of God</u>.

For who among men knows the thoughts of a man except the spirit of the man, which is in him? <u>Even so the thoughts of God no one knows except the Spirit of God</u>. <u>Now we have received</u>, not the spirit of the world, but <u>the Spirit who is from God, that we might know the things freely given to us by God, which things we also speak, not in words taught by human wisdom, but in those taught by the Spirit, combining spiritual thoughts with spiritual words.</u>

<u>But a natural man does not accept the things of the Spirit of God</u>; for they are foolishness to him, and he cannot understand them, <u>because they are spiritually appraised</u>. But he who is spiritual appraises all things, yet he himself is appraised by no man. For who has known the mind of the Lord, that he should instruct Him? <u>But we have the mind of Christ</u> (1 Cor. 2: 6-16) (See John 14:26, 15:26, 16:7-15, Eph. 4:30-5:2).

In the beginning before there was time, before there were stars or moons, the Wisdom of Yahweh prepared everything for our benefit. His Wisdom took on flesh and lived among us (John 1:1-3). Wisdom formed the earth and the heavens. Now we have the mystery made known through the Holy Spirit as He teaches of Jesus Christ.

Only the Spirit within God knows the heart of God. If a man has receives the Holy Spirit, he is free to know what God gives him.

Tree of Life

The Holy Spirit combines the Spiritual LEGO of the Bible and with the Spiritual LOGOS of Jesus Christ. The Holy Spirit searches the depths of the man and the depths of the Godhead and considers the complete picture as He reveals the Wisdom of Life in Jesus Christ. Without the Holy Spirit's sealing, such knowledge is impossible. If a man joins as one to Jesus Christ, the Holy Spirit reveals all the good in Jesus Christ and makes it available to that man and the man shares Jesus Christ's inheritance because he shares Jesus Christ's Life.

In the Old Testament days Yahweh spoke to us through the prophets with a precept here and a demonstration there (Heb. 1:1-2). The Holy Spirit used men to record the lessons given through the prophets (1 Peter 1:20-21). We often think of prophets as people who tell the future, but their mission is to reveal the mind and heart of Yahweh. Prophets did not have special spiritual gifts of their own. They were average men and women who spent time with Yahweh. Sometimes Yahweh gave an account of what He was going to do. His purpose for recording what would happen was to show that He knew what was going to happen before it happened. Yahweh's primary motive was to communicate His thinking, not to predict the history of Israel before it happened. Scripture records the historical deeds of the Creator, with His thinking, so we could understand His Love.

In the present day of man's history, Yahweh is speaking through His Son (Heb. 1:1-2). It's not a new message but the same message of the Old Testament said in a different way. It is still the same thinking. The medium has changed from words to the example of Love shown in the life, death, and resurrection of Jesus Christ. The Holy Spirit is still actively working to make the Father known to us. Instead of miracles presented by prophets bearing a message of God's judgment, we have the Message of Love presented by Jesus Christ.

Who can know the mind and heart of "I AM," outside the Spirit of "I AM?" (Rom. 8:26-27). The Holy Spirit bridges the chasm that divides Yahweh from man. His thoughts are wise and so much higher than ours and He sees so much clearer than we do (Isaiah 55:7-9). Our thoughts are not like His thoughts and we could never grasp them on our own.

In The Beginning was the LOGOS of God

The Author of the Scriptures tutors us in the Scriptures
    The Holy Spirit knows the original intent behind the words in the Bible because He is the One who directed men to write the Bible. With the Holy Spirit's help, we can understand the original, intended meaning (LOGOS) of the parables and portions given to us in the Bible. The Holy Spirit searches the heart of Yahweh and searches the heart of men. He knows both sides of the story. He is interceding for us with groanings too deep for words (Romans 8:26-31). Jesus Christ is the clear expression of an unseen God. He takes that which is unknowable and makes it knowable. He gave us the Comforter (Holy Spirit) as a tutor so we would never be on our own again (John 14:16-18 and 26, 15:26-27). Unguided, we are just as helpless as we were before we accepted our new life in Jesus Christ. With His guidance, we have the power to understand. Our understanding is not all at once or as fast as we would like. Remember, His teachings are difficult to understand and even more difficult to practice! It is understandable that we do not change overnight.

    The Holy Spirit knows the design of what our life, our inner being, should be like and how to live according to the design. He has the Words of True Life. Even in difficult times, the Holy Spirit brings us Life full of joy, love for one another, and the comfort of His companionship (Rom. 5:1-5). Seek and you will find, knock and the door will opened, ask and receive. The Father knows how to give good gifts to His children (Luke 11:1-13, Matt. 7:7-14).

    To understand the LOGOS of the Scriptures, we must know the Author of the Scriptures. Only the Author can give true meaning to the Scriptures (2 Peter 1:20-2:3). We have the Holy Spirit sealed with us until the day of redemption (Eph. 1:13-14 and 4:30). He makes a bridge between Yahweh and His people. He helps us understand that which eye has not seen and ear has not heard. His thoughts enter our hearts.

    LOGOS is not available to those outside His companionship. When we try to explain LOGOS to others, they cannot understand what we are saying because they must understand spiritual ideas by applying what is available to them, a worldly thinking. The Holy Spirit applies the spiritual mind of Jesus Christ to the spiritual ideas exemplified in real life. It is impossible for the world to understand the most important message ever delivered in the history of

Tree of Life

humanity, because they are not fellowshipping with the only One who can explain it to them. That is just as true for those who claim to be born-again believers as it is for atheists. Men will interpret the Word of God to suit their own situation because they apply thinking that comes from the Tree of the Knowledge of Good and Evil. They cannot do anything else because they have denied the Truth (LOGOS). They deny the only source of true understanding by denying the Creator of the Universe. If you shut off the only source of water, where can you get water to drink?

Those who believe in the Son of Man as the LOGOS of God naturally walk inside His companionship. They have access to the resources the Holy Spirit provides to know the heart of God. He allows us the privilege of understanding the depths of Love, which develops into trust (faith) based on His Love, and we believe that He will make all things work out to the good in ways we cannot imagine (Romans 8:28). We trust the Wisdom of the His Blueprint.

We do not always see the purpose and the wisdom of the His design. On the last day, when we enter His presence and we hear, "Well done, my good and faithful servant. Enter your rest" (Matt. 25:15-30), we will see that everything had a purpose, a reason, and timing. Our shortsightedness can only see a few years at best. But He looks from the beginning to the end. We only see a few relationships from us, but He sees every relationship, how they connect and how they react to each other. He accounted for everything when He predetermined everything from before the beginning of time.

We look through a glass darkly (1 Cor. 13:8-13). Paul wrote these verses in 1 Cor. as an illustration to remind us that we cannot know the depths of I AM. It will take longer than we have on this earth to do that. Even with the help of the Holy Spirit, no one man can know the depths of God, but the Father knows what is most important and makes it available. We cannot know all, but we can know what He has chosen to reveal. Those who understand His Love have much confidence in His Love. Could we have more confidence? (Faith) Yes! As we yield to the Spirit, we agree that He is the One who can help us grow in our confidence toward our Savior and Lord. We continue to grow as long as we companion with Him in the Light of Love.

In The Beginning was the LOGOS of God

The more we incorporate His thinking into ours, the more He renews us by transforming our mind, which becomes our spiritual service of worship (Rom. 8:29, 12:1-3, 2 Cor. 3:17-4:7, Col. 3:1-17). The more the Holy Spirit reveals the thinking of God, the more we realize just how special He is. The fairness of His judgments draws us. It amazes us that He loves and cares for men even those who least deserve it. We are awed by the power He can muster while at the same time being gentle, kind, and attentive to our needs.

Nobody can know the thoughts of another man, or know the depths of his feelings. So it is with the Eternal God. We cannot reason His thinking out by using artificial knowledge. Yahweh gave everyone enough knowledge to begin the journey (Romans 1:18-22). We cannot find the Most High Sovereign God without the Holy Spirit's help. True believers want the same mind as Jesus Christ and not the mind of a man, no matter how godly a man he is. Men do not naturally have the knowledge of Life in them, only what the Holy Spirit has revealed. They share among themselves what the Holy Spirit reveals. They can learn from each other as the Spirit leads them together through the path of Life. Yet no one thinks they are better than another, no matter how able he is to teach or preach. It is the Holy Spirit who has enabled the gifts in each of us. One gift is not more important than another, but God gives the gifts for the benefit of the body and not the one who bears the gift (1 Cor. 12:1-7, Rom. 12:1-21).

The Holy Spirit is our only teacher,
    HE may use the voice of men to teach other men

It is true that many men come claiming to hear truth from the Holy Spirit when they only hear themselves. They draw many away in error by their cleverly designed speeches and grand-sounding talk. Those who follow such men into error have no one to blame because they were not listening to the Holy Spirit in the first place. If they were listening to the Holy Spirit, they would not remain under a false teacher's influence.

Yet, it is also true that God uses His people to teach His followers. The Holy Spirit used men to record His thoughts in the scriptures. It was not the thinking of men that they recorded and they do not get the credit for what they wrote. He uses men today to make

Tree of Life

known His thinking, but they do not get the credit either. If the writers of the scriptures did not fully know what they were writing but longed to see its fulfillment (1 Peter 1:10-12), then those who teach are no more able to explain it then the ones who wrote it.

Only the Holy Spirit can reveal the truth to a man when another person speaks to Him. Yes, new believers need guidance from older Christians and men receive gifts of understanding to help guide His flock. But Yahweh intended only one man to be the authority behind His message. He intended the Bible to be His written Word (LEGO) and Jesus Christ to fulfill it (LOGOS). Jesus is the only Way, the only Truth, and the only Life. No other man is a facilitator between Yahweh and His people! Each man is responsible for the Light shining on him and is responsible before the Lord for receiving the friendship He offers. No one will stand before the Creator to give answer for another man other than Jesus Christ the Advocate. We cannot point to someone else and claim that they led us astray, for we are all responsible to know Yahweh through the Holy Spirit. Yes, we have a commandment to give an answer for the hope that is in us (1 Peter 3:12-18). But it is the Holy Spirit who gives hope by the words we speak. He gives a heart of Love to share the Good News. It is not about debating. It is about sharing what the Holy Spirit taught us and how that changed us.

Children, it is the last hour; and just as you heard that antichrist is coming, even now many antichrists have arisen; from this we know that it is the last hour. <u>*They went out from us, but they were not really of us; for if they had been of us, they would have remained with us; but they went out, in order that it might be shown that they all are not of us.*</u>

<u>*But you have an anointing from the Holy One, and you all know*</u>*. I have not written to you because you do not know the truth, but because you do know it, and because no lie is of the truth. Who is the liar but the one who denies that Jesus is the Christ? This is the antichrist, the one who denies the Father and the Son. Whoever denies the Son does not have the Father; the one who confesses the Son has the Father also.*

<u>*As for you, let that abide in you which you heard from the beginning. If what you heard from the beginning abides in you, you also will abide in the Son and in the Father.*</u> *And this is the promise*

In The Beginning was the LOGOS of God

which He Himself made to us: eternal life. These things I have written to you concerning those who are trying to deceive you.
     And as for you, the anointing which you received from Him abides in you, and you have no need for anyone to teach you; but as His anointing teaches you about all things, and is true and is not a lie, and just as it has taught you, you abide in Him. And now, little children, abide in Him, so that when He appears, we may have confidence and not shrink away from Him in shame at His coming (1 John 2:18-28).

    False teachers argue that we cannot depend on the average person to understand the scriptures; that people need leaders to guide them in their search. They will justify their existence and convince others they know the right way and all others are wrong. The Holy Spirit tells you in 1 John 2:27 that you are able by His help to understand the meaning of the Scriptures. You need no one to teach you anything. Jesus Christ gives the Helper and seals Him in you to stay with you forever. Will all learn at the same pace? No! But all will learn who listen to the Holy Spirit's voice.

    He may be using someone else's voice, or a book like this one, or a preacher in the pulpit, or a dear beloved friend in the Lord. But it is always the Holy Spirit who is revealing the heart of God to us. We need the Holy Spirit at home, in our spiritual house, guiding us daily regarding what we hear from other sources. We are not alone, struggling to understand what others are saying. He is our Tutor and our constant companion. God promised the Holy Spirit to us and He never breaks a promise.

May the Holy Spirit's guidance be as a Tree of Life to you.

Tree of Life

Chapter 15

Scripture Comes with its Own Meaning

The Holy Spirit gave us the Bible,
    we can understand it by His power

And so we have the prophetic word made more sure, to which you do well to pay attention as to a lamp shining in a dark place, until the day dawns and the morning star arises in your hearts. <u>But know this first of all, that no prophecy of Scripture is a matter of one's own interpretation, for no prophecy was ever made by an act of human will, but men moved by the Holy Spirit spoke from God.</u>

But false prophets also arose among the people, just as there will also be false teachers among you, who will secretly introduce destructive heresies, even denying the Master who bought them, bringing swift destruction upon themselves. And many will follow their sensuality, and because of them the way of the truth will be maligned; and in their greed they will exploit you with false words; their judgment from long ago is not idle, and their destruction is not asleep (2 Peter 1:19-2:3).

To understand the truth, we must first agree with this: no Scripture came about as matter of man's determination, and is not subject to man's interpretation. It is for people to listen, with more than ears, to the words given to them by the Creator Himself. His thoughts will guide the path of the righteous during a time of little understanding until He reveals all.

What I am about to say is very important, maybe the most important point made in the book! Jesus Christ is the **only** Way, the **only** Truth, and the **only** Life (John 14:1-14). No other man can make that claim. I mean, no other man can make a claim like it. He is different from all other men who ever lived. Other men claim to know the way, or the truth, or the life. But Jesus Christ is the "Personage" of the Way, the Truth, and The Life. No one can go to the Father except through Him.

Truth is not a matter of what I believe. If it were about what I believed, it could change as I change. It would be up to each individual's interpretation who reads the Bible. Each generation

In The Beginning was the LOGOS of God

would need to rediscover the meaning to the Scriptures according to their generation's needs. There are those who use this shaky reasoning when they interpret the words of the Bible. Since they assert that each generation must discover the Bible's meaning, they can assign whatever meaning serves them best, allowing them the freedom to act as the wish. They teach their false doctrine convincing themselves and others that they are on the right path. The more people they get to agree with them, the more right they appear and the more confident they become in their own thinking.

Without the Light shining from the Word of God, we are in total ignorance of the Truth. The warnings of pending judgments and everlasting separation from God are something we should not take lightly. We should listen closely to the declarations of His Love and benevolence that can change the nature of our souls. We must understand that it was for our benefit that God penned the words in the Bible. But they can only be a benefit if they have His intended meaning. Putting a different twist to His words will only destroy the benefit. If the words are the words of eternal life, twisting the meaning will take out the eternal life.

The Word of God has a special meaning

The writing of the Scriptures was not an act of the human will. Reading the Scriptures to get the true meaning is not an act of the human will either. It is an act of "Spiritual Guidance" when the Holy Spirit makes known the true meaning of the Scriptures. These are prophetic words from the mind and heart of God Almighty. They are the tender and stern words of a Father to His children. They are the passionate words of love passed between a Bridegroom and His Bride. As the blood is to the body of men, so is the meaning behind each word to the body of believers. The meaning behind these words is the Life source of the Church.

In the beginning was the Word, and the Word was with God, and the Word was God. He was in the beginning with God. All things came into being by Him, and apart from Him nothing came into being that has come into being. In Him was life, and the life was the light of men (John 1:1-4).

Tree of Life

Remember that Jesus Christ is the LOGOS of God. He is the special meaning behind the words. Our God poured out His heart into the Person of His Son for our benefit. Before we even existed, He knew what He wanted to say to us. He has put His thoughts into the hearts of His people. Only those led by the Holy Spirit can speak the truth to His people. He makes known those who speak according to His will for our benefit. **He does not to honor the one speaking. He honors the one listening.**

There are those the Holy Spirit has warned us about, who introduce destructive heresies. He tells us in 2 Peter 2:1-3 that they wish to exploit us for their own gain. Think about the time these deceivers spend begging for money. As they ask for more money, they teach that God was not able to fund the ministries He called into being. It is easy for me to believe that it is the money they are after. The more money and the more prestige they receive, the more they deceive to get more money and prestige. Matthew 6:25-34 tells us not to worry about our daily needs. God knows our needs. He will provide according to His will. He provides us with what we need to carry out His plan and not what the ministers need to carry out their plans. False Teachers will not put the future of their ministry into the hands of God by allowing Him to limit them financially. They take charge and start fundraisers and canvass the believers and the unbelievers alike. Light in partnership with darkness is never a sign of resting in the Lord.

Ministries that walk according to the intent of God's Word understand that they are not in charge of the ministry. They know it is their God's responsibility to provide the wherewithal to carry out His work. If He does not supply, then to continue will be to fall out of His will. Understanding who He is, what makes up His character, and where we fit in enable us to trust in His ability to provide. Therefore, if the provision is not forthcoming, we must accept the limitation as His will serving His purpose.

Man did not imagine the story of God, for it is too wonderful

Understanding what Yahweh intended to say is critical to believing that He is who He says is! "I AM Who I AM"(היה **hayah**) sent a love letter personally carried and explained through His Son, Jesus Christ. It is not a figment of our imagination. The story of the

In The Beginning was the LOGOS of God

cross is so different from man's thinking that we cannot fully grasp what His death meant (Romans 5:8-10).

I ask you, "What myth has ever described a self-sacrificing deity who put mortal man ahead of Himself?" The answer is that no religion has described a god with a character like the character of Yahweh. The concept of the only all-powerful being in existence laying His life down and taking ours as His own is too foreign for mankind to grasp, let alone devise. The religions of the world are all centered on works done by the followers so as to gain the right to ascend to a Higher Level. Man wants to be the victor and progress to Yahweh's level. A religion made up by a man would leave man in charge of his own destiny. It would not have men yielding themselves to another being. It would not have men relying on another being to make them acceptable.

The story of Jesus Christ tells of the Creator descending to our level because it was impossible for us to ascend to His. This truth is not acceptable to most. We would never create such a story on our own. No, without a doubt, the more we understand the thinking behind the sacrifice of Jesus Christ on the Cross, the more we believe it originated from His heart of Love, and not the thinking of men.

The message sent to us through Jesus Christ tells us about being lost in a maze of right and wrong thinking that we can never find our way out of. He tells us that, without Him, we remain lost and on a path of spiritual death. But with Him, we are on the path of everlasting life. Those who recognize the truth about their situation find the story of Jesus Christ to be so amazing that it affects their souls. Realizing how fantastic He is humbles the believer and causes him to follow.

The message in the story of Jesus Christ's death is not an act of human will (2 Peter 1:20-21). It is the most important message ever given in Heaven and on Earth, in every dimension that exists (whatever that might be), in this time, in the time before, or all the time that ever will be. The meaning behind the story of Jesus Christ on the cross is the most important message any soul could ever receive. The story of Yahweh's love is like a light shining is a dark place (Psalms 119:103-106). It is the difference between life and death, love and hate, goodness and wickedness. Those who walk according to the Message of Love have Life in them.

Tree of Life

We know the Holy Spirit wrote the Scriptures and that only He can properly teach their meaning. His teachings help us love our families, friends, and enemies more. How grateful are those who have the Message as a Light. Their lives have changed forever. The Message does not embarrass them so they proclaim it to whoever will listen.

The Bible is not about private interpretations!
But just as it is written, "Things which eye has not seen and ear has not heard, and which have not entered the heart of man, All that God has prepared for those who love Him." For to us God revealed them through the Spirit; <u>for the Spirit searches all things, even the depths of God</u>.

For who among men knows the thoughts of a man except the spirit of the man, which is in him? <u>Even so the thoughts of God no one knows except the Spirit of God</u>. Now we have received, not the spirit of the world, but the Spirit who is from God, that we might know the things freely given to us by God, <u>which things we also speak, not in words taught by human wisdom, but in those taught by the Spirit, combining spiritual thoughts with spiritual words</u>.

But a natural man does not accept the things of the Spirit of God; for they are foolishness to him, and he cannot understand them, because they are spiritually appraised. <u>But he who is spiritual appraises all things</u>, yet he himself is appraised by no man. <u>For who has known the mind of the Lord, that he should instruct Him? But we have the mind of Christ</u> (1 Cor. 2:9-16).

We do not think like God. He is not like men and does not bounce ideas off us to see what our take is. We cannot intelligently talk with Him about anything that He is doing. We cannot even understand what He is doing. We have an infant's understanding compared with Him and can only understand His thinking in a primitive way. But we do have the mind of Christ so the thoughts we do have can be like the thoughts He has. I speak "arithmetic" while He speaks "calculus" but we are both speaking mathematics. I cannot understand all He understands, but what I know can be in harmony with what He knows. The Spirit we share with Jesus Christ can align us with His thinking.

In The Beginning was the LOGOS of God

The Voice of Almighty God moved men to write the Word of God. Therefore He can move men's thinking to understand the original intent of His message. The message of the LOGOS of God is not an artificial effort at defining the universe. It is a communication from the depths of the heart of God. If what we seek is not an act of human will, it will take something more than an act of human will to understand it. It will take the same "Voice of the Living God" moving in us to give the understanding He wants us to have.

He can help men in the lowest social strata as well as the most educated and admired. He made the Gospel simple enough for a child to understand, yet its implementation is so complex that one will need a lifetime to learn how to live it. The Lord does not hide the gospel from men's minds because it is hard to understand. Men miss it because they do not wish to pay the cost of living it daily. The Scripture was not written as a matter of human interpretation. We cannot read it as a matter of human interpretation and we cannot live as a matter of human interpretation.

My words are not enough!

There are many voices in the world claiming to know the way. The competition is intense among the many false preachers and teachers. They look for our time and our money (mostly our money). Many claim to have a truth that no one else has. They can make up anything they want, because the truth is not important to them. They only need to convince people that what they say could be true. They do not need to prove anything. What they say only needs to sound reasonable.

Good writing is not a skill that I possess and how I wish that it was. I wish there was a way to craft the perfect sentences into the perfect paragraphs and then assemble them into the perfect chapter that shows how importance this message is. The words I have are not enough to explain the truth that waits inside the Scriptures. The words of the Bible alone are not enough to give the understanding hidden within its pages. No one can unlock the meaning of the words for another. Only a talk with the Author Himself can make what He is saying clear to the heart of a believer.

I wish everyone already understood why I say the tree of the Knowledge of Good and Evil is a set of teachings centered on the

Tree of Life

righteousness or wickedness of man. And why I say that those who elaborate on such teachings will evaluate the virtue and sinfulness of their followers. I wish all could see these preachers base acceptance on getting it right and those who do not agree with them are forced out. Their love is conditional, based on the character of the one they give love to. If they do well, they are loved and if they do not, then they lose the love given. This is not True Love. This is why churches split over the smallest of matters. Members fight over the controls and they argue about doing it right according to their own thinking, instead of acting through Yahweh's love. They find it hard to yield the control over to a God they cannot see.

I would wish everyone already understood why I say the Tree of Life is about Yahweh's love. Why I say that it is about Love based on the character of the one giving Love and not the character of the one receiving love, making acceptability a nonissue. True friendship comes from the relationship the one giving Love has with God. We base our friendship solely on the example Jesus Christ displayed to us when we were in hateful opposition to Him.

I would wish everyone already understood why I say we whom He is changing into His likeness, are to also demonstrate the same Love. We cannot understand such Love on our own and cannot demonstrate such Love on our own. It is by the power of the Holy Spirit that we are able to love in the manner that He loves. The degree to which we are able to love as He loves is the same degree to which He lives His Life in us.

Are you ready to walk and talk with the Author of Life? He is ready to enter a relationship that is impossible for you to have with anyone else. It is face-to-face, with no one between, communing with an awesome God. That is what it takes to know the truth. It will take leaving your own life and becoming a part of His. When you understand the Message of the Cross, that God the Father loves you just the way you are, and there is nothing you can do to improve on that love, then you can trust that He will take care of the rest also.

May the likeness of Jesus Christ be in you
                        and may it be a Tree of Life to you.

In The Beginning was the LOGOS of God

Chapter 16

God so Loved the World

Jesus Christ reveals the Love of God to us
And as Moses lifted up the serpent in the wilderness, even so must the Son of Man be lifted up; that whoever believes may in Him have eternal life. <u>For God so loved the world, that He gave His only begotten Son, that whoever believes in Him should not perish, but have eternal life</u>. For God did not send the Son into the world to judge the world, but that the world should be saved through Him. <u>He who believes in Him is not judged; he who does not believe has been judged already</u>, because he has not believed in the name of the only begotten Son of God. <u>And this is the judgment, that the light is come into the world, and men loved the darkness rather than the light; for their deeds were evil</u> (John 3:14-19).

But Jesus was saying, "<u>Father, forgive them; for they know not what they are doing</u>" (Luke 23:34).

In the movies, the one who becomes the leader is the one who is the strongest or the bravest or the smartest or the fastest, or has some other great trait that people respect. At the time Jesus Christ walked the earth, the people of Israel were looking for the Messiah to save them from Roman rule and sit on the throne of David. They were looking for Yahweh to rescue His people, something He had not done for more than 150 years. They were looking for someone to capture the imagination of the people and to gather an army that could overthrow the Roman Empire. When Jesus Christ started His ministry, some believed He was the Messiah. The religious leaders did not because of their misinterpretations of the prophetic portions of Scriptures (John 7:11-53). They refused to accept that Yahweh was behind what they were witnessing. Others did not know what to think.

He went about teaching and doing miracles as men debated about Him being the Messiah. They were not looking for Yahweh to draw them close by giving His only begotten Son. If they were to write the story, Yahweh would draw them by might and supernatural power. They would have flashing bolts of lightning with great signs

Tree of Life

and miracles that removed all opposition to His authority. He would prove His worth by destroying the Romans. Israel would be the new Empire ruled by a supernatural force. The nations of the world would be too afraid of them to wage war any more.

They forget that God used those methods in the Old Testament days and His people's hearts were hard and faithless to the point He could not lead them. Men did not change their way because they saw miracles. The book of Exodus is about men reacting to His power and miracles. They complained to the point of rebellion and returned to serving idols at the drop of a hat. Even in the presence of a column of smoke by day and of fire by night, the false prophets worked against Yahweh, within His people!

Yahweh is the owner of everything created. He wanted something more than overthrowing the Roman government. Even now, He works toward a greater purpose. Sometimes what happens in our lives does not make much sense. That is because we are looking for God to fulfill our individual expectations. He is not working to accomplish our individual goals! He is completing a plan He implemented at the very beginning. Yahweh decided He wanted to draw all men to Him. He prepared the plan and the Message. The Message did not come about as a response to anything that happened after creation. It was a part of the Blueprint from the start. That is why Jesus never did overthrow the Roman government.

God so Loved the World

Godhead so loved men that He allowed them to crucify Him as Jesus Christ. He then forgave those who sin against Him and those who crucified Him. The Godhead so loved the world that He bore their iniquities (Isaiah 53). Contained within the story of His life and death is the Message, "I love you so much there is no end to what I would do for you." "I will never leave you or forsake you" (Deut. 31:6, Heb. 13:5, John 14:16-18). Jesus Christ's death on the cross is an everlasting symbol of Love and devotion.

If we look on the Cross of Calvary, we find The Tree of Life. He spoke the Words of Life there: *"Father, forgive them; for they know not what they are doing" (Luke 23:34)*. The Shepherd calls us to follow Him from there (John 10:1-5 and 26). The Shepherd came to this place of judgment, at the proper time, to put forth a show of

In The Beginning was the LOGOS of God

Love unequaled in the history of humanity. He gave an example for all men to follow. If men followed this example, there would be no more war or hatred or suffering. It is here on the cross that the LOGOS of the Godhead speaks with deep meaning. We find all that Yahweh wanted to say from the beginning of time, right here on the cross. The power to overcome sin and our ability to receive cleansing from all unrighteousness comes from the work of Jesus Christ.

He summons us to join him in the likeness of His death (Romans 6:1-11). Our joining Him on the cross is to walk the narrow path of Truth (Matt. 7:13-14). Here is the door to the sheepfold in which the Shepherd enters through (John 10:1-18). If the Shepherd comes in through the door of the cross, the sheep must use it also as they leave with the Shepherd. We who hear His voice are ready to follow Him and to be obedient to Him even to death, death on a cross (Philip. 2:5-11).

Jesus said to him, 'I am the way, and the truth, and the life; no one comes to the Father, but though me (John 14:6).

When Jesus said this, He was talking of Himself. He was not talking about His teachings, or some wonderful idea. He was not saying, "The deeds I do are the way, so do as I do." He was saying that He, Himself, was the path to the Father. It is here at the cross that He summons you to join Him and share Him (Luke 9:23, Romans 6:3-11). If you wish to share in His Life, you must also be willing to share in His death.

For while we were still helpless, at the right time Christ died for the ungodly. For one will hardly die for a righteous man; though perhaps for the good man someone would dare even to die. <u>But God demonstrates His own love toward us, in that while we were yet sinners, Christ died for us</u>. Much more then, having now been justified by His blood, we shall be saved from the wrath of God through Him. <u>For if while we were enemies, we were reconciled to God through the death of His Son, much more, having been reconciled, we shall be saved by His life</u>. And not only this, but we also exult in God through our Lord Jesus Christ, through whom we have now received the reconciliation (Romans 5:6-11).

Tree of Life

In their meditations, many Christians skip over the "God so loved" part and go right to the "everlasting life" part of Romans 5:8-10. Many Christians do not recognize what this verse says about their Creator and who He is. They miss out on the perfectness of His character. They think only about "being saved," as if salvation was the most important item on their agenda. Therefore, the eyes of God's people turn away from the person of Jesus Christ. They are blind and see not their God. They misunderstand His action and do not credit Him with an act of Love. When God said to Moses, "My name is "I AM", He was alluding to something that makes Him who He is. When Jesus said, "I am the Way, and the Truth, and the Life," He was also alluding to something that makes Him who He is.

"God so loved us" is a phrase used so often that we do not give it our attention. Here on the Cross of Calvary, the LOGOS of God displayed for all men to see an announcement of such importance that it took an act of *great* consequence to give it *great* meaning. Nothing in front of Yahweh had a greater importance than the welfare of His people. The issue here is spiritual life and death. It was so important that He came Himself, in the person of the Son, to announce it. Yahweh loved the world so much that He decided to prove His love toward us by taking our place in judgment, a judgment that He should have carried out *against* us. He became the owner of our sin and stood in our place to receive the punishment that was to fall on us (Isaiah 53). He paid the full and horrendous price to say to us "I LOVE YOU."

He did everything with this announcement in mind. All the teaching about sin and the Law of Righteousness He gave to help us understand the problem, so we might **value** the solution.

At the right time, Jesus Christ died for us
For while we were still helpless, at the right time Christ died for the ungodly (Romans 5:6).

At the right time, Christ died. He did not come for the righteous but for the sinner (1 Tim. 1:12-16, Luke 9:51-56, Matt. 9:9-13). Those who believe they are good cannot understand the meaning in this verse, only those who see their ungodliness can value the state they were in when Christ died. He died for the ungodly when we

In The Beginning was the LOGOS of God

were yet sinners and while we were His enemies. He died for us when what He found deep down in our hearts was against Him (Romans 3:10-20). He knows our coming and our goings, our risings and our laying down (Psalms 139). Every thought we think, He knew before we thought it. He knows the number of hairs on our heads (Luke 12:4-10). He wrote down the number of our days and the outcome of our lives while we were yet in our mother's womb And He loved us before time began. With all the knowledge of how unworthy we are, He still died for us. He knows what makes us ashamed about our lives. He knows the sins and the terrible thoughts that make up our daily existence. When we think about Him knowing our ugly thoughts, we squirm, ashamed of our inner beings. He loves us despite what is wrong with us. There is no need to hide our shameful selves from Him. He has already accepted us in our shameful condition and wants to help us out of our circumstance and put us into a place of hope and glory. **This is the heart of the Message delivered by the LOGOS on a Cross of Reconciliation.**

    Now it is important that we admit the truth about the condition of our lives when He died. One would hardly die for a righteous man, but some would die for a good man. How many men would give their lives for someone who hated them? Jesus Christ does not base His love on the goodness He found in the people. He bases it on His Love for them, regardless of what person they are.

    Many see Romans 5:8 as a salvation verse. They limit their understanding to Jesus Christ taking their sins. They miss that His dying for their sin was a demonstration of Love and therefore misunderstand His Love. But if the Father sent His Son to the cross and Jesus Christ was willing to go while we were the worst person possible, is there any reason to think the Godhead would stop loving us now? If we were the worst person we could be and He loved us, then after He reunites us can we be bad enough for Him to reject us? No way! We can trust that He will love us always, for His love has passed the test already. We can believe what the Holy Spirit said through Paul in Romans 8:38: there is nothing that can separate us form the Love of God. If He loved us so much that He would bear the penalty for our sins no matter what, what could we possibly do that would cause Him to stop loving us after we become close to Him?

Tree of Life

He paid a debt He didn't owe, to silence us all

He communicates the Message (LOGOS) of Love, when we were at the most unworthy time of our lives. This is to silence all those who take credit for being good. He performed the act of saving us from our sin while we were His enemies. We could not get any further away from Him. It was at the right time that He died for us. If we believed that God proved His Love because we were worthy and ready, it would lessen the depth of Love shown to us. On the cross, we see a comparison of our unworthiness to receive love and God's Love for us. Jesus Christ, the Lamb of God, never sinned and was never guilty of sin. We have sinned from the beginning of our lives. No one forced Him to go to the cross for us and nothing obligated Him to take our place. He could have delivered the right and lawful judgment against us and He would have remained pure and without sin. No one could have accused Him of wrongdoing, for He must deal with sin. It was because of Love that God the Father sent God the Son to bear the load of sin and shame and we have received the benefit for what He has done.

And when you were dead in your transgressions and the uncircumcision of your flesh, He made you alive together with Him, having forgiven us all our transgressions, having canceled out the certificate of debt consisting of decrees against us and which was hostile to us; and He has taken it out of the way, having nailed it to the cross (Col. 2:13-14).

First He took the charges that were waiting against us and removed them (Col. 2:8-14). Then He made us alive by sharing His perfect Life with us. The method Yahweh uses to save us is a marvel to contemplate, but it does not change the person we are. When we think about the reason behind His method, it changes us deep inside. The more we think of His Love, the more we become like His Love. If we believe we deserve His Love, His death will do us no good. It is when we think of the truth about our sinful condition the truth becomes real to us.

His ways are not our ways and His thoughts are not our thoughts (Isaiah 55). We begin to see the gulf that exists between the kinds of people we are and the person He is. The "I AM Who I AM" displayed on the cross what makes Him worthy of being our God and

In The Beginning was the LOGOS of God

Master and Lord. No one else is worthy, for no one else can love to the depths of His Love. We can have a love like His, if we are willing to join Him on the cross. We join Him in the likeness of His death so we can join Him in the likeness of His Life. We walk in the likeness of His Life so we can walk in the likeness of His Love. Not that we love God, but that He first loved us (1 John 4:10).

May your understanding of the certainty of His Love
                                         be a Tree of Life to you.

Chapter 17

No Longer I, but Jesus Christ Lives in Me

We have confidence before God because of LOGOS
For if while we were enemies, we were reconciled to God through the death of His Son, much more, having been reconciled, we shall be saved by His life. And not only this, <u>but we also exult in God through our Lord Jesus Christ, through whom we have now received the reconciliation</u> (Romans 5:10-11).

We can trust Yahweh's dedication to us for He showed a commitment to us when there was nothing in us that would compel Him to make such a commitment. He makes His pledge as an outpouring of who He is and not on who we are. When it comes to gaining approval, it is not about what we do or how well we do. It is about God's faithfulness to fulfill His promise. He has declared us acceptable and has announced His proclamation from the cross. Therefore, our thinking should change about our companionship with our Maker and Master. We no longer evaluate how good we are or are not becoming. Instead we evaluate how good He is and how undeserving we are. We can never become deserving. Our evaluation of ourselves helps us see how deserving He is.

There was a wall of selfishness dividing us from Yahweh's Love. When Jesus Christ died for us, He proved the division was not because of what He thought of us. He showed that we made the wall from materials of what we thought of Him. Those of us who understand the reconciliation He offers have changed our opinion of God. Having received the Message of Reconciliation, we learn the depths of Yahweh's love. Now we take pride in Him and focus our attention to His faithfulness instead of our unworthiness. We rejoice in knowing Him. We do not rejoice in our knowledge of Him for it is not about our intellectual knowledge. It is the Person of the Godhead we experience everyday in whom we glory.

Now to the one who works, his wage is not reckoned as a favor, but as what is due. <u>But to the one who does not work, but believes in Him who justifies the ungodly, his faith is reckoned as righteousness</u> (Romans 4:4-5).

In The Beginning was the LOGOS of God

Trying to earn acceptance so we may enter the presence of God by doing good demands doing the deeds we do perfectly. Any deed that is not good earns non-acceptance. To come up short in such an effort would be disastrous for it would end in the outer darkness forever (Matt. 25:14-31, Rev. 20:10-15, Matt. 22:1-14). Try this with your creditors or on your tax return. Pay only 95 percent of what you owe and see how long they accept it. Earning 99.99 percent of the right to appear before Yahweh is the same as earning 60 percent. A person must earn 100 percent or it is all for nothing. Only Jesus Christ can claim a life that earns 100 percent of the right to appear before God based solely on merit.

If Yahweh accepts us into His presence as a gift in response to the life of Jesus Christ, then it is not a right, but a privilege to stand before Him. If we have received this privilege as a gift, we no longer need to work for it. Our acceptance is a gift Yahweh gives freely without regard to merit. Why, then, should those who have received the gift of acceptance spend time worrying about God accepting them? Those who trust the announcement made by the Master on the cross no longer need worry about the results of their deeds (Luke 12:21-38, Matt. 6:19-34). They trust the perfect Love of Jesus Christ and His Father. Perfect Love cast out fear (1 John 4:14-5:1, Col. 3:12-17).

Trust in the witness the Father bore about His Son

If we receive the witness of men, the witness of God is greater; <u>for the witness of God is this, that He has borne witness concerning His Son</u>. The one who believes in the Son of God has the witness in himself; the one who does not believe God has made Him a liar, because he has not believed in the witness that God has borne concerning His Son. And the witness is this, <u>that God has given us eternal life, and this life is in His Son</u>. He who has the Son has the life; he who does not have the Son of God does not have the life (1 John 5:9-12).

God the Father gave this announcement about His Son. If one does not trust in the Message of His announcement and continues to worry about his acceptance before Him, he declares to God's face that He is not trustworthy. The person claims the One who created

Tree of Life

him cannot continue to love him under all circumstances. If our God is trustworthy, then we must believe with our hearts that we are now free from our fear of sin and death. We can now relax about how righteous or unrighteous we are. We can enjoy the goodness and righteousness of Jesus Christ our Redeemer. When it comes to our salvation, our sin and our goodness are no longer the issue. For if, while we were sinful creatures, Christ proclaimed His acceptance by dying for us, there is no other act we need to add to His death. Instead the question becomes "What will we do with this man named Jesus Christ? (Matt. 27:22). What are we doing with the promise He has given to us? He has accepted us as someone He loves. Have we accepted Him as someone we love? That is the question we must answer and it is a life and death question!

    The purpose of His death and His willingness to pay the penalty for our sins was to show us how much He loved us. He did not sacrifice His goodness and righteousness to accept us. Instead He sacrificed His own well-being to make it possible for Him to cleanse us from our sin. Stop and think about that. **He put Himself in our place, literally**. This is not some nice saying that you read quickly and pass over to the next line. Jesus Christ sacrificed His own well-being to improve our well-being.

    Just how much do we value the truth of that last paragraph? We shared in the Tree of the Knowledge of Good and Evil and failed to control that knowledge, which created a need for repair. Our problem, combined with the cost of the solution, shows God's Love. He did not love with words only. He showed the depth of Love with the actions He took. Soak it in! Take the time to linger on this thought: the thinking of Tree of Life is in the depth of His love. Thoughts and meditations, with prayer, about His love will be a Light that reveals our inner being and will change our lives, and has already changed many lives down through the centuries. These are not new thoughts, but we must put them center stage and think about them more often.

    Can a woman forget her nursing child, And have no compassion on the son of her womb? <u>*Even these may forget, but I will not forget you. Behold, I have inscribed you on the palms of My hands;*</u> *Your walls are continually before Me (Isaiah 49:15-16).*

In The Beginning was the LOGOS of God

In Isaiah, Yahweh compared His love to a mother's love, because it is something we can understand. But even a mother's love is not a good enough example. It would take the Cross of Love to explain it. After the cross, when Jesus showed Himself to the disciples, He showed the wounds on His hands, feet, and side (Luke 24: 38-39, John 19:20). Those marks will be visible, for eternity, as symbols of Love.

Yahweh is not a God of hateful judgment and destruction. He does not wish for anyone to perish, but wishes all could have everlasting life (1 Tim. 2:1-6, 2 Peter 3:9). He proved that He is willing to sacrifice Himself to better His people.

He is for us and He will save us by His life

If all this is true, the issue of sin is no longer a problem, right? *Well, not exactly.* He removed the need for punishment, but not the need for cleansing! He restores us by His death and He saved us by His Life (Rom. 5:10). He has shown His willingness to suffer much for the good of His people. Do you think He will grant entrance into His Heaven to those who stubbornly continue in their destructive lifestyles? He knows they would destroy His people just as they do on Earth today. **No!** He will not allow sin to continue in His presence forever, for it will take away the gift of Life. Take time to reason this out! With complete diligence, He will strongly guard the gift that cost Him so much. If the issue of sin was so important that Jesus Christ laid down His Life, it is too important to leave sin unchecked in Heaven.

Therefore it is foolishness to believe that a God of Love will let anyone into His presence based on His Love only. He must recreate our spirit (John 3:1-8, 1 Peter 1:1-5 and 1:17-25). He has made a way to bring sinners into His courts to fellowship but they must enter using the path He has provided. No other path will do, for no other path will cleanse men of their sins. He does not want to damn anyone for eternally and He has provided a safe path. Those who refuse His gift damn themselves.

<u>Or do you not know that all of us who have been baptized into Christ Jesus have been baptized into His death</u>? Therefore we have been buried with Him through baptism into death, in order that as

Tree of Life

Christ was raised from the dead through the glory of the Father, so we too might walk in newness of life.

For if we have become united with Him in the likeness of His death, certainly we shall be also in the likeness of His resurrection, knowing this, <u>that our old self was crucified with Him, that our body of sin might be done away with, that we should no longer be slaves to sin; for he who has died is freed from sin</u>.

Now if we have died with Christ, we believe that we shall also live with Him, knowing that Christ, having been raised from the dead, is never to die again; death no longer is master over Him. <u>For the death that He died, He died to sin, once for all; but the life that He lives, He lives to God</u>. Even so consider yourselves to be dead to sin, but alive to God in Christ Jesus (Romans 6:5-11).

I have been crucified with Christ; and <u>it is no longer I who live, but Christ lives in me</u>; and the <u>life which I now live in the flesh I live by faith in the Son of God</u>, who loved me, and delivered Himself up for me (Gal. 2:20).

The Creator of the Universe calls us to join Jesus Christ in the likeness of His death. Jesus Christ died for the sin of the world. We are guilty and could not pay the full judgment for our own sins let alone for anyone else. Therefore we cannot join Him while He paid for the sins of humanity. <u>Since we cannot join Him in the likeness of His death for redemption's sake then we must join Him in the likeness of His death according to His demonstration of Love</u> (Romans 5:8-10).

If by death we join ourselves to His demonstration, then by His resurrected Life, we live out the same demonstration. If He lived His Life to show His Love for us while we were enemies and we are joined to His Life, then our lives must reflect His Life of Love by loving our enemies. He calls us to share in His demonstration in our reaction to those around us in Love (1 Cor. 13:4-8, 1 John 3:11 and 23, 4:8 and 20). We cannot continue to live the old life that was full of hateful acts. We must take on His Life as our renewed life. We do not start living our old life in a new way, but we join Him in the likeness of the Life He lives. Now that He lives His life us, it is no longer our life to live as we like. We can no longer remain separate from His spiritual being. He must join us to Him by sealing us in the

In The Beginning was the LOGOS of God

Holy Spirit. It is no longer our life to live, but it is His life to live through us. It is not about us any longer. It is all about Him.

Love is the fundamental nature of God

God is Love (1 John 4:8). Love is not just an action that Yahweh takes. It is an expression of what makes Him who He is. He loves, for it is the natural outpouring of His nature. Jesus Christ is the image of Yahweh (2 Cor. 4:1-7, Col. 1:15 and 3:1-15) and Love's expression. He transforms us into the image of Jesus Christ by changing the way we think (Romans 12:1-21). He calls us to love as a natural outpouring of our new nature.

Jesus Christ fulfills the Law (Matt. 5:14-20, 1 Cor. 15:1-4) and there is no Law against Love (Rom. 13:9-10, Gal. 5:16-26, Rom. 5:10-13). Therefore joining Jesus Christ in His Demonstration and sharing His Life cause us to live according to the Law, by the Spirit of Life in Christ Jesus (Rom: 8:1-8). We would no longer be in violation of the Law of Righteousness, for where there is no Law, there is no violation of the Law (Rom. 4:15). If it is no longer we who live, but Christ Jesus who lives within us, then we cannot take the old life with us, for we cannot put new wine in old wine skins (Luke 5: 30-39, Mark 2:18-22, Matt. 9:10-17). We must become lesser and lesser as He becomes greater and greater (John 3:22-36).

What, you are not comfortable with this idea? You want the new life to reflect your old life? You want Him to accept you into His favor while doing your own thing, your way? **It will not work that way**, for He grants a man one life and after that judgment (Heb. 9:24-28).

It is time to agree with the Creator. The life you have lived on our own is a hateful, self-centered example of what is not acceptable in the presence of God. This is true of every person who has ever lived, except Jesus Christ. To hang on to your old way of thinking is to hang on to your death sentence. Jesus Christ is the only path available that will take you to everlasting life. He created the way for your acceptance into the Father's presence, but He paved that way through the <u>Cross of His Father's Love</u> (Rom.5:1-13).

To gain acceptance into the Father's presence, we must share in the Life He lived without sin. We must be willing to share in the likeness of His death to share in the likeness of His resurrection. This means for there to be His Life in us, there must be a death in us (John 12:23-28). We must die to sin or die because of sin. Either Jesus Christ dies for us or we die for us. If we live our own lives, we die our own death. Are you prepared to bet that you lived a 100 percent acceptable life before God?

Praise God, since Jesus Christ died for us, it is also necessary that He live for us. When we join Jesus Christ on the cross, we turn responsibility for our sinful lives over to Him. He suffered the natural consequences for our actions. Our old lives died when He died. His Life did not die for it was free from sin. We can only continue to live if we live in His Life. There is no other life to live for our old life die because of sin. Now we live the perfect life He lived and since it is not ours, He must live it for us by living His Life through us.

If He was willing to love us based on the goodness of His character, and He is living His Life through us, we must then love others as He loves them based on the goodness of His character. If we cannot love the ones He was so willing to die for, how can we be sure we love the One who died? (1 John 5:1). Remember that, as often as you do something for the least of His brethren, you also do it for Him (Matt. 25:31-46).

This truth is hard to grasp. If you let go and do not try to control the events of your life and you do not try to make them end in a way that pleases you, your life will end in a way that pleases you. If you do not let go and try to control the events of your life, making them end in a way that pleases you, then your life will end in a way that is not pleasing to you. In other words, you will fail.

For who ever wishes to save his life shall lose it, but whoever loses his life for my sake, he is the one who will save it. <u>*For what is a man profited if he gains the whole world, and loses or forfeits himself?*</u> *(Luke 9:24-25).*

Finding our way through the maze

There is a way that seems right to a man but leads to destruction (Prov. 16:16-25 and 14:12). Learning to live our lives properly is like finding our way through a maze. There is the One who created the maze and knows it's every turn and knows the path that successfully weaves its way through to the end. There are the ones wanting to find their own way out of the maze. Those who

In The Beginning was the LOGOS of God

follow the Creator of the maze do not rely on their own understanding (Prov. 3:5-14) but trust the Creator to lead them through. They do not argue about what is the best path for they trust that He knows what He is doing.

Others trust their own understanding or listen to men who claim to know the path. They get more lost in the depths of the maze. They find danger from those who have given up hope of escaping the maze and live off those unlucky enough to meet them. When given the chance to join the followers of the Creator, they refuse, for they want to go their own way. Their end is sure, for without His help, they will never find their way through.

To put everything into Jesus Christ's hands is not such a risk after all. Jesus Christ is the only one to live a perfect life. His people throw away old useless garments that cannot cover them properly and gain new, perfect garments that fit properly. Before they could put on the new man they put off the old (Eph. 4:17-27, Col. 3:1-10, Rom. 6:1-6). Jesus Christ set the example for us in that He did not think equality with the Father something to hold on to, but became obedient even to death (Phil. 2:5-7). If anyone had the right to do it His way it would have been Jesus Christ. He did not. Instead, He followed the instructions given to Him by His Father (John 12:49, 8:42, 14:10, and 16:13). Therefore, He expects us to have the same attitude as He did.

Is it fair for the Great "I AM" to expect us to live His way? Yes it is, for He also walks the same path we walk. He shared in our life of sin so we share in His Life of sinless behavior, which distinguished His Life above all others. Those who are in the Light will love as He loves. Those who claim to walk in the Light but who walk according to the teachings of men, walk in darkness still (1 John 1:5-10 and 2:4-11).

"A new commandment I give to you, that you love one another, even as I have loved you that you also love one another. <u>*"By this all men will know that you are My disciples, if you have love for one another"*</u> *(John 13:34-35*

May Jesus Christ live His Life through you
                          and may it be a Tree of Life to you

Tree of Life

Chapter 18

God Cannot Ignore Sin

The fact is we were sinners and sinners are separated from God

I permitted Myself to be sought by those who did not ask for Me; I permitted Myself to be found by those who did not seek Me. I said, 'Here am I, here am I,' To a nation which did not call on My name. I have spread out My hands all day long to a rebellious people, <u>Who walk in the way which is not good, following their own thoughts, a people who continually provoke Me to My face</u>, Offering sacrifices in gardens and burning incense on bricks; Who sit among graves, and spend the night in secret places; Who eat swine's flesh, And the broth of unclean meat is in their pots. Who say, <u>'Keep to yourself, do not come near me, For I am holier than you!'</u>

These are smoke in My nostrils, A fire that burns all the day. <u>Behold, it is written before Me</u>, I will not keep silent, but I will repay; I will even repay into their bosom, Both their own iniquities and the iniquities of their fathers together, "says the Lord."... (Isaiah 65:1-7).

The need to deal with sin is real and the Shepherd of Love cannot ignore it. The outcome of sin is harmful to all those involved. Even the innocent are damaged by the sin of others. We have already noted the condition of this world after eating from the wrong tree. I know of no one who would want to use today's world as a pattern for what they would like heaven to be like. We would expect something much better than we now have on earth. If the Lord allows people to continue in sin and then enter Heaven, how can the result be better than it is here on Earth?

He cannot allow sin to happen in Heaven, for the sake of the citizens of Heaven. Therefore He must do something about sin. He must contain it. So, if He leaves the condition of man as it is, they must remain forever separate from the presence of Yahweh. Otherwise Yahweh must consider rape and war and drive-by-shootings acceptable and not evil. What is our real expectation of a loving God? Can He send people to hell because they didn't get it right in this earthly life? Should a God of Love throw people into hell at all? Should a Loving God separate people from Him just because

In The Beginning was the LOGOS of God

they rejected His Son? These questions are only hard to answer when approaching them from the wrong perspective, which is the thinking of the Tree of the Knowledge of Good and Evil. Our God thinks differently and has a different perspective.

After Adam and Eve ate of the forbidden fruit, Yahweh allowed their sons to work the issues of sin out on their own (Gen. 4:1-12). God told Cain that he needed to master the sin that was "crouching" at his door. The result: Cain killed Abel because his deeds were evil and Abel's were good (Jude 1:11-16, 1 John 3:11-13). Cain was only able to cause earthly harm to Abel's body but not to his soul. On the physical plain, Yahweh confines the results of sin to this earthly life. On the eternal spiritual plain, the harm Cain caused could have Able had everlasting results. If the Lord allowed such a thing, Cain's attitude could turn into actions that would turn Abel's heaven into hell. In eternity, there are many who are like Cain and many who are like Abel. What would heaven be like if the God of Love did not separate them? Jesus prayed that it would be on earth as it is in heaven, not the other way around (Matt. 6:10).

Woe to them! For they have gone the way of Cain, and for pay they have rushed headlong into the error of Balaam, and perished in the rebellion of Korah. <u>These are the men who are hidden reefs in your love feasts</u> when they feast with you without fear, caring for themselves; clouds without water, carried along by winds; autumn trees without fruit, doubly dead, uprooted; wild waves of the sea, casting up their own shame like foam; wandering stars, <u>for whom the black darkness has been reserved forever</u> (Jude 1:11-13).

These are grumblers, finding fault, following after their own lusts; they speak arrogantly, flattering people for the sake of gaining an advantage. But you, beloved, ought to remember the words that were spoken beforehand by the apostles of our Lord Jesus Christ, that they were saying to you, "<u>In the last time there will be mockers, following after their own ungodly lusts.</u>" <u>These are the ones who cause divisions, worldly-minded, devoid of the Spirit.</u>

But you, beloved, building yourselves up on your most holy faith, praying in the Holy Spirit, keep yourselves in the love of God, waiting expectantly for the mercy of our Lord Jesus Christ to eternal life (Jude 1:16-21).

Tree of Life

The ones who are empty of the Spirit will cause division because of their selfish behavior. The Holy Spirit is harsh in His description of these people. How do you want the God of Love to handle these Cain-like people? Remember as you answer this question that you also fit this description, unless the Message of Love is at work in you (Eph. 2:1-10). All have been selfish in their undertakings, **all of us**. All have sinned and have fallen short, **all of us** (Rom. 3:9:18). What a spot we are in. We cannot answer the question about what to do with Cain-like people without condemning ourselves. If we lower the standards so we might get into heaven, then heaven will be like earth and we live in an everlasting hell polluted by Cain-like people.

Jesus Christ has already made it known that He will separate the sheep from the goats. (Matt. 25:31-46). He has decided not let people like Cain have the power to ruin eternity for people like Abel. Which side do you want to be on? There is only one way available that results in your being on the side of the sheep. You must be the results of the His handiwork. If you insist on finding your way through the "Maze of Truth" or by following the thinking of men, you will find yourself on the side of the goats saying, "LORD, LORD did I not do _____ in your name?" (Matt. 7:13-23) He will answer, "Go away I do not know you!"

What should a Holy, Loving God do?

A Holy and Loving God cannot allow the behaviors that now commonly happen on earth to happen in Heaven. God cannot let those who would destroy life on earth to enter a holy place with such behavior, so they may destroy it also. Yet He loves us and does not want to separate us from Him forever. The Creator of the Universe decided to correct the problem and He needed to do two things: 1) satisfy the judgment for sin, 2) cleanse the sinners from sin so they may enter in a clean state. There is, however, a cost involved, a very expensive transaction that results in personal pain and suffering. The truth is, sin causes pain and suffering. The sinner is not the only one who bears the results of their sin.

We were due the death penalty on a spiritual and eternal level. God so loved the world that He was willing to bear an "eternity of death" for us. Don't like that statement? Do you want the cost of

In The Beginning was the LOGOS of God

your sin to be less than His eternal death? Do you want to believe that Jesus Christ suffered a partial payment as a token for the penalty you would have suffered? Do you believe the penalty He paid for your sin was less than the penalty you would have paid for the same sin?

This is like the God of Justice taking 10 percent payment on every dollar of penalty we owed. Men would rather think that our salvation was some bargain-basement deal at sale prices. **It does not work that way!** Our salvation was like court where the judge gives justice to the victims and punishment as retribution for crimes committed. Show me where the scriptures say that Jesus Christ did not bear the full weight of our sin and the total retribution due us!

I believe He bore the complete cost for our sin and the cost for bearing our iniquities was great. We need to compare His Love with the greatness of the cost. The more we lessen the cost of sin, the more we underestimate the depth of His Love. I think human beings do not want to admit the true value of their gift. It is an awesome price, which makes it an awesome gift. To miscalculate the cost of our salvation is to misrepresent of the length, breadth, and depth of His Love.

The God of Love knows that to tolerate sin is the same as not loving. The condition of this earth is a perfect example of why a Loving God must judge sin. God is Love. His nature is Love. Sin opposes His nature. He will not tolerate a sinful man to continue to sin because sin is hateful and uncaring. Therefore a sinful man is a hateful man and the one who the Shepherd separates from His sheep.

Sin is the opposite of Love and therefore is anti-God. Just as light and darkness cannot exist together, Love and sin cannot exist together. Those who continue in their sinful ways cannot live with God. If Yahweh is Love then He must remove sin from the presence of His people. He must change their hearts and renew them to the thinking of Love. He will separate those who cling to their sinful practices from those who are willing to live for the common good (Matt. 25:31-46). The ones trained by the Holy Spirit join the Life of Jesus Christ and are willing to live according to the common good. Those not trained by the Holy Spirit continue in their sin. They think of the Cross of Calvary as foolishness and practice their own

Tree of Life

righteousness based on their own good works. They are the ones who want to do things their way, even if it harms another.

We are to trust in someone outside ourselves. We are to believe there is someone who loves us so much that He is willing to put Himself in our place, in harm's way. We must trust that He is working with us. We need to trust that He intends to do whatever it takes to clean us of all unrighteousness (1 John 1:9). We must trust that all He allows to happen in our lives is for our good. We must trust that He turns the wrongdoings of others into our benefit (Rom. 8:22-33). We must trust He sent us the only One who can lead us through the "Maze of Knowledge" and present us to Yahweh fully cleansed.

Why would He suffer so much on our account, if He knew that He was going to fail to complete His work? He will not fail, for God is Love and Love never fails (1 Cor. 13:8). You can trust the perfect Lamb of God to set you free because He blazed the trail that leads to Yahweh's presence with His own blood. He made a covenant with us and sealed it with His blood so those who believe in Him shall have everlasting life (John 3:16).

Not the way man thinks

When man imagined his idea of what the gods were like, we got religions like the Roman and Greek mythologies. Man imagined his gods as evil and deprave as himself. The notion of a God who would lay down His Life for the sheep (John 10) was unheard of anywhere else. Man rejects the idea that he needs Yahweh to be all-powerful and knowing. People reject the idea that Yahweh already knows what He needs to do and that He has the right - **no**, the duty - to demand the final say. Mankind rejects the idea that all authority and truth lie with his Creator.

The Lord God Almighty looks at you right now and sees the innermost thoughts of your heart. He can see your rebellion, humility, grief, sorrow, lust, jealousy, anger, hate, love, kindness, and every other emotion you might have. He looks past all of that and sees the finished work: your character, His workmanship in you. (Eph. 2:8-10, Phil. 1:6 and 2:13). He does work that brings out the best of what you are and what you have to offer. He looks for you to respond to Him. Accept the gift of Life found in the Person of Jesus

In The Beginning was the LOGOS of God

Christ. Understand who we are in the presence of Yahweh. It is important for us to come honestly before the God of Love and Righteousness.

Think about what we have said in the book so far.

1) We must admit the world is in a desperate condition of evil and hate for one another. The life humans live today is not what the Creator designed them for.

2) We have had a part in making this world a dangerous place to live in. We help make the lives of those around us less like heaven and more like hell.

3) From the start, God knew what He was going to do and what He needs us to know. Every action He has taken is by design and is not in response to anything we have done.

4) Jesus Christ expresses what God intended to say and showed His Message of Love on the cross as a Light in a dark place.

5) There are those who try to convince us of something different and try to lead us away from Jesus Christ. They want to be our light and to receive honor and glory from us.

6) God so loved us that He sent Jesus Christ to reunite Himself to us. He has forged the path for us to follow. Everyone who wishes to enter Yahweh's presence must enter through Jesus Christ's Life and death on the cross as a narrow gate allowing us to share in His resurrection.

No one can mimic what Jesus has done on the cross or what He is going to do for you in your life. He is not a religion that you can follow. You cannot change His teachings to fit your life style. He is the Master of the Universe and what He has said will last forever (Luke 16:15-16, Matt.24: 29-39). He wants to do good work for your sake. He is someone you must deal with, either now where He can change your destination or after you're dead when He will need to separate you as goats from the sheep.

But just as it is written, Things which eye has not seen and ear has not heard, And which have not entered the heart of man, All that God has prepared for those who love Him (1 Cor. 2:9).

Tree of Life

Anyone who knows the heart of Yahweh will love Him and His people. It is the natural outcome of having Him in our daily lives. You cannot conjure Him up by an act of your will. You must yield to Him and let Him be your God. No one can respond to the offer Yahweh has given unless He chooses them, for He said, "Many are called, but few are chosen" (Matt. 22:1-14).

Words, words, and more words

I wish for a language we could use to communicate without words. Words seem to be two-dimensional. They have length and width but no depth. Without the meaning behind the words, they are not useful. I look at the words I put together and wonder, "How is anyone ever going to understand the depth of what I say?" We are earthly beings who think earthly thoughts and live earthly lives. Without the Holy Spirit, we are like the words with two-dimensional lives. It is not until He adds the meaning of Jesus Christ to our lives that we have real depth. He adds the meaning to our beings by the experiences we share with the God of the Universe as we live with Him. We watch Him work in our lives; He is the one who gives true meaning to our lives.

We might find something on this planet that fulfills our need for a short time, but they can only help in this earthly life. To give meaning to our spiritual lives we need the spiritual meaning of life, which we cannot find in the teachings of any religion, even if that religion is about Jesus Christ. Teachings alone cannot make man complete. Knowledge alone will not give depth to our souls. Knowledge of where to locate food may make one comfortable, but unless they act on their knowledge they will still be hungry. We are not talking about a truth of intellectual fact that one can use in a Bible study or a debate. We are talking about knowing the most wonderful individual anywhere at any time.

Get away from the hype surrounding Jesus Christ and instead look at Him as a person. If you seek Him, He will make Himself known to you. You cannot go to Him, He must come to you. You do not know where to go, but He can show you. His path leads you through the Cross of Calvary. He intends it to remove sinful thoughts from your mind, your heart, and your soul. He will wash you clean and you will no longer sin. You will be a new creature with a new

In The Beginning was the LOGOS of God

mind transformed from the likeness of this world of death and destruction to the likeness of Life in Christ Jesus (Romans 12:1-3 and 8:29, Col. 3:10 and 1:15, 1 Cor. 15:49).

May Yahweh deal with your sin
                          and may his work be a Tree of Live to you.

Tree of Life

Chapter 19

A Perfect Life is Ours

Jesus Christ shares His perfect life with us

Before Jesus sealed us with the Holy Spirit, our behavior was not always valuable to those around us. As we lived according to the flesh, we helped to shape the world as it is today. We were not able help ourselves, for we knew what was right, but we lacked the spirit to do them (Matt. 26:38-47, James 4:17).

Now He has sealed us in the Holy Spirit and He empowers us to live according to the Spirit of God. Jesus Christ lives in us according to the will of the Father. Every act that Jesus Christ causes to happen within us carries out the Blueprint. Since every work He performs within us is in accordance to the Father's will, He commits no sin in us (Gal. 2:20). Therefore, it is to our advantage that we yield the control of our lives to Jesus Christ through the Holy Spirit.

We have never been in "control" of our lives. We have always lived as slaves to someone. Either a slave to Satan, who uses lies to lead us into an everlasting death by his example of hate, or Jesus Christ, who tells the truth to lead us into everlasting life by His example of Love.

For we know that the Law is spiritual, but I am of flesh, sold into bondage to sin. For what I am doing, I do not understand; for I am not practicing what I would like to do, but I am doing the very thing I hate. But if I do the very thing I do not want to do, *I agree with the Law, confessing that the Law is good*.

So now, no longer am I the one doing it, but sin which dwells in me. For I know that nothing good dwells in me, that is, in my flesh; for the willing is present in me, but the doing of the good is not. For the good that I want, I do not do, but I practice the very evil that I do not want. *But if I am doing the very thing I do not want, I am no longer the one doing it, but sin which dwells in me.*

I find then the principle that evil is present in me, the one who wants to do good. For I joyfully concur with the law of God in the inner man, but I see a different law in the members of my body, waging war against the law of my mind and making me a prisoner of the law of sin which is in my members.

In The Beginning was the LOGOS of God

Wretched man that I am! Who will set me free from the body of this death? Thanks be to God through Jesus Christ our Lord! <u>*So then, on the one hand I myself with my mind am serving the law of God, but on the other, with my flesh the law of sin*</u> *(Romans 7:14-25).*

In Romans, Paul claims that since he chooses to do good, yet he still sins, that it is no longer he who is doing what he believes is wrong, but sin is working wrong in him. If it is sin that works the wrong and if we disagree with what is happening through us, we are not in control of our actions! When we do what we do not want to do we are slaves to sin!

If you say that you are in control of yourself and you agree that sin is wrong, then why do you still sin? If you are in control of your life, you need no one to gain control for you. (Luke 5:30-32). If you sin and you are in control of your life, you willingly choose sin and become guilty for that sin (Gal. 5:13-25).

If you sin, because you lack control over your life and you wish to gain control, then you should willingly put your life into the hands of One who has gained the victory. By turning over the control of your life to Holy Spirit, you gain control over your life through Him. It is like someone who wishes to get control over their finances by turning over the control of their spending to a financial counselor. The counselor must have the authority to stop the bad spending habits and channel resources toward resolving the debt. We must turn our lives over to the Spiritual Counselor who must also have authority over our lives.

Jesus Christ lived a perfect life and is now sharing that perfect life with His Body. If it is true that it is no longer we who live but Christ Jesus who lives in us, then He exercises within us the power not to sin (Gal. 2:20, 1 John 2:1). He has sealed us with the Holy Spirit, so it is not our power over our sin but His. He lives a Life of Love so as we become like Him, we also live in the likeness of Love, which is perfect and without sin (Rom. 13:8-14).

Now, after the sealing, we are free from doing what we do not want to do. But if the Holy Spirit is working through us, it is no longer we who do the work, but the Spirit of Jesus Christ who is working through us. The new life we gain is not ours. It belongs to the Lord Jesus Christ. He allows us to share in the glories of the Life

Tree of Life

that He lives. We are dead to the old life of sin and alive to the perfect Life of Jesus Christ. It makes no sense to hang on to a life that was not ours anyway. We are not only laying down our lives but we lay down the life of sin that is in us.

Make no mistake, Jesus Christ cannot sin. The Holy Spirit cannot sin. If sin abounds in our lives, then Jesus Christ does not. The God of the Universe does not sanction sin. He understands our weakness but does not overlook willful sin. If we do sin, we are not lost, for we have Jesus Christ as the Advocate (1 John 2:1) yet our freedom does not give an excuse to sin. If we continue to make sin our habit, then it is not Jesus Christ who lives in us, but the life of sin we claim to have left behind.

Sharing Christ's Perfect Life changes our outlook

For the love of Christ controls us, having concluded this, that one died for all, therefore all died; and He died for all, that they who live should no longer live for themselves, but for Him who died and rose again on their behalf. Therefore from now on we recognize no man according to the flesh; even though we have known Christ according to the flesh, yet now we know Him thus no longer. Therefore if any man is in Christ, he is a new creature; the old things passed away; behold, new things have come.

Now all these things are from God, who reconciled us to Himself through Christ, and gave us the ministry of reconciliation, namely, that God was in Christ reconciling the world to Himself, not counting their trespasses against them, and He has committed to us the word of reconciliation. Therefore, we are ambassadors for Christ, as though God were entreating through us; we beg you on behalf of Christ, be reconciled to God. He made Him who knew no sin to be sin on our behalf, that we might become the righteousness of God in Him (2 Cor. 5:14-21).

We are to no longer see one another as we are in this physical life, but we are to see one another as we are in the spiritual life, as we would see Jesus Christ. We need to see one another through the eyes of Jesus Christ and see one another as He sees us. We look past the weaknesses of each other's lives, and look forward to the completing work that Jesus Christ is performing in our lives. It is no longer a

In The Beginning was the LOGOS of God

question of "How are we doing?" Instead it is a question of "How is Jesus Christ doing in our lives?" The responsibility for righteous living no longer rests on our shoulders but instead rests on the shoulders of Jesus Christ. We no longer judge one another according to the flesh, but according to the spiritual Life of Jesus Christ.

Those who have yielded to the Holy Spirit have found that they are not slaves without choice. When Christ lives His Life through our lives, He enriches us personally. We have a joy that is present even in the midst of great difficulties, because we have His companionship. We have not lost anything. Instead we have gained what was not possible before. We have Love for one another that was not there before. There is an oneness with those we have never met, based solely on our common oneness with Christ.

But the one who joins himself to the Lord is one spirit with Him (1 Cor. 6:17).

We are one with each other because we share in the same mind and body, which is Jesus Christ (1 Cor. 12:7-14, Eph. 4:1-7). We are in the Lord and can feel the Holy Spirit commune with others through us. We can feel the Love He has for others when He reaches out to them using our minds and our bodies and our circumstances and our lives. It may not be for our blessing, but nevertheless we share the blessing He has given to another. In doing so, the Life Jesus Christ made available enriches us.

There is a Fork-In-The-Road

Some of you are confused about the life that you are living. Some of you are wondering if sin controls your life or if the Spirit controls it. If you believe all things are working for your eternal good, then believe that Yahweh is faithful in all circumstances. Receive all that comes at you as from His hand, whether you can prove it or not. He will not fail you! You cannot will His control over your sin. You can only trust in His faithfulness to conquer it on your behalf. We will talk more in Part 3 of the book about our shared life in Christ.

Some of you are not willing to believe that anything can control you and want to believe that you have full control over what you do. Men believe the lie that Satan has told them since the days of

Tree of Life

Adam and Eve. Satan lies to us through the world, but also through the pulpits of the church. He wishes to take our eyes off of Jesus Christ and move the focus to our own righteousness. If he can get your eyes off of Jesus, he can control you through your sin. We have only two choices. We can walk a path that leads to destruction or a path that leads to a perfect Life.

Have you heard of the "Cardinal Christian" teachings? This is a person who is supposed to be "saved" but is living according to the flesh. This teaching is a lie, for we are either on the broad way of destruction or the narrow path of Life. We cannot walk both paths for they travel in different directions. They are not parallel so we cannot jump from one to the other at will. You may think you can jump back and forth, but if both travel in the same direction, then both paths travel to the same destination.

Taking the path that leads to Life will not make you perfect (complete, mature) on the day you take your first step, but it will lead you in the right direction. The longer you walk, the closer to becoming the finished work that He has planned you to be. You cannot continue to live for yourself and walk this road. You either follow Jesus Christ or you do not. Hanging onto the control of your life will cause you to lose your life. For the sin in your life is keeping you bound to a life of slavery. Sin is killing you. Therefore you are hanging onto what is causing your murder. A "Cardinal Christian" is not living in the likeness of Christ's death! You cannot bring the old life with you. You must lose it at the cross. He must find you in the likeness of His death for Him to find you in the likeness of His resurrection. Let go of your life, for it leads to your spiritual death (Mark 8:36). Cling on to the Life that will result in a spiritually everlasting life. Jesus Christ has already won the prize and shares it with you.

How does sharing Life with Jesus Christ work?

When you join Him on the cross, you join to Him your wicked way of life. He joins to you His Righteous Life. He shares your sin and bears your death. You share His virtue and inherit all that is His. Take time and think about what I am saying here. Salvation has a process to it and it is not just a bunch of words. What "I AM" did on the cross must work on the spiritual plain of your life.

In The Beginning was the LOGOS of God

It cannot be a bunch of words that sound good to the ear but not affect the rest of the body. The reality of everlasting salvation must overcome the destructive nature of sin. It is not enough that Jesus Christ died on the Cross and paid the debt owed by the world. His death must conquer the sin in the one who receives salvation. First salvation must happen and next the cleansing must take place.

Jesus Christ lived a perfect life without sin. This is a critical point because, if it were not for Jesus Christ, all who sin would go to the Lake of Fire. Without Him, there would not be one who lived a perfect life, and there would be no human beings in Heaven. Jesus Christ lived a perfect life and stood before the judgment seat and the Judge declared Him innocent. When the Judge declared Jesus innocent, He also declared all those who are in Him innocent. For if the Head is innocent then the feet and the hands are innocent also. Jesus Christ is the Head of the Church and we are His arms and legs (1 Cor. 12:11-31). The Judge does not judge the arms and legs only but the whole body according to the works of the head. We know that His works are acceptable and therefore our acceptance is assured.

We were not able to prepare ourselves so Jesus Christ could join Himself to our goodness, so He made Himself one with our wickedness, thus making Himself a party to our sin. Although He did not sin Himself, He became guilty of our sin, because He became one with us and shared the responsibility for our sin. He took our sin onto Himself and stood before the judgment seat, in our stead, guilty. Jesus Christ cannot lie. Therefore, He cannot admit to a crime He did not commit. After he became one with us, there was no longer any distinction between Him and us. He became equally guilty as us. He shared in our sin as if He had committed it, yet He remained faultless in His own Life. He became sin on our behalf (2 Cor. 5:21).

After He presented Himself as sinless and was judged innocent of any wrongdoing in His own Life, He stood in our place before the Father, guilty of the sin found in our lives. The great "I AM" poured the complete penalty for our sins into Jesus Christ and the penalty for sin is death. He did not die as Jesus Christ but as _____ (fill in your name). A human being can only die one death, so when Jesus Christ shared our lives, He died our spiritual death. Therefore, death no longer controls us for we already died in Him (Heb 9:27-28, 1 Cor. 15:51-57). Jesus Christ defeated

Tree of Life

death and caused us to live in Him. His Life, already acceptable before the judgment seat, became our life and we are now acceptable through Him. When we share His life, we share in a life that is in Heavenly Places. We cannot return to our old lives living for the flesh, for it died as part of the judgment. To resurrect the "Old Man" would be to nullify the work Jesus did on the cross and we would still be liable for our sin, which is not possible - for Jesus Christ died. For those who have received Him, the "Old Man" is gone. The "Cardinal Christian" is gone (Heb. 6:1-6).

If you are trying to live your own life, then the "Old Man" is not gone. The Judge has yet to consider your case. Your deeds and not Christ's will be on trial as you stand judgment in the upcoming Judgment Seat (Rev. 20:10-15, Dan. 7:9-13 and 22). The Judge will find all guilty as charged, for no other man has lived a perfect life (including you).

If your life is in Christ Jesus, then He has judged you already and found you not guilty, when He found Jesus Christ not guilty. Because Jesus Christ is one with you, He took the full fury of the wrath of God and you remain safe, just as Noah and his family were safe in the Ark while God's judgment passed over. Just as the Hebrews where spared during Passover, your life is safe in Jesus Christ through the blood He shed on your behalf. He stood between you and your judgment, saving you from you. Why would you want to go back to face the judgment alone? In truth, you cannot go back if you have made the journey, for the "Old Man" is gone and all that you have left is Life in Christ Jesus.

Those of us who have made the journey will never want to go back for He is the treasure we are looking for. He is our salvation, He is our all in all, and He has become the center of our lives. His is the Life we want to live. We have left behind all that makes life miserable and gained what makes life valuable. Not that we have already finished the course, but we see Jesus Christ and push forward to gain our prize (Philp. 3:7-14). He is our guarantee that we will complete the course, for He seals us in the Holy Spirit.

So then, you will know them by their fruits. Not everyone who says to Me, 'Lord, Lord,' will enter the kingdom of heaven; but he who does the will of My Father who is in heaven. Many will say to Me on that day, 'Lord, Lord, did we not prophesy in Your name, and

In The Beginning was the LOGOS of God

in Your name cast out demons, and in Your name perform many miracles?' And then I will declare to them, 'I never knew you; depart from Me, you who practice lawlessness' (Matt. 7:20-23).

Not everyone walks along the right path just because he says he is. What other men think will not be of much use when we reach our destination. It is what God thinks that will matter. If we walk in friendship with Jesus Christ, we will also join Him in Love's demonstration. The message entrusted to the LOGOS of God is entrusted to those joined to His death, in whom He has made His home (John 14:23). The result of having God's thoughts dwelling in us is our transformation into His image. He recreated us by renewing our minds in the power of Love as found in Jesus Christ (Rom. 12:1-3).

Again I point out to you that we are not talking about a nice idea, but spiritual life and death. All men must make a choice between two competing ideals. The Lord God has made a statement about His Son. He has declared that His Son has prepared a way for our redemption. Any choice that does not accept the offer made by the Father through the work of His Son is a choice of death.

For whoever wishes to save his life shall lose it, but whoever loses his life for My sake, he is the one who will save it (Luke 9:24).

It is your choice. As far as I can see there is only one choice to make.

May Jesus Christ's death of on the cross be a Tree of Life to you.

Tree of Life

Chapter 20

Pointing to the Right Source

Paul discourages us from following other men's thinking
But we have the mind of Christ (1 Cor. 2:16).

And I, brethren, could not speak to you as to spiritual men, but as to men of flesh, as to babes in Christ. I gave you milk to drink, not solid food; for you were not yet able to receive it. Indeed, even now you are not yet able, for you are still fleshly. For since there is jealousy and strife among you, are you not fleshly, and are you not walking like mere men? <u>*For when one says, "I am of Paul," and another, "I am of Apollos," are you not mere men?*</u> *What then is Apollos? And what is Paul? Servants through whom you believed, even as the Lord gave opportunity to each one. I planted, Apollos watered,* <u>*but God was causing the growth. So then neither the one who plants nor the one who waters is anything, but God who causes the growth.*</u> *Now he who plants and he who waters are one; but each will receive his own reward according to his own labor. For we are God's fellow workers; you are God's field, God's building (1 Cor. 3:1-9).*

Even in Paul's day, men of the Christian faith were divided according to the teachings of men. Paul reminds us that we are only workers in the field and it is the Holy Spirit's task to work in the hearts of Christians. The Holy Spirit allows us to be His helpers so we may see His work within the flock and honor Him. Men who become leaders without instruction from the Holy Spirit are "the blind **leading the** blind and both fall into a ditch" (Matt. 15:14, 23:1-36). Those who follow other men's thinking are "the blind **following** the blind," giving honor to men instead of God.

It is not Yahweh's will that His people divide over the issues of doctrine (1 Cor. 1:10, 1 Cor. 11:17-19). He expects the body to have the same mind but the same mind as whom? (Eph. 4:1-7). What good is having a group of people with the same mind, if the Author of Life does not share the same mind with them? We have the Mind of Christ (1 Cor. 2:9-16). We are not one because we agree in our beliefs. Our oneness comes about because of the person we have

In The Beginning was the LOGOS of God

placed our trust in. Each has different levels of knowledge and maturity, but all trust in Jesus Christ alone.

The "Mind of Christ" is in the Message communicated through the LOGOS of God. What is our response to this revelation? Is it to raise controversies we cannot resolve and make our thoughts about them more important than the doctrine of Love? We do not show the Mind of Christ by waging verbal warfare with one another. We can only make the teachings of the Most High God confusing. Yes, the verses are there in the Bible and false teachers will twist them any way they want to further their own thinking. They turn the Mind of Christ into the thinking of man. They change the meaning of God's words to meet their own agendas because they do not fear Him and their fearlessness leads them to their own destruction.

We are to focus on the Scripture in proper perspective

"The eye is the lamp of the body; so then if your eye is clear, your whole body will be full of light. "But if your eye is bad, your whole body will be full of darkness. <u>If then the light that is in you is darkness, how great is the darkness!</u> "No one can serve two masters; for either he will hate the one and love the other, or he will be devoted to one and despise the other. You cannot serve God and wealth (Matt. 6:22-24).

Jesus is not talking about a physical eye but the eye of the spiritual body. He speaks about our thought life and how it affects our spiritual well-being. These verses are part of the Sermon on the Mount. In Matt. 6:25-34, Jesus points out that too much attention paid to our everyday lives could get in the way of our knowing Him. To be excessively anxious about what we are going to eat or how we are going to get our clothing takes our focus off of Christ and puts it onto the temporal things of this life. The Holy Spirit is our clear eye filling us with the creator's light.

We must attend to our daily lives, but we ought to maintain it in proper proportion to our spiritual lives. In Matt. 6, God claims that He will provide. If we trust Him to provide what we need, we can clear our mind to hear the Holy Spirit teach us the important aspects of life. If we do not trust Him, we will spend too much time working out the details of how we are going to meet our needs. We will spend

Tree of Life

valuable resources and time on plans that may never happen. How many times have people worried about circumstances in life that worked out O.K. by themselves? Many times we thrashed over problems that we cannot control and should not control. We waste our time thinking about what is outside our ability to change.

If we trust that our God loves us and has a plan that He is achieving for our benefit, then we can trust that He will provide for us even before we see those provisions. Since we trust in Him, we are free from worry about the burdens and toils of our lives. We are free to aim for the knowledge of God. If our thinking is chiefly on the thinking of God, then worldly things become undesirable. If our thinking is mainly on the world, then the thinking of God will appear strange and undesirable. If we do not listen to the Holy Spirit's guidance, we will feel lost in a maze of men's thinking.

The true student of LOGOS sees a great worthiness in Yahweh. We trust Him because of the worthiness we see. We know the Creator of the Universe has set standards for our own good. We want the boundaries He has lovingly set for our benefit. Parents know the limits of little children. Who would leave an infant alone to fend for himself? We would consider it child abuse in a court of men's law. We would rightly become angry when we hear of such. Even when the child gets older and thinks, "I am old enough to take care of myself," the parents know whether his statement is true. If a child drowns in a swimming pool and the parents had left the child alone, unattended, we would think them reckless and the outcome unavoidable. Parents set boundaries for their children because they love them and wish to protect them. Where would we be without guidance from the One who loves us and who has blazed the path before us? True students of the Word know that He has the words of Life (John 5:39, 6:64-70) and they want those words as others want gold and silver, regardless of the boundaries they set.

Many who claim to seek wisdom find a look a like wisdom. But it is folly. *"There is a way which seems right to a man, but its end is the way of death" (Proverbs 14:12).* The Lord holds teachers to a higher standard than others, so do not quickly wish to be a teacher (James 3:1-2). There are many teachers in this world. They each claim to have the truth. A true teacher of God's Word will fear and honor God (Luke 12:1-10). Jesus Christ is the truth. Without

In The Beginning was the LOGOS of God

Him, you have nothing (John 14:6). Any who teach others to follow another way, other than the way provided by the Godhead, teach doctrines that are from the Tree of Death. They are words of poison to all who listen.

Jesus Christ did not come on His own initiative

The Godhead is the only one who understands Truth. He created the universe based on Truth. Those who follow Yahweh's teachings do so by living out His truth according to the design of the Creator. If anyone wishes to know "Truth," he must first know Jesus Christ. The Holy Spirit is the one who will reveal Jesus Christ to him.

"When the Helper comes, whom I will send to you from the Father, the Spirit of truth, who proceeds from the Father, He will bear witness of Me (John 15:26).

When the Spirit of truth comes, He will guide you into all the truth; for He will not speak on His own initiative, but whatever He hears, He will speak; and He will disclose to you what is to come. He shall glorify Me; for He shall take of Mine, and shall disclose it to you (John 16:13-14).

Jesus said to them, "If God were your Father, you would love Me; for I proceeded forth and have come from God, for I have not even come on My own initiative, but He sent Me. Why do you not understand what I am saying? It is because you cannot hear My word" (John 8:42-43).

"I can do nothing on My own initiative. As I hear, I judge; and My judgment is just, because I do not seek My own will, but the will of Him who sent Me" (John 5:30).

"For I did not speak on My own initiative, but the Father Himself who sent Me has given Me commandment, what to say, and what to speak" (John 12:49).

Notice the Holy Spirit will glorify the Messiah and not Himself. The Holy Spirit is not self-centered, but rather Christ-centered and promotes God the Son. Also notice what Jesus Christ said: His actions and sayings were according to what the Father had shown Him and not His own thinking. Jesus Christ does not work according to His own will, but is living within the will of the Father.

Tree of Life

He does nothing on His own initiative but follows the commands of His Father. Jesus is pointing to His Father and not toward Himself. He willingly submits Himself to the Headship of God the Father (Phil. 2:1-11).

A true disciple of the Holy Spirit will follow the example set by the Godhead. He will point to the Holy Spirit, who points to the Son, who in turn points to the Father. The Holy Spirit points to the Son of God when He educates a true disciple. When a true disciple speaks of what he has learned from the Holy Spirit, he will also point to the Son of God and to the Holy Spirit, but not to him. When a true disciple leads another to Christ, he wants the one he leads to grow spiritually and not to follow him. He wants others to hear the Holy Spirit for themselves so they may learn on their own. Here then is how we know truth from lies. If teachings honor men over Yahweh or dishonors one man to uplift another, it is not following the example of Jesus Christ and the Holy Spirit.

With the Holy Spirit, we have the mind of Christ

And in the same way the Spirit also helps our weakness; for we do not know how to pray as we should, but the Spirit Himself intercedes for us with groanings too deep for words; and <u>He who searches the hearts knows what the mind of the Spirit is, because He intercedes for the saints according to the will of God</u>. And we know that God causes all things to work together for good to those who love God, to those who are called according to His purpose. For whom He foreknew, He also predestined to become conformed to the image of His Son, that He might be the first-born among many brethren. (Romans 8:26-29).

<u>For who among men knows the thoughts of a man except the spirit of the man, which is in him? Even so the thoughts of God no one knows except the Spirit of God</u>. Now we have received, not the spirit of the world, but the Spirit who is from God, <u>that we might know the things freely given to us by God</u>, which things we also speak, not in words taught by human wisdom, <u>but in those taught by the Spirit, combining spiritual thoughts with spiritual words</u> (1 Cor. 2: 11-13).

In The Beginning was the LOGOS of God

Our walking in the Mind of Christ forces us to admit that we have weakness. We do not know how to come before a Holy God. We do not know the real meaning of His word. Other people and their difficulties do not move us, for we know not how to love as He loves us. When we pray, the Holy Spirit searches our hearts and presents our petitions before God, communicating the way we feel and think. We are not able to put into words all that we wish to bring before the throne of God. The Holy Spirit connects us to our God with an unbreakable connection. He translates our thinking for the Father and the Father's thinking for us by combining spiritual thoughts with spiritual words. The thinking of God flows through us like a spring of living water (Isa. 58:1-11, John 4:9-14 and 7:37-39, Jer. 2:13 and 7:13). We are now free to explore the mind of God by the bridge He has made between us. We now have the proper food to eat. The manna from Heaven is now available to us and we can gather it in plenty!

As well as having a connection to the Father through the Holy Spirit, there is a connection to those who share the connection to Him. We feel this connection most when meeting people we have never meet before. He draws us to each other, even though we have nothing in common except our love for our God.

The right source is not in finding the right religion. It is not in finding the right group of people. It is not in finding the right ministry. And it is not in finding the right teacher. The only true source lies in a proper shared connection to the Creator through the Holy Spirit.

May the connection to the Holy Spirit be a Tree of Life to you.

Tree of Life

Chapter 21

We Can Know Who the False Teachers Are

Holy Spirit warns us of false teachers

Beloved, do not believe every spirit, but test the spirits to see whether they are from God; because many false prophets have gone out into the world. <u>By this you know the Spirit of God: every spirit that confesses that Jesus Christ has come in the flesh is from God</u>; and every spirit that does not confess Jesus is not from God; and this is the spirit of the antichrist, of which you have heard that it is coming, and now it is already in the world.

You are from God, little children, and have overcome them; because <u>greater is He who is in you than he who is in the world</u>. They are from the world; therefore they speak as from the world, and the world listens to them. <u>We are from God; he who knows God listens to us; he who is not from God does not listen to us. By this we know the spirit of truth and the spirit of error. Beloved, let us love one another, for love is from God; and everyone who loves is born of God and knows God. The one who does not love does not know God, for God is love</u> (1 John 4:1-8).

There is a spiritual battle going on for the minds of men that Satan started in the Garden of Eden (Gen. 3:1-5). The battle is real and the combatants fight it out on the streets and in the media. The Holy Spirit tells us to test the spirits. Be watchful of those who try to put thoughts into your mind. Some spirits come over the airwaves, in movies, by the Internet, or in print. They honor lustful living and selfish behavior. Offering wisdom, they lead those who listen into sensual pleasures at the expense of what is worthy and good. People involved with mediums that communicate with the dead or use tarot cards, astrology, séances, and other such practices allow the spirit of darkness direct access. Such associations bring people into fellowship with the antichrist. Eat no spiritual thoughts without considering their source.

Satan told Eve that if she ate of his tree, she would become like God knowing good and evil. She ate and did become like God, but only in knowing good and evil - not in handling that knowledge.

In The Beginning was the LOGOS of God

Man-made religions offer the same lie: a way to ascend on one's own merit. It is the same thinking that motivated Satan to overthrow the throne of God. He wanted to raise himself up to the same level as God and sit on the throne of God. Consider what the evil of Satan stands for. Be grateful that our God – and not Satan - sits on the Throne of Authority. Think what it would be like if the ruler of the universe was like Hitler or Saddam Hussein. Their thinking directed men down a path of hatred and destruction.

We can identify these evil spirits by their unwillingness to confess Jesus Christ as Lord (1 John 2:15-19 and 4:1-6) and their inability to love as Jesus loves. They oppose Jesus Christ as the LOGOS of God. They do not want the Light of Love to shine and will attack it any way they can. They succeed to influence the world because the light bearers in the Church are asleep and the salt is less salty (Matt: 5:11-16).

We need to test the thinking of those who want to influence us. We need to be aware of the thoughts that we allow into our minds and challenge them with the Bible (2 Cor. 10:3-5, Col. 2:6-10). Then we must ask the Holy Spirit for the right answer. That answer will always be compatible with the life Jesus Christ lived. It will always fit on the cross and will be full of forgiveness, understanding, and Love; never self-centered, always God centered.

Give credit to your Teacher and honor Him

<u>Do not love the world, nor the things in the world.</u> If anyone loves the world, the love of the Father is not in him. For all that is in the world, the lust of the flesh and the lust of the eyes and the boastful pride of life, is not from the Father, but is from the world. And the world is passing away, and also its lusts; but the one who does the will of God abides forever.

<u>Children, it is the last hour; and just as you heard that antichrist is coming, even now many antichrists have arisen;</u> from this we know that it is the last hour. <u>They went out from us, but they were not really of us; for if they had been of us, they would have remained with us</u>; but they went out, in order that it might be shown that they all are not of us.

<u>But you have an anointing from the Holy One, and you all know.</u> I have not written to you because you do not know the truth,

Tree of Life

but because you do know it, and because no lie is of the truth. Who is the liar but the one who denies that Jesus is the Christ? <u>This is the antichrist, the one who denies the Father and the Son.</u> Whoever denies the Son does not have the Father; the one who confesses the Son has the Father also.

<u>*As for you, let that abide in you which you heard from the beginning. If what you heard from the beginning abides in you, you also will abide in the Son and in the Father.*</u> *And this is the promise which He Himself made to us: eternal life. These things I have written to you concerning those who are trying to deceive you.* <u>*And as for you, the anointing which you received from Him abides in you, and you have no need for anyone to teach you; but as His anointing teaches you about all things,*</u> *and is true and is not a lie, and just as it has taught you, you abide in Him (1 John 2:15-27).*

Some say they know the truth, but they lie. They will tell you that understanding the truth is something they are helping you do in your life and that you should honor them for it. Man is not the one who can teach you. When you read a book or listen to someone on a tape or the radio, the Holy Spirit is there to guide you in your understanding. The Holy Spirit helps you discern the true disciple from the false. He will help you know if someone is rightly interpreting the scriptures (Heb. 5:11-14 and 4:12, 1 Tim. 4:1-11). Since false teachers mix the truth with lies, the Holy Spirit can use false teachers to train you for His own purposes (even if they are using the Word of God to lift their own ego). If they taught lies only, others would easily see them for who they are. Therefore, the Holy Spirit can use the truth in their false teachings to improve your understanding of the truth He is revealing.

You can know they are false teachers because they want you to follow them. They work hard to control the events surrounding them. They strive to get others to recognize they are correct in their beliefs. They do not strive to live out those convictions in their own lives. They do not care for you. Instead, they want attention and acknowledgment from you to lift their own egos. They want the credit for teaching you what you believe. Once they have you, they will not want to let you go. They want to be your examples and become jealous of anyone else the Holy Spirit uses.

In The Beginning was the LOGOS of God

Jesus is our only true example. Those who belong to Him grow into His likeness and the Holy Spirit uses them to help us better understand the One who died for us. The Holy Spirit's followers do not strive to be an example and may not know that they are being used by the Holy Spirit as examples. When approached, they always point to the Lord as the one true example.

Lifting men in the place of Jesus Christ, works against the truth. If you lift others up, as the example of righteous living, you point others toward a man's understanding. Then if they fall, you have helped a false teacher to deceive. A man's understanding is flawed at best, so you could be leading them away from the True Light and away from the only path (2 Tim. 3:1-9, 1 Thess. 2:13-16). You would be opposing the Light and effectively murdering those you helped to deceive. Do not raise men to take Jesus Christ's or the Holy Spirit's place in another person's life. Look at your motives. The heart of a man is evil. You may want others to agree with you, so they honor you and not Yahweh. What an awful feeling it will be if the one you thought you were working for finds you are working against Him.

The words of many false teachers are basically true. You should do what they tell you to do, but they also want you to worship them and set them on the throne of your heart, which you must not do (Matt. 23:1-13). They will mix their error with the truth to deceive you. They lead with words of honey and enslave with good works. Their goal is to be the source of your faith and the object of your love.

They are the ones you hear of who return to their wicked ways. They are the ones who abandon their faith for worldly lusts. All those who build their faith on a man will have that faith crumble when the man fails (Matt. 7:15-27). All men stumble at some point, so set your faith on one who never fails. He has already lived a perfect life and is willing to share that perfect life with you. God the Father Himself testified that He has given you everlasting life through His Son, Jesus Christ (1 John 5:9-15). You need no one to intercede for you or teach you (1 John 2:27).

Why would men want to exchange the truth for a lie? It is because they hate the truth and they hate the Holy Spirit who is revealing the truth! They will face an angry God, for they are

Tree of Life

powerless to help His sheep and they interfere with those He has sent (Matt. 23:13). Because of jealousy, the false teachers work against the witnesses of God. They confuse the multitude for their own selfish gain. Be sure their time is short.

<u>Beware of the false prophets, who come to you in sheep's clothing, but inwardly are ravenous wolves.</u> You will know them by their fruits. Grapes are not gathered from thorn bushes, nor figs from thistles, are they? Even so, every good tree bears good fruit; but the bad tree bears bad fruit. A good tree cannot produce bad fruit, nor can a bad tree produce good fruit. Every tree that does not bear good fruit is cut down and thrown into the fire. So then, you will know them by their fruits. <u>Not everyone who says to Me, 'Lord, Lord,' will enter the kingdom of heaven; but he who does the will of My Father who is in heaven.</u> Many will say to Me on that day, 'Lord, Lord, did we not prophesy in Your name, and in Your name cast out demons, and in Your name perform many miracles?' And then I will declare to them, 'I never knew you; depart from Me, you who practice lawlessness.' (Matt. 7:15-23). (See also: Luke 6:39-49.)

Jesus said there would be those who come to Him and falsely call Him, Lord. He will not accept them, for they were not His. It will take more than words when men come before a Holy God. They are not going to play word games with Him. The truth is what will count. One is not a disciple of Jesus Christ because they say or think they are. If Yahweh does not have an affect on the choices made in the life of a disciple then that disciple follows in vain.

There are only two possibilities for each person who has ever lived. There is the Tree of Life and the tree of the Knowledge of Good and Evil. You either receive instruction about the true meaning of the Word of God (LOGOS) revealed by the Holy Spirit or you receive training according to man's thinking. False teachers are everywhere looking for their next victim. Beware.

**May your test find the Spirit of Truth
                      and may He be a Tree of life to you.**

The LOGOS of God is the

Tree of Life

A Journey to Discover the Heart of God

Part Three

Walking in the Fellowship of Love

A choice we must make, a question we must answer.

But you did not learn Christ in this way, if indeed you have heard Him and have been taught in Him, just as truth is in Jesus, that, in reference to your former manner of life, you lay aside the old self, which is being corrupted in accordance with the lusts of deceit, and that you be renewed in the spirit of your mind, and put on the new self, which in the likeness of God has been created in righteousness and holiness of the truth
 Ephesians 4:20-24.

Tree of Life

Walking in the Fellowship of Love

Chapter 22

The Goal of God's Instructions is Love - I

The Tree of Life is about Friendship of the Light

As I urged you upon my departure for Macedonia, remain on at Ephesus so that you may <u>instruct certain men not to teach strange doctrines</u>, nor to pay attention to myths and endless genealogies, <u>which give rise to mere speculation</u> rather than furthering the administration of God which is by faith.

<u>But the goal of our instruction is love from a pure heart and a good conscience and a sincere faith</u>. For some men, straying from these things, have turned aside to fruitless discussion, wanting to be teachers of the Law, even though they do not understand either what they are saying or the matters about which they make confident assertions (1 Tim. 1:3-7).

One of them, a lawyer, asked Him a question, testing Him, "<u>Teacher, which is the great commandment in the Law?</u>" And He said to him, "'YOU SHALL LOVE THE LORD YOUR GOD WITH ALL YOUR HEART, AND WITH ALL YOUR SOUL, AND WITH ALL YOUR MIND.' "This is the great and foremost commandment. "The second is like it, 'YOU SHALL LOVE YOUR NEIGHBOR AS YOURSELF.' "<u>On these two commandments depend the whole Law and the Prophets</u>" (Matt. 22:35-40).

"<u>A new commandment I give to you, that you love one another, even as I have loved you, that you also love one another.</u> "<u>By this all men will know that you are My disciples, if you have love for one another</u>" (John 13:34-35).

I have a vision of the person who would continue reading this book. I feel a closeness to the person I see in my mind. For me, our relationship is more than author and reader. I feel friendship toward you because I believe you desire the Tree of Life (John 6:31-58). If it is true - that you want to be a True Disciple of the Tree of Life - then you must learn to love as Jesus has loves you"

A disciple of any given discipline takes on certain characteristics of that discipline. A true disciple of Jesus takes on His likeness and therefore His temperament. When you think of certain groups of people, you think of them as having a likeness that distinguishes them from others. I want you to think about the Pilgrims who came over from England. What do you picture in your mind's eye? Most likely you picture a certain style of clothing, maybe a Thanksgiving Dinner, their speech and mannerisms, perhaps the culture they came from, or their faith in God.

Today, we can tell ethnic groups by the clothes they wear, their accents, and the style of food they eat. If I say "Mexican Restaurant," it most likely causes you to picture a different style of cooking than Italian cuisine or Chinese food. That's because everything has characteristics that we relate to them by. People in America think and act differently than people in Africa. Their priorities are different, because they, as a people, are different. The circumstances they face daily are different because of location, history, culture, and opportunity.

Christians need to "Love as Jesus has loved" because that is what Christians do. That is the culture we are joining. When Jesus gave a sign to distinguish His true disciples from those who claim to be His followers, He gave the characteristics of Love. He did so because Love speaks of His character living within them. A true disciple of Jesus Christ takes on the characteristics of Jesus Christ because it is the expected outcome of their companionship. If they do not take on His characteristic of Love, He does not live within them. Love is the fruit of His labors, which He has born within the heart of His people.

The Creator created us according to His plan. The Holy Spirit actively fulfills the plan. The goal of Yahweh is to create within us a love that is like His Love. He wants us to have Love, issued from a pure and clean heart of sincere faith. Jesus Christ is Love. His people inherit His likeness as He becomes greater and greater in their lives and they become lesser and lesser (John 3:26-36). They shine the Light that is within them because they cannot contain Jesus Christ and stop the Light from shining (Luke 8:16-18, 11:33-36).

Notice in John 13:34-35 that Jesus Christ changed the Second Greatest Commandment. Until that time, the only example men had to compare their love for each other was the love they had for themselves. According to the Second Greatest Commandment, a man would ask, "Would I feel loved, if someone did this to me?" After

Walking in the Fellowship of Love

Jesus, a man should ask, "Is this the way Jesus showed His Love to me?" We might take this a step further and ask, "If Jesus was me, is this the way Jesus would show His love? Would He treat someone the way I am treating the other person?"

There is a major difference between these two types of questions. Normally when I ask myself about my feelings, I reveal a self-centered and selfish tendency. When I compare my actions to the Demonstration, my thoughts are about Jesus Christ's sacrifice and His unwarranted acceptance of me and of others.

The goal of Yahweh's instruction is Love

In 1 Cor. 13, the Holy Spirit uses Paul to define Love. We should think about this definition every day. His definition of Love is deeper than it might first appear. It is one thing to agree intellectually with such a definition - and another to live it. We cannot humanly manufacture such Love by forcing ourselves to overcome our sin nature. It can only happen if it is the nature of our being. Jesus Christ has joined Himself to us, through the Holy Spirit, so Love is to be our natural impulse as He becomes more of who we are.

Love is the meaning Yahweh intended and it empowers His words. The cross of Jesus Christ defines Love as, "While we were His enemies, Christ died for us." He is the example we are to follow (Rom. 5, 1 John 4:6-21). How does one learn to love as Jesus Christ loves? Only He can provide the ability to overcome our sin and overcome our natural inabilities to be helpful through oneness with Him.

What is Love? Many would define Love as a passion, a commitment, a feeling, or the will of the mind. They would learn to love by willing themselves to feel good toward others and perform acts worthwhile to others. Yet, any attempt to force an act of love that is contrary to our nature, will be a product of our flesh (works). A mindset on the flesh is in opposition to Yahweh and the Message He sent (Rom. 8:5-10).

In truth, Love is a condition of the soul. It is the material the Holy Spirit uses to build Christian character. To love as Jesus loves, we must change our thinking (Rom. 12:1-3). We need Him to rebuild our souls with the materials of Love. We were all lost, marred by our selfish hateful ways (Eph. 2:1-10). The Holy Spirit in us changes us.

Tree of Life

One learns to love as Jesus Christ loves by abiding in Love and by having Love abide within (1 John 15:1-18). To love as Jesus loves, it must become our nature to love because it is His nature to love.

Our natural response will always align with what comes from the depths of our souls. We need a rebirth and the image of the Person of Christ must grow in the deepest areas of our beings (John 3:3). His Love must grow in us like a Tree of Life or Spring of Living Water. Then we will love, naturally, without planning our action. When our natural responses originate from a heart of selfish wants and hate, the actions we commit toward others are self-centered and without compassion. We introduce our worst behavior to even those who lovingly care for us. When the natural responses originate from a heart of Love, we commit other-centered actions full of compassion. We expose our best behavior to those who spitefully use and hate us.

Only the blood of Jesus Christ, which is symbolic of the Holy Spirit, can clean us of our unrighteousness and hate by giving us a new heart of flesh and replacing of our hearts of stone (Eze. 11:19, 36:26). We are the branches who receive life-giving substance from the Vine (John 15:1-18). The branches bear the fruit but it is the Vine who makes it possible. Good fruit comes from a good tree and evil fruit from an evil tree (Matt. 7:12-23). The Holy Spirit causes His fruit to be obvious in us and it is a sign of His handiwork in us (Eph. 2:10). Just like a tree which was planted as a seedling, our fruit does not appear on the first day we believe. As we mature, we will have the fruit of His labors (Matt. 7:12-20, Gal. 5:13-25).

For us to be recreated anew, God must do His work in us

For while we were in the flesh, the sinful passions, which were aroused by the Law, were at work in the members of our body to bear fruit for death. But now we have been released from the Law, having died to that by which we were bound, so that we serve in newness of the Spirit and not in oldness of the letter (Romans 7:5-6).

In the same way the Spirit also helps our weakness; for we do not know how to pray as we should, but the Spirit Himself intercedes for us with groanings too deep for words; and He who searches the hearts knows what the mind of the Spirit is, because He intercedes for the saints according to the will of God.

Walking in the Fellowship of Love

And we know that God causes all things to work together for good to those who love God, to those who are called according to His purpose. For those whom He foreknew, *He also predestined to become conformed to the image of His Son*, so that He would be the firstborn among many brethren; and these whom He predestined, He also called; and these whom He called, He also justified; and these whom He justified, He also glorified. *What then shall we say to these things? If God is for us, who is against us? (Romans 8:26-31).*

For we are His workmanship, created in Christ Jesus for good works, which God prepared beforehand so that we would walk in them (Eph. 2:10).

Our God predestined all to work out for our good. He does not allow events to happen to His chosen ones that are harmful to their eternal well-being. He needs us to face "all happenings" as if they come from Him. He allows stuff to happen to cleanse us of our bad habits and to create Love within us. He intends to release us from our bondage to a selfish hateful nature, which causes us to sin, and give us a new nature of Love (Gal. 5:19-26, Rom. 13-8-10). The classes can be exacting and frustrating as we struggle under His tutelage. His instruction has purpose to it. It takes time, practice, and commitment to incorporate that purpose into our lives.

When we come to the Tree of Life, we gain far more than knowledge. We gain a day-to-day communion with the "I AM." He is LORD God Almighty and we have the privilege to travel with Him on a spiritual walk of faith, a faith that we base solely on His Love. Those who come to Jesus Christ have total confidence in His Love. We know the Demonstration cost Jesus Christ greatly. We cannot grasp the total personal grief and suffering that He endured for us. We know that after paying such a ransom, He is not willing for His mission to fail now. The work that He has begun in us He will finish in us (Philip. 2:12-15 and 1:6). It is not by works of the flesh that we boast in, but is the product of the Artist skillfully applying His hand to our lives (1 Cor. 1:15-29).

If Jesus Christ, through the Holy Spirit, does not create in us a Spirit of Love then we have no hope. Yet, He has started the good work in us and He will finish the good work in us, guaranteed! We place our faith in the trustworthiness of Jesus Christ because we

Tree of Life

believe in His Love. The responsibility for our reconciliation rests on His shoulders and we have confidence in His ability to carry out His goal (Isa. 55:8-11).

Those who eat from the Tree of Life learn to view life from Jesus Christ's viewpoint. As He walked on this earth, He showed Love to His enemies and will do so as He continues His walk through us. He desires to show Love to His enemies through us. He longs for us to join Him by demonstrating the same Love He showed. We no longer live as the judges of men, deciding fair or unfair, righteous or unrighteous. Our lives have a new purpose. We interact with other people according to His Love. The skill we need to Love comes from the power of the Life He lives in us.

The Holy Spirit is like spiritual blood that flows through the body of believers, which brings nourishment to each cell and takes away the waste. The Holy Spirit teaches us with lessons that nourish and cleanse our souls. He uses common everyday experiences to change our thinking into His thinking. We need to learn to receive hardships as a time to lean on the Lord, to act according to His Love. And we need to seize times of ease as opportunities to use our prosperity for the benefit of others. To be like that, we must stop focusing on what we are doing and begin to focus on who we are in comparison to Jesus Christ. We know that we will never fully love as He loves. Yet, it is true: to the degree that He has formed us into His image, we love as He loves.

The Holy Spirit, through Paul in 1Timothy 1:3-7, directs us to stay away from the meaningless controversies that confuse, an all-too-common hindrance among the elect. We are to focus on the instructions that teach us about God's love. Remember, not all teachings about Love are from God the Father and are therefore misleading. We have revelations from the Holy Spirit, which reveals to us the LOGOS of God as spoken of in the Bible.

It is the skill of the Potter that shapes the clay according to the Potter's will. The clay does not help the Potter create the shape of the pot (Jer. 18:1-10, Isa. 64:6-9, Rom. 9:14-21). The Potter does not tell the clay what He is doing and why. The clay does not question the Potter about the proper time go into the fire. It is the skill of the Potter taking the correct action at the proper time that results in His will being carried out. We cannot do the work of salvation. It belongs

Walking in the Fellowship of Love

to the Godhead and Godhead alone. God must to do the work in us and we must yield to Him as He does His work. What we can do is value what we see happening to us and those around us. We can rejoice in our inclusion into Communion of Love, rejoice under all circumstances, and look for the chance to show Love from a clean and sincere heart.

Studying the teachings of God's Love

The Holy Spirit teaches us that our God's nature is Love. The nature of His disciples will mirror His nature as they grow into His Image (2 Cor. 3:18, Rom. 12:1-3). According to Jesus Christ, Love fulfills every good represented by the Law (Matt. 22:34-40, Rom. 13:8-10). If our character becomes like His character, we would naturally fulfill what is good in the Law.

Read 1 Cor. 13. As you read, remember that God is Love. Try reading Yahweh's name or Jesus Christ's name wherever you see the word Love. Love seeks the benefit of those around them. Love sacrifices His own well-being to promote another. Love does not keep a tally sheet or an account ledger. Love seeks the best for all involved. Those who follow Love are careful that pretenders, who are like wolves in sheep's clothing, do not fool them. Those who follow Love do not hate the pretenders. Instead, they grieve for the pretender's souls, because the followers of Love know they were once pretenders also.

1 Cor. 13 describes the person you are joining your life to. Because of Love, Jesus Christ took onto Himself our sins and the penalty due us as sinners. We believe the promise of Love. We proclaim the promise is true. We study His demonstration to understand the depth of our sin, so we might know the depth of His Love. We do not judge ourselves as worthy or unworthy when we search the depth of our sin. We search so we may be thankful for the Love shown to us by our God. The more we see the difference between Him and us the more we see our need for change and the more we understand the cost for what He has done on the cross. We understand the depth of our sins, so we are humble when dealing with other people's sins. If our study is for any other purpose than to know Love, then we are noisy gongs and clanging cymbals. We

Tree of Life

make much noise but no one can understand what we are saying (1 Cor. 13:1-4).

In Matt. 22:35-40, Jesus said that two commandments sum up everything LOGOS is teaching. First is our love for our God, which has its foundation on His Love for us (1 John 4:6-12). The other is our Love for the brethren, which is an outpouring of the Holy Spirit from within us (1 John 4:20-12). I can tell you about Love, but I cannot cause you to understand the meanings behind its teachings. The true meaning is much deeper than words. This is why it takes fellowshipping with Yahweh Himself and the study of His heart, through the Holy Spirit. It is in the heart of God (LOGOS) where one finds the meaning to the words of God (LEGO). All wisdom is in the pages of the Bible, but it takes joining our lives to the Author of the Bible before those words make sense to us, for they are understood spiritually (1 Cor. 2:10-16).

Love must be an ingredient of our inner being. It must be something that makes us who we are. It is more than an act performed in a "loving way" toward someone. It is incorporating the thinking of Love into our thinking. Then, what comes from us is a natural expression of Love. Just like when our God said, "I AM WHO I AM" to Moses, LOVE IS WHO LOVE IS (1 John 4:8). It is necessary that "WHO HE IS" should also be "who we are," since we are a part of His Body. Therefore "LOVE SHOULD BE, WHO WE ARE."

We are a small part of a big picture

A body does not go anywhere it wants. Where the head goes, so goes the rest of the body. If the Head of the Church is thinking Love and exists as Love, then His Body must also think Love and exist in Love. Our reactions to the ebb and flow of everyday life originate from our inner being. If we fill our souls with hateful selfish thoughts, then what flows out of us is selfish and hateful and Jesus Christ is not our Head (Matt. 15:18-19). If our inner beings conform to the thinking of Yahweh's Love, and Yahweh's Love becomes an integral part of who we are, then we will handle life without needing to think about how to Love. Love happens when our Head does our thinking for us.

Walking in the Fellowship of Love

You see, God is Love. Love is what makes Him who He is. He does not have to become aware of having a hateful thought to overcome it by an act of His will. His thinking is the materials of Love. His "Nature of Love" comprises His purpose and the motivation for all His actions. Our old nature could not love as God loves for God loves naturally as an expression of Himself. We commit acts of love that were contrary to our true nature of hate. We force ourselves to act lovingly by overcoming our old nature, which we often fail to do. Our real self will eventually show itself when the stress of life overcomes us and we act naturally from the store of our inner thoughts.

We need a new nature that He builds up with materials of Love. The more the transformation takes place, the more we act according to our new nature of Love. He takes our hearts of stone and makes them into a heart of flesh (Eze. 11:19). He removes the hardness of our hearts. He gives us sensitivity to other people's feelings.

To do this, we must move away from man's selfish viewpoint when we try to understand the events we find ourselves in. We must stop analyzing in detail who is right and who is wrong. We must see the event from Our Master's viewpoint, a view of Love so strong that it includes the Creator subjecting Himself to His creation nailing Him to a cross for His creation's sin. We must stop thinking according to the worldly method of thinking, which we have grown up with and have come familiar with. We must become aware of, and accept as our own, the eternal view of the One who created us (Isa. 55:8-11).

May the Holy Spirit's instructions be a Tree of Life to you.

Tree of Life

Chapter 23

The Goal of God's Instructions is Love - II

The Message He teaches is about Love

This is the message we have heard from Him and announce to you, that God is Light, and in Him there is no darkness at all. If we say that we have fellowship with Him and yet walk in the darkness, we lie and do not practice the truth; but if we walk in the Light as He Himself is in the Light, we have fellowship with one another, and the blood of Jesus His Son cleanses us from all sin (1 John 1:5-7).

The one who says he abides in Him ought himself to walk in the same manner as He walked. Beloved, I am not writing a new commandment to you, but an old commandment which you have had from the beginning; the old commandment is the word which you have heard. On the other hand, I am writing a new commandment to you, which is true in Him and in you, because the darkness is passing away and the true Light is already shining.

The one who says he is in the Light and yet hates his brother is in the darkness until now. The one who loves his brother abides in the Light and there is no cause for stumbling in him. But the one who hates his brother is in the darkness and walks in the darkness, and does not know where he is going because the darkness has blinded his eyes (1 John 2:6-11).

Beloved, let us love one another, for love is from God; and everyone who loves is born of God and knows God. The one who does not love does not know God, for God is love (1 John 4:7-8).

The Godhead is Light. The Godhead is Love. The goal is of His instruction is Love. We cannot have communion with Light if we have hate in our hearts (1 John 2:9). God is Love and in Him there is no hate at all, just 100 percent Light of Love. Fellowshipping with the God of Love is a spiritually revealing place to be, for there is no shadow to hide in. Those who join Him expose themselves to His Light. When the Light exposes attitudes not characterized by Love, we must confess them as the sin of hate.

Since we walk in companionship with Yahweh, we can expect Him to have certain influences on us. As we walk in the

Walking in the Fellowship of Love

newness of Life, the blood of Jesus Christ (the Holy Spirit) cleanses us by the communion of His Love. Those of us who trust the Message of Yahweh do not fear His Light. We do not fear He will expose our shame. Rather, we come as one would come to a doctor. We hope the Light will make known our need, so He can cleanse us from all unrighteous, unloving ways.

The purpose of the Holy Spirit's writings in 1 John is that we may not continue to sin (1 John 2:1). All who will come into agreement with the Light about sin confess the sin and He cleans them from all sins (1 John 1:8-9). But the message in 1 John focuses not on our failure to achieve perfection. It focuses on our hateful acts of selfishness, and our lack of love for others. From Yahweh's viewpoint, actions that are not beneficial are hateful. We hate when we don't care, when we disrespect, when we are dishonest, or when we take what is not ours. Stop and think about it: if someone treated us the way we treat other people, it would hurt. If we are not making life better, we make it worse. One may try to overcome acts of sin, but if there is hate in the heart, then one can only overcome the outward show of sin. In their heart, there is still sin.

He must increase, but I must decrease

As Jesus Christ makes His home in us, we remain in Him and abide in His love (John 15:9-17). As we remain in His love, He increases as we decrease (John 3:30). As Jesus Christ's influence increases within us, so His Love increases within us. As we walk in accordance to His Love, our hate decreases until we become like Him and there is no darkness in us at all. Jesus Christ cleans our heart from the source of our sin. That is, He cleans us from our hate, which is our self-centeredness and pride. He replaces our motivation for sin with a motivation for goodness, based on the other-centeredness of Love.

Again I emphasize that it is not something we produce outwardly. Selfish attempts to fix what is wrong by doing that which is contrary to our nature, are not useful and do not cleanse us from sin. Only pure Love, which is plentiful in communion with Jesus Christ, can set us free to love as He loves. We are His handiwork, created for the good works that He had planned for us from the foundations of the world. When we begin to be Light as He is Light,

Tree of Life

it is not to our merit. It does not increase our worth in the Kingdom of Heaven. On the Cross of Calvary, Jesus Christ forever set the exchange rate that fixes our worth: His Life for ours. Therefore, He equates the value of our souls to be like His own.

It is the handiwork He has completed in us that causes us to lift the name of Jesus Christ. As we grow in our understanding of where we were (Eph. 2:1-3) and where we are now, our estimation of His worth increases (Eph. 2:4-6). As our estimation of His worth increases, our estimation of our own worth increases because of the value He places on us. We are the results of His effort and not a product of our own doing. We boast of Him and not of ourselves.

What the Holy Spirit is saying in 1 John 2:6-11 is not a new idea. It is a commandment given in the Old Testament (Deut. 6:5, Lev. 19:18) and elaborated on by Jesus Christ (Matt. 22:36-40). Some wish to water down what He is saying and in doing so circulate a lie (Matt.24:24). Some want to believe that we can live a Life of Love while wallowing in hateful feelings. Beloved, this cannot be! A fountain cannot give freshwater and saltwater at the same time (James 3:8-4:4). If we say we are in the Light, having confessed our sins, and still have hateful feelings toward another, we are in the darkness still. We confess with our mouths but not with our souls (1 John 2:9-11). We must be careful not to make the same mistake Adam and Eve made when they chose to believe Satan and not God. Hate is hate, no matter how small and insignificant it is. Hate injures and divides while Love bridges the gaps.

So I'm thinking, because you are still reading this book, that you agree with the Light of Love. That is, you agree that you are a sinner and you cannot overcome sin without the Love of God in you. Remember page 54? I am thinking that you can join me by putting your name in the blank. "I, _____, have helped to make this world a harder place to live in and have contributed to the condition we now find on this earth." I'm thinking that you are willing to admit to your sin according to 1 John 1:8-9. Therefore, He is working out the promise He made in those verses in you.

1 John 1:8-9 says that He is faithful and true to clean us of all unrighteousness. Because it says He is faithful and true to decontaminate our soul from sin, it is not up to us to purify ourselves. He purifies us by cohabiting in us. 1 John 2:5-6 uses the word

Walking in the Fellowship of Love

"abiding" to refer to the companionship we have with the Light. Our abiding is "in" Him. Our abiding is not around Him as if we were "together but separate." We abide in Him as a branch abides as part of the Vine (John 15).

The Greek word translated as abiding is **μένω menō** (Strong's 3306) and it has the meaning of staying or remaining with. Our walk in the light is not part-time. We cannot be friends with the world and have friendship with the Light (James 4:4). Those who walk in a partnership with Light become humbled by what they find there. Complete cleansing does not happen on the first day. Our transformation takes time. It might be better to think of it as growing and maturing spiritually, like wheat for the harvest or vegetables in the garden. We are not all ready in the spring but must wait until the fullness of our season. Not all the fruit and vegetables in the garden reach maturity at the same time, each wait for their own season, when they are ripe.

Each opportunity we face challenges us to Love or hate. Each challenge is used by the Holy Spirit for our good and the good of those around us. We mature in a way that cleanses our sin by the scrubbing action of each opportunity to love. There are troubles we wish we did not have to go through and troubles we wished our friends or family did not have to go through but they are for our benefit. We trust in the goodness of our God that they are necessary and good. It is our chance to display a character of love.

Walk in a true walk of Love

It is not too much for me to say again: be careful not to turn the Message of Love into a message of works. Fellowshipping in the Lord is a one-on-one walk of abiding in Him. No one can love the God as He deserves. We break His heart every day by the attitudes we have toward Him, but He will consider the Love we show to one another as Love given to Him (Matt. 25:32-45). We should love the person Jesus Christ abides in. How can we be a benefit to Yahweh whom we cannot see, if we cannot be a benefit those we can see who have His Spirit? (1 John 4:12).

It is not about performing acts of kindness to God but that He has shown grace to us. We respond to His Love by loving those around us. How can we respond to Love if we never experience it?

Tree of Life

We experience Love by spending time with the One who loves us and gave His life for us. We experience Love when we fellowship with others who also walk in His Light. As others love us the same way He loved them, we experience the fullness of the love He intended for us.

Our time spent with Him is a "living-in-with" partnership, a sharing of our souls with the One who made us. Not only are we in a partnership with our Maker, we are in partnership with everyone who is partnering with Him. It is awesome to watch His leadership and see the craftsmanship of His work in each of us. As we walk in the Light together, we should focus more on the wonder and the power and the Love of our Master, Jesus Christ, in the lives of those around us.

We must recognize that He accepted us into His life while we were impure in heart and that acceptance came about by His good grace alone. We must recognize that He accepted others the same way. We must remember to accept those whose hearts He has yet to purify, as He accepted us before He made our hearts pure. We once separated ourselves from the Body and we have to start somewhere (Eph. 2:1-6). It is OK to be weak in the faith as long as we are maturing toward the goal. Fellowshipping with those who are fellowshipping in the Light will strengthen those of us who are weak in the faith. As our weakness in the faith matures, we encourage others to mature in their faith also. We should encourage one another other, bear one another's burdens, and lift one another up (Gal. 6:1-5).

We can know who lives in Love by their understanding of the grace of God. We see their understanding of the damaging power of sin and the damaging power of their sin in the lives of those around them. They know forgiveness and, more importantly, they understand their need to forgive those who have sinned against them (Matt. 6:6-15). They are cleansed of their hate by having Love endure in them. Their good works are a natural outpouring of Love from the nature of Godhead within, with no thought of how it would benefit them personally or spiritually. Remember, the quantity of knowledge one possesses does not make one mature in the faith. It is how well one lives according to the knowledge he has that makes him mature in the faith.

Walking in the Fellowship of Love

Set aside time from daily life to fellowship with other believers
Therefore, brethren, since we have confidence to enter the holy place by the blood of Jesus, by a new and living way which He inaugurated for us through the veil, that is, His flesh, and since we have a great priest over the house of God, <u>let us draw near with a sincere heart in full assurance of faith, having our hearts sprinkled clean from an evil conscience and our bodies washed with pure water</u>. Let us hold fast the confession of our hope without wavering, for He who promised is faithful; <u>and let us consider how to stimulate one another to love and good deeds, not forsaking our own assembling together</u>, as is the habit of some, but encouraging one another; and all the more as you see the day drawing near (Heb. 10:19-25).

If you are looking for washing from the Holy Spirit, spend time with people who give credit to Yahweh for changing them. Look for ones who walk in Love, who yield their lives to a Sovereign God and give Him the steering wheel of their lives. These verses sum up the reason to search out their fellowship and to stimulate one another. We need others to stimulate us to Love and good deeds. Those who stop having fellowship with other believers suffer like a plant without water.

Fellowship must be honest and center on the Lord and not on meetings. We should avoid meetings for meetings' sake. Fellowship for entertainment is a waste of time. We need fellowship that encourages us to seek after the Lord. That makes Him better known to us, encourages us to exchange the childishness of selfish behavior for a mature behavior, and prepares us to dwell in the presence of God Almighty.

The fellowship we seek should be an instruction with Love as the goal. Fellowship should be available in a corporate setting, like a planned, organized meeting of a worship service. But it should also be daily as we live together, in the homes we live in. Find fellowship that has the encouragement that stimulates people to Love, which results in good deeds. Daily fellowship with those who actively live a life of faith encourages us to also actively live a life of faith, believing the promise made to us from the Cross at Calvary.

Tree of Life

Do not wait for someone to reach out to you. Be someone who reaches out. Maybe it is a short visit, a long visit, a card, or a phone call - but it will say, "I am thinking of you." Acts of Love can be taxing and come at a personal cost. But what would you give in exchange for an eternal soul? So do not stop living in Love when it does not reward you. If you reach out in Love to those around you, you will receive Love from the One who is in you, and the power of Love will set you free.

May the Fellowship of Love be a Tree of Life to you.

Walking in the Fellowship of Love

Chapter 24

Relationship between Yahweh and His People

We are to be the People of Yahweh

If you review the relationship Yahweh has had with His people, I think you would agree that it has been rocky. From Adam and Eve to the flood, mankind and Yahweh have not been close. Yes, there were men like Enoch (Gen. 5:223-24), who walked with his Creator. And Noah (Gen. 6:8) found favor with God. But most did not please Him. Yahweh describes mankind before the flood as a people continually full of evil in their hearts. Yahweh declared that He was sorry that He had made them (Gen. 6:5-7).

After the flood, man's response to his Creator did not improve, even after starting out with such a faithful and righteous man as Noah (Eze. 14:12-23). Generations later, men built the Tower of Babel (Gen. 11:1-9) to get a name and so they would not scatter throughout the land. They paid no attention to the commands the Lord gave to Noah and his descendants to go forth and populate the land (Gen 9:7, 1:27-28). Man focused on his agenda and not on God's will (Matt. 16:23 and Mark 8:33).

The story continues with the nation of Israel, which is about an agreement Yahweh made with Abraham and again with his descendants. Yahweh spiritually separated Abraham's descendents from the rest of the world. If they lived according to the agreement, He would be their God and they would be His people. Israel continually broke the conditions of the agreement. Even in the best of times, when they were faithful to their covenant, they were not faithful to their Creator. Idol worship was common among the people and they treated their Creator as if He was one of their invention. They treated their God as if He was one of their idols. They came before Yahweh with the same fake worship they used to worship their fake gods.

The Babylonian Exile, described in the books of Jeremiah, Daniel, and Ezekiel, cleansed the nation of Israel from idol worship, but did not improve the way they treated their God. They still treated Him as if He was not real, as if He were a system of religious beliefs born from the hearts of men. They began to worship their laws and

Tree of Life

boast of their separateness from the rest of the world (who they looked down on as lost for eternity). Even after Jesus Christ died on the Cross, many Jewish Christians believed and taught that Christ's death on the Cross was only for the Jewish Nation. Controversies arose about whether Gentile believers had to obey Jewish Laws to gain salvation (Acts 15:1-5).

Adherence to the commands of God was an improvement over ignoring Him altogether. But He is looking for more than obedience to a set of rules even if they are His rules (1 Sam. 15:22, John 14:15-27).

The Creator of mankind is not to be treated as an idol

The covenant that Yahweh made with Abraham, and later confirmed with the nation of Israel under Moses, was that He would be their God and they would be His people. They were to remain separated to Him alone. Later, Jesus Christ renewed the same covenant with His blood. The agreement the Lord made with His people was about something that was to happen between His people and Him. Most of the time, Yahweh's people approached Him incorrectly. The wanted the relationship to reflect them instead of Him.

Today, His people still wish to approach Him in a way that emphasizes them, not Him. Some want to believe the covenant is about obeying the Law through Grace. They want salvation to be a gift, but they want their friendship with Him to be about works of faith. Some in today's church have fashioned His Word into a false god by twisting the meaning of His words. People use their religion as if it was a genie in a bottle. If you rub the bottle the right way you can get your wish. Christians rub the bottle of prayer looking for Yahweh to pop out to do their bidding. They pretend to look for God's will, but pray for what they want. They teach that if you approach God the right way, He will do what you ask. They make it sound as if Yahweh wants to hold back the good things and only gives in if they ask in the correct way.

They want their God to respond to them instead of responding to Him. This thinking is like the way the Jewish people of old approached their idols and it comes from the Tree of the Knowledge of Good and Evil. They act as if the original plan was their idea and

Walking in the Fellowship of Love

that Yahweh does not have a plan of His own. They think He makes decisions based on their prayers and not according to the Blueprint. They act as if He is evaluating each person, with each decision based on who is asking, how well they live their lives, and how well they do the asking.

They treat Him as if He is a powerful force who has no real direction of His own, as if they are redirecting a spiritual force to do their will, like the force in Star Wars. Such thinking takes the sovereignty and dominion away from Yahweh and transfers it to the "worshipper." The one asking becomes the god and the one being asked becomes a servant forced to do their will. Such teachings become obvious in the practice of many in today's world of Christian religion. Keep to the rules, approach in the right manner, and pray believing; then God will grant what you ask. Such teaching sounds a lot like the Eastern Religions including witchcraft.

The covenant is about a relationship

Our God is not looking for people who focus on themselves when they come before Him. He is looking for something much deeper. What He looks for is not much different from what we would look for. How many stories and movies are about a rich, important person, like a king or a princess, who wants assurance the person he has fallen in love with, can love him in return? They fear the attention they receive is because they are rich and powerful, not because of the person they are inside. We want others to accept us for who we are and not for what we might provide the other person.

The story of Cinderella was about a prince who fell in love with someone he met at a ball. He wanted to marry her even after he found out she was a servant girl living in the house of her stepmother. The Prince and the Pauper is about a man who showed loyalty to the future king, before he knew he was the future king. He was loyal to the person the prince was with and it had nothing to do with status or gain. There are stories of kings who dressed up as peasants to go out among the people to find out what the people thought of them. How about the story of the king who fell in love with a young woman, so he dressed up as a peasant to see if she could love him even if he were not the king.

Tree of Life

Humanity is full of true stories that play out such ideas of true love, a love that transcends all the circumstances and prevails over everything else. We, as humans, want pure love to succeed. Love stories break our hearts. They make us cry, cause us to rejoice, and restore our faith in humanity. We find irresistible stories of love that succeeds while overcoming all obstacles. They leave us feeling a little bit better about life.

The story between Yahweh and His people is a story of everlasting love. His love prevailed even though the ones He loves are stubborn and rebellious toward Him. It is a story about of a love so powerful and true that it remains unhindered, no matter what His people do (Eze. 16:1-63). The story starts in the Garden of Eden and will end with the Marriage Feast of the Lamb.

The story of Jesus Christ becoming a man and dying on the Cross is not just about victory over sin. It is a story of God's Love for His people, which caused Him to take the punishment for their sin onto Himself, making it possible for Him to restore the ones He loved. We can use the cost He endured as a measure for the depth of His Love.

Sadly, His Love story is not the story that is in most churches today. Yahweh's people stop telling the story and focus instead on receiving salvation. They miss the love story.

God so loved the world that He gave His only begotten Son (LOGOS) *that who should ever believe in Him might have everlasting life (John 3:16).*

You cannot find a more perfect love than the Love by which Yahweh loves. He does not want us to follow Him solely for the purpose becoming a better person, which is personal gain and selfish. He wants us to follow Him because we see His worth. He wants our love for Him to be true, like the love He has for us. We do become better people, but that must be a secondary reason for following Him.

Many Christians hold their love for God captive, releasing it depending on how well He performs. They feel depressed and frustrated because He does not carry out His will the way they want. Their faith in Him dwindles when He does not use His power according to their will. They would be upset if they found out that their friends or family or spouse or children loved them that way. No

Walking in the Fellowship of Love

one wants love based on performance. We want others to love us regardless of our successes and failures, our weaknesses and strengths. We want to receive love the same when we are poor as when we are rich.

Our God wants a love relationship with us that has nothing to do with personal gain. He offers to us the same Love He looks for. He showed the love He is looking for on the cross. We should love Him the same, whether life is wonderful or life is horrible. The difficult events of our lives should pale in comparison to the wonder and joy of knowing our God. The willingness in our hearts to go where He leads, no matter the cost, is a sign of our love for Him. Our lives are no longer a reflection of who we are, but they are a reflection of WHO HE IS.

Headship is an illustration of what Yahweh is taking about

But I want you to understand that Christ is the head of every man, and the man is the head of a woman, and God is the head of Christ (1 Cor. 11:3).

But as the church is subject to Christ, so also the wives ought to be to their husbands in everything. Husbands, love your wives, just as Christ also loved the church and gave Himself up for her, This mystery is great; but I am speaking with reference to Christ and the church (Eph. 5:24-25 and 32).

What relationship is Yahweh looking for from His people? He created the family to teach us about the relationship He is looking for. He created parent-child and husband-wife relationships to show a unity and togetherness that represents His relationship to His people. Human beings crave friendships and want to interact with one another in positive, loving ways. He wants the Church to be a suitable Helpmate. He created Eve to become one flesh with Adam, to show us that He created us to become one person with the Creator of the Universe.

It would be an illusion for me to believe the doctrine of headship is not a controversial subject to raise here. Nevertheless, the headship of Yahweh over Jesus Christ is scriptural (1 Cor. 11:1-5, Phillip. 2:5-8). Christ's headship over the Church is also scriptural (Col. 1:13-20). The husband and wife represent the headship of

Tree of Life

Christ over His Church (Eph. 5:22-32). Jesus Christ is the head over the man and the man is the head over his wife. By taking a good look at Biblical headship and the Church's role as the Helpmate, we can better understand the communication Yahweh gives through Jesus Christ.

Nothing speaks of our relationship with Yahweh like marriage. Paul calls it a great mystery of Christ and His Church. When Paul used the Greek word for mystery, **μυστήριον mustērion** (Strong's Number 3466), in Ephesians vs. 1:9, 3:3-4, 3:9, 5:24-25, 5:32 6:19, he was not speaking of a mystery that was hard to understand, but rather about a mystery that reveals something. The doctrines found in scripture are important and preordained for understanding by those given to the Holy Spirit. He did not previously reveal them and, therefore, people did not fully understand them until the LOGOS of God was revealed. They are no longer a mystery. They are understandable now in our time.

God instituted marriage and He uses it to explain His role in the relationship and to explain the relationship He looks for from His people. He has placed a special message into the marriage institution, one we can only see in a proper relationship between husband and wife. A man should leave his mother and bond to His wife and they shall become one flesh (Gen. 2:18 and 22-24) just as Jesus Christ left His throne to become one with us. The man is to love his wife in the same way that Christ loved the Church (Eph. 5:25-32). God wants to bond with us in the same way the husband bonds to his wife.

The Holy Spirit uses the family that surrounds such a marriage to teach of Yahweh's character. The man portrays both the image of God as a husband and the image of God as a father. The woman portrays the image of the Church as Yahweh's Bride, who takes care of His children, His sheep. The message embedded into marriage is very important, for it helps to explain the heart of Yahweh. Marriage is not only about the people. It is also about God.

Back to the Garden for the illustration

Do you remember Adam and Eve in the Garden of Eden? Remember they ate of the fruit of the Tree of the Knowledge of Good and Evil, which God told them not to eat? That was only part of their story. There is a portion of their story that takes place before

Walking in the Fellowship of Love

they disobeyed God. It is the story of the first union of man and woman. We could say it is the beginning of Yahweh's Love story in the Bible.

Think of the proper marriage relationship as a play the Holy Spirit wrote and directed a play that teaches us about God's heart. He handpicks each person to act important roles. Yahweh made the choice for us about which gender we would be (Psalms 139). No human decides if they are going to be a man or a woman. Yahweh decides and He does not get it wrong! He crafted the man to love his wife in the same way that He loves the Church. He crafted the woman to respect her husband, as the Church needs to respect Her God. I believe the role the woman plays is more important than the role the man plays. It is the Church's role. It is the one that needs improvement. The Lord has always performed His role perfectly. We need to better understand the Church's role so we might better live as His Helper. Confusion about the woman's role creates confusion about the Church's role. Adherence to the model of marriage, as set forth by Creator, results in two spiritual souls united.

This is not man's idea and he cannot change it when it is convenient. It is not an old-fashioned idea that we may ignore and replace with other ideas. He made us according to His design. Failing to live according to the design causes a sick society full of lawlessness. You do not put diesel fuel in a gasoline engine because burning diesel is not its design. Society fueled by improper marriage unions will fail, in the same way the gasoline engine fails when filled with diesel fuel.

Satan has another play performing out on the human stage. It is diesel fuel of selfishness for a society designed to use the gasoline of other-centeredness. Satan wrote it, worldly influences directed it, and billions act out the parts each day. Marriages that use this script for their play fall apart because they depart from the model Yahweh presented. Those who do not know the Creator cannot live according to His design.

Satan works hard to destroy the scriptural image of one man properly unified to one woman. His goal is to take everyone's eyes off from message found in the Biblical Institution of Marriage. He does this by attacking the roles of men and women that God ordained within the marriage relationship. He bombards society with

Tree of Life

conflicting doctrines about what marriage is. He distorts the truth on one side and then attacks his distortions on the other.

As I write this page in 2004, a fight rages in the political world to define marriage. What was unheard of just a generation ago, people are considering and implementing before our eyes. Governments sanction marriages between members of the same gender, yet the Creator does not recognize them. The weakness in the family today comes from a missing marriage foundation. Satan is out to destroy the picture of Yahweh and His people, so he attacks marriage with everything he's got.

Satan works to destroy the proper family structure because he does not want the husband and wife relationship to show Christ's Love for His Bride. He sends into the world teachings that destroy the roles of husband, wife, father, and mother. This is so he might confuse the message found deep in the symbolism of the proper marriage relationship. So confused is the Church that She helps Satan teach his lies. Satan confuses the message by moving the husband-wife relationship from the center of the family and replacing it with the parent-child relationship. If we make the children the center of the family in place of the bond between husband and wife, we lessen the Message. We work against Yahweh. We try to block Him and prevent Him from revealing His heart. The mystery about Christ and the Church remains because we never think about it. By promoting the role of children in the family Satan teaches them to think in a self-centered way, lovers of self instead of lovers of others.

Satan has used the Women Liberation Movement to confuse the roles husband and wife by setting women against men. He designed the sexual revolution to destroy the marriage bond in general. What men call liberalism and open-mindedness is Satan's plan to bury in the mist of "social injustice" the message God intended to reveal through marriage. Satan uses teachings from the Tree of Death to convince men to lord the scriptures over their wives for selfish control. Husbands became disobedient to Yahweh and put themselves into His place in the family hierarchy. Next Satan worked on the women's thinking to raise them up against the men's injustice and, by doing so, they joined the men in their rebellion.

Now both the men and the women are taking on the man's role and trying to portray God in the pageant. Few portray the

Walking in the Fellowship of Love

Church. The Church leadership of today does not teach effectively regarding the roles within the family. They fear this teaching would cause controversy. If they taught about the roles in the family, they would need to teach about roles within the Church also. The Church today teaches its members to ignore their God-given role. They encourage them to "ad lib" their roles and redefine them as they go through life. Thus spiritual oneness between the man and the woman is weakened. They replaced oneness with individualism and each doing it their way (Judge 17:6 and 21: 25, Deu. 21:9, Pro. 12:15 and 21:2).

    The Church can counter this attack by being more conscientious about living out proper Biblical roles. The difference between how the Church lives and how the world lives should be easy to see by those on the outside. How can we ensure that we have a true friendship with the Creator if we work against His Message? If we live according to the world's model, we are opposing His. He is looking to His Church, His Helpmate, to assist Him in doing His will. We do this by living out the demonstration He gave us. Marriage is His idea. He gave it to communicate a particular message. We help make that message clearer by living it in our homes.

    The question is, "How important to the Church is the picture Yahweh paints?" In other words, "How real is the God they claim to follow? Do we believe He set marriage aside for His purpose? Or do we believe human beings determine the definition of marriage?"

    We must turn from the teachings of the world and return to Yahweh's original intent. We must start by forgetting the lie taught by Satan about "the war between the sexes." There can only be a war when couples live outside their God-given-roles. When husband and wives accept their roles from God, there is no need to fight. Let the world fight husband against wife, but the Church needs to stop.

How is it going for you?

    Take time now to evaluate your treatment of Yahweh. Why are you following Him? Are you following Him because you want your life to straighten out? He will do that for you, but it is the wrong reason to follow Him. Are you following because you want to feel better about yourself? You will feel better about yourself, but it is the

Tree of Life

wrong reason to follow Him. Is it because you see worthiness in the God who would go to Cavalry for you? Yes! He is worthy of your devotion. Are you drawn by His love for you?

He is looking for a love given freely, one not affected by how life is going. He is looking for love that responds to the character of the person you see in Him. He does not want your works, goodness, or holiness to be the center of the relationship. He does not want you to be His follower because He is powerful nor does He want you to follow because you are trying to escape hell. He is not looking for a man-centered relationship. When the relationship between a man and Yahweh is about the man, the man treats Him the same way he would treat an idol. When the number of people coming to worship in a building is more important than the quality of the worship, it is reduced to idol worship. When we need music to worship, the music lulls us into false worship. If you work for the ministry and the ministry's success makes you or breaks you spiritually, it is the ministry and not God that you serve.

You must ask yourself, "Why do I follow my God?" Do I follow an illusion of a god that I have created for my own purposes? Is what the Lord holds dear to His heart the same for me? Do I preserve my beliefs to hold me up and make me comfortable with me?

He wants you to love Him and to love His people in the same way He loves you, with no conditions. Jesus Christ came as the LOGOS of God to explain what Holy Spirit is talking about. He wants to continue His demonstration in us as we walk together toward eternity. He wants us to trust in His Love, no matter the circumstances. He wants a friendship that is true and forever.

Relationship means interaction with those around you. The relationship we have with others should reflect the values of the God who remains within us (the Tree of Life) and not the values of the world (The Tree of Death). Our agreement to live His message in our marriages is a way to do that.

May your relationship to Yahweh be as a Tree of Life to you.

Walking in the Fellowship of Love

Chapter 25

Christ's Relationship with His Bride

Yahweh's Love Story

Then God said, "Let Us make man in Our image, according to Our likeness; and let them rule over the fish of the sea and over the birds of the sky and over the cattle and over all the earth, and over every creeping thing that creeps on the earth." <u>God created man in His own image, in the image of God He created him; male and female He created them</u> (Gen. 1:26-27).

There was a time when Adam and Eve were perfect their knowledge of good and evil was limited to only good. They were in direct companionship with their Maker, and applied themselves to the task He gave them which they performed according to His will. They were in a perfect state to model the union Yahweh wishes to have with His people. We did not get to see their perfect model for long because they ate of the Tree of the Knowledge of Good and Evil.

Ever think about the sequence of events Yahweh followed when He created Adam and Eve? Hove you ever wondered, "Why did He choose to create them separately, one at a time, and not together at the same time? Why didn't He breathe life into Eve's nostrils as He did Adam's? Why did He use a rib from Adam to create Eve? Why did God first look for Adam's mate among the animals, when He knew He would not find a suitable mate among them? What did He expect to accomplish by creating man and woman with the sequence of events He selected? **What is the message that He intends to communicate?"**

Remember Yahweh had a Blueprint and each event happened to communicate the Message. It was His objective to create a need in Adam that only the proper mate could fulfill. When Yahweh said, "It is not good for man to be alone," it was the first time that He said that something in creation was not good. I believe He chose these events to communicate something about Himself. The story of the Creator creating Adam and Eve is the first revelation of His heart, the first story with a message. Since the Lord used Adam to represent

Tree of Life

Him, we will want to review the sequence of events the Lord followed in creating him, looking for indications of what He is revealing about Himself. Since Eve represents the Church, we will want to review her creation and her union to Adam, looking to understand what Yahweh is revealing about our union to Him.

Then the LORD God formed man of dust from the ground, and breathed into his nostrils the breath of life and man became a living being. The LORD God planted a garden toward the east, in Eden and there He placed the man whom He had formed (Gen. 2:7-8).

<u>God created man in His own image, in the image of God He created him; male and female He created them</u> *(Gen. 1:27).*

Notice that Yahweh created man in two parts, male and female. As we will see, the male is not complete until the Lord adds the female. Yahweh chose to create man in a way that was different from the rest of His creation. Adam was a lump of dirt, an object without life. He had no soul. The Lord God personally formed Adam then breathed life into him. He did not speak Adam into existence like the rest of creation. Yahweh passed life to Adam through His own breath of Life, which made Adam unique in the garden. (Note: Yahweh passed life to Adam. Parents pass life to their children through conception. Life from the father mixes with life from the mother and is passed on to the child.) Yahweh created someone with like nature to His, someone with feelings, creative abilities, and the capacity to do right or wrong.

Then the LORD God took the man and put him into the Garden of Eden to cultivate it and keep it. The LORD God commanded the man, saying, "From any tree of the garden you may eat freely; but from the tree of the knowledge of good and evil you shall not eat, for in the day that you eat from it you will surely die" (Gen. 2:15-17).

While Adam was alone and before there was Eve, the Lord assigned Adam the task of tending the garden to cultivate it and received instructions about the Tree of the Knowledge of Good and Evil. There is no record of a conversation between Yahweh and Eve about these instructions and no record of Adam telling Eve. Even so, Eve knew what Yahweh said to Adam about the tree, but not

Walking in the Fellowship of Love

accurately (Gen. 3:2-3). Scriptures call eating the forbidden fruit "Adam's sin" not "Eve's sin." Adam had the responsibility to do right. Yahweh placed on Adam the same responsibility He has. Adam failed to perform his responsibilities, but God never fails (1 Cor. 13:8). The Creator placed the leadership responsibilities on males but it is not because they are men. It is because He created males to represent Him, the great "I AM." Males who fail to take up their responsibilities rebel before the One who created them. Yahweh created Adam in His image and He expects Adam's descendants to live up to it. It is not a male's choice to be a male or a female's choice to be female. It is their choice to accept the definition He gives defining manhood and womanhood, or to accept the definition as Satan gives from the Tree of the Knowledge of Good and Evil.

Then the LORD God said, "It is not good for the man to be alone; I will make him a helper suitable for him." Out of the ground the LORD God formed every beast of the field and every bird of the sky, and brought them to the man to see what he would call them; and whatever the man called a living creature, that was its name. The man gave names to all the cattle, and to the birds of the sky, and to every beast of the field, <u>but for Adam there was not found a helper suitable for him</u> (Gen. 2:18-20).

Since Adam is in the image of Yahweh, he symbolically stands in Yahweh's place. The Creator did not create Eve at the same time He created Adam because He wanted to say these words, "It is not good for man to be alone." Why? Here, in the second chapter of the Bible, He makes known the reason He created His creation. It is significant when Yahweh declares that it is not good for man to be alone for it speaks of Himself also. Could He be saying that it is not good for God to be alone? I believe the answer is yes. Yahweh is saying that He is creating for Himself a Helpmate. His wish to have companionship with someone like Himself is the reason He created creatures that could sin against Him.

Notice that He did not run off and create Eve for Adam's sake at this point, so there is more to His Message. He showed Adam all the creatures and had Adam give them names. They found no Helpmate among the living creatures available for Adam to commune with. Yahweh created all the living creatures in heaven and earth. None are like Him. Adam is the closest to Him because he was created in the image of God, but he could not become one with God. Is it possible that Yahweh is telling us why He created the universe, knowing the results would include sin and evil? Could it be He needed the right environment in which He could create the one who would be His companion?

Listen to what Yahweh says in this story. Do not let arguments for or against the doctrine of predetermination confuse you. He has full control and full knowledge of what He is doing and why. He predetermined His actions in creating His Bride. He knew there would be sin and evil and that He would die on the cross because of sin. But for the Bride to be "bone of My bone and flesh of My flesh," the Bride must have a nature of Love like Yahweh's nature Love. It is His choice to do as He pleases and the arguments of man are no use. What He has done He has done and what He is doing He is doing! (Jer. 18:1-10, Rom. 9:14-23, Isa. 29:13-16, and 45:5-12). He sealed His purpose in the Blueprint before He took one act of creation. Leave the endless debates behind (1 Tim. 1:3-7 and 3:5-11) and grasp what He is communicating through Adam and Eve. He created us to have the image of His character and to come alongside as Helpmates.

We become one with our Husband

So the LORD God caused a deep sleep to fall on the man, and he slept; then He took one of his ribs and closed up the flesh at that place. The LORD God fashioned into a woman the rib which He had taken from the man, and brought her to the man. The man said, "This is now bone of my bones, And flesh of my flesh; She shall be called Woman, Because she was taken out of Man."

For this reason a man shall leave his father and his mother, and be joined to his wife; and they shall become one flesh. And the man and his wife were both naked and were not ashamed (Gen. 2:21-25).

If Eve is the answer to Adam being without a helpmate and God created Eve to represent God's called ones, then He brings us into the Body as His Helpmate. Do you see yourself as the Helpmate of God? Are you developing spiritually as a companion to the

Walking in the Fellowship of Love

Creator of the Universe? Everything that has happened from the day of the first act of creation was to fulfill the will of Yahweh.

Why a rib and what significance does the rib have? The rib stands for Jesus Christ. Notice that Yahweh did not breathe life into Eve Why didn't He do it the same for Eve as Adam? Where did Eve get her life? She received it from Adam. Like the rib of Adam, God the Father sent His Son, Jesus Christ, the second Adam (1 Cor. 15:42-49, Rom. 5:10-21) to create the Bride, the Church. We receive our spiritual life through Jesus Christ the same way Eve received physical life through the rib.

No one has lived a perfect life except Jesus Christ and no one has defeated death except Jesus Christ. Only one physical human being will stand sinless before the Father's throne, Jesus Christ the Righteous. When He stands before the throne He will bring all those who abide in Him. Those who have refused to abide in Him will stand before the throne on their own merit. We do not want to be standing on our own merit. We need to be in Christ standing on His merit.

You may hear it said that God will one day ask you why He should let you in to Heaven. They tell you to reply, "Because Jesus Christ died for my sins." If you hear Yahweh asking you this question, your condemnation draws near. For if you were in the Body of Christ, your inclusion as a member of His Body would cause Yahweh to accept you when He accepted Jesus Christ. If you hear the question, He will judge you for your deeds. You have lived your own life for you. You were not sharing in the Life Jesus Christ was living. If you share the Life Jesus Christ is living, then when the Father asked Jesus Christ the question, He will accept you as He accepts Jesus Christ. When He accepts the Head, He accepts the rest of the Body also. He does not accept the feet separately from the elbows. If the head has met the requirements then the eyes and the hands also meet the same requirements. Everything that is true about Jesus Christ is also true about the rest of His Body.

The male and the female are to be become one man and that teaches us that we are to become one with Jesus Christ (Gen. 2:22-24). Eve received life from the rib and therefore shared in the life Adam lived, just as the Church receives True Life from Jesus Christ and shares in the Life He lives. Adam said, "Bone of my bones, and

Tree of Life

flesh of my flesh," because Eve came out of Adam. Therefore Eve joins herself to Adam and they shall become "one soul." This teaches us that Yahweh is creating a Bride with a rib that came from Him, Jesus Christ. He joins us to Him and we become one the same way the individual Eve became one with the individual Adam. He created Eve for a purpose and that was to help Adam. She was to be where Adam was and help Adam do what he needed to do. There is no recording that Yahweh gave Eve any task other than to be Adam's helper, nothing to suggest that Eve did her individual responsibilities while Adam did his. This teaches us that we are not to do our work while Yahweh does His. He expects us to help Him in carrying out His plan.

    When Yahweh planned the sequence of events by which He created man, He purposely did not create Eve at the same time He created Adam. He wanted to show Adam's need for Eve as a Helpmate, as his companion. God gave Adam and Eve as a portrait painted in words to illustrate Yahweh's reason for creating His Bride. She is to be His companion and Helpmate. Those who fellowship in the Light should be looking for ways to assist their God in every incident they are in and not spend time looking to do their own ministry. No matter how worthy the ministry is, it will be counterproductive to His work. The only way we can be productive is if we come alongside the one we are to be helpmates to. The Church should not be looking to have Her own career or try to do Her own works of faith. She should be looking to help Her Husband, as He directs. She helps Him perform what He has predestined in His Blueprint. Together the Church and Her Husband stand on principles found in the Blueprint and not on what she has set aside for herself.

    Those who are Yahweh's helpmates will want to join Him by living out the pattern He has set. We should want to make His Message known by the lives we live. At the Cross of Calvary, we find a picture of the love Yahweh has for us, His enemies. The picture given in the Garden of Eden, when God created Adam and Eve, helps us understand the Love exchanged between Yahweh and His people.

    Take time to note that Yahweh did not create a slave for Adam. He was not looking for someone to serve Adam at his beck and call. God created man male and female (Gen. 1:27). Alone,

Walking in the Fellowship of Love

Adam was half a man. He was only male and not what God planned for him to be. Yahweh created Eve to complete Adam, to be his companion and assist him in completing his assignment from God.

Put away the old ways of thinking. Do not listen to the lies of the devil. When Adam ate of the Tree of the Knowledge of Good and Evil, he received Satan's teachings that stained the picture of Love, making it hard to see. Satan's teachings will keep you from experiencing the beauty of the proper relationship of the Church to Her God. Join Yahweh in living out His Message of Love.

Both men and women are members of Wife of Christ

It may be easier for the female to see herself as the Helpmate to God. The male must study the female role to understand his place before Yahweh. The female's role in the earthly marriage is the same as her spiritual marriage to God, as she stands before Him in prayer. This should make it easier for her to switch between her earthly and spiritual roles. The male's role is different in his earthly marriage than it is in his spiritual marriage to God, as he stands before Him in prayer. In the earthly marriage, the male is the head of the female and of the family. While he is in prayer, God is his head. It is easy for the male to approach God in prayer with an attitude. He can forget that he is not the head of God but God is his Head. His prayer life can reflect this wrong attitude and we can see it in how he exercises his leadership role.

Because the Church has modeled itself more according to the male's role, the Church has become arrogant before Her Creator. She has fallen into the same thinking Satan has, which is a wish to be equal to God. The females of the Church have added to the rebellion of the males by disrespecting their role in the church and wanting the male's role. Churches who adopt the male's role approach God as if they have the steering wheel in their hands. They act as if He needs their guidance on how to continue.

It is time the Church Body embraces a role that is like Eve's role, which Jesus Christ also lived out (Philp. 2:5-11). It is time for women in the Church to accept their true role and demonstrate it to their husbands, their family, and the Church. It is time for men to begin to learn from the proper example the women are to give and approach their God as Helpmates and not as equals. Together, both

Tree of Life

genders should humble themselves and approach their God as they should approach the Shepherd of their souls who is ready to direct them according to His predetermined course.

However, in the Lord, neither is woman independent of man, nor is man independent of woman. For as the woman originates from the man, so also the man has his birth through the woman; and all things originate from God (1 Cor. 11:11-12).

Have this attitude in yourselves that was also in Christ Jesus, who, although He existed in the form of God, did not regard equality with God a thing to be grasped, but emptied Himself, taking the form of a bondservant, and being made in the likeness of men (Philip. 2:5-7).

The attitude of the Bride of Christ should be like the attitude displayed by Christ. Whether male or female, equality with each other is not something we hang onto. Instead, we are to empty ourselves and take on the form of Jesus Christ and become a bond servant. To be a part of Love's demonstration is a privilege He offers us. Remember the example He set: for he who wishes to be first must be willing to be last and serve the many (Matt. 20:17-28). Jesus Christ was the one who washed the disciples' feet. Men are to take on the attitude Christ has and become like a bond servant to their wife and family (Philp. 2:5-8). The male's attitude toward the female's role should be one of honor and respect because it represents his personal role before Yahweh. Women are to take on this role and embody the attitude of Jesus Christ by the way they submit to their husbands. The woman is the male's Helpmate and is assuming mankind's place in the demonstration. This allows the man to embody Christ's role. He cannot clearly represent both sides, so she helps him fulfill his duty. She is representing the Church as the Bride and the male is a member of the Church. Therefore, he must stand before God as a member of the Bride. Everything she represents in her role is true of both her and of him. The male represents God in the family, but in no way is able to be God in the family. In this representation of God and His people, everything the male represents is true of God and not himself. The example he sets is not displaying anything about him as a man. That is his

Walking in the Fellowship of Love

Helpmate's job. The example he is to set is only completely true about the Lord.

When the female sees the male as her head, she is to look past him and see her Head, Jesus Christ (Eph. 5:21-24). When she looks at the male's role, she is looking at Yahweh's initiative and His continual Love for her (Eph. 5:25-32). When the male looks at his wife, he is not to see her personally; for she represents him. He is to look at her submission as a mirror, so she might remind him of his own submission to his Head. The Creator gave the male authority over his wife symbolically only. Therefore he is to use his unique relationship with his wife to display the truth about Christ. The male's authority over his wife is representative of Christ's authority over the Church. He should allow her to remind him that he has no authority of his own. It is his Head's authority working through him. He should treat his wife the same way Christ has treated him and give himself up for her.

As we look at the role of the woman, we must realize she is like an actor. She is acting out mankind's state of affairs before God. Because she is a member of the family of man, she is also acting out her own part. Nevertheless, when the Scripture teaches the woman to be submissive to her husband, it has nothing to do with her as a person, but rather it is because of her head, her husband. Her submission is in recognition of the will of the Creator. Her submission recognizes people's need to submit to Yahweh.

Women, this is not your husband's idea and it is not yours. Yahweh predestined it before the beginning of creation. It is His will that you are the gender that you are. He chose you to take on a specific role in marriage, which helps Him communicate His Message to others. If you engage in His demonstration, the world will attack you, for you will undermine their teachings more so than the male. The world will encourage you to strive to show your equality with your husband, thus acting out the part of rebellion. Strive instead to join Christ in the attitude He had, which did not hold onto His equality to the Father but emptied Himself by becoming a bond servant (Philp. 2:1-8). When women treat their husbands the same way they should treat their God, they properly display the correct attitude the Church is to have before God. Remember, do everything as to the Lord because He is worthy, not because your husband is worthy.

Let us talk about the meaning of the head covering

For a man ought not to have his head covered, <u>since he is the image and glory of God</u>; but the <u>woman is the glory of man</u>. For man does not originate from woman, but woman from man; for indeed man was not created for the woman's sake, but woman for the man's sake. Therefore the woman ought to have a <u>symbol of authority on her head</u>, because of the angels. However, in the Lord, neither is woman independent of man, nor is man independent of woman. For as the woman originates from the man, so also the man has his birth through the woman; and all things originate from God (1 Cor. 11: 7-12).

Boy, there is no subject as taboo in the Christian Church today as head coverings. Satan has done a good job of confusing this message. He did so by getting us to look at our fleshly world for understanding. We have become so tuned into wrong teachings that this teaching insults us. The Holy Spirit, through Paul, calls the head covering a symbol of authority. Whose authority? God's authority! I know, I really do know, that many of you thought the head covering symbolizes the wife's submission to her husband and his authority. Yes and no. Remember, man has no authority of his own. He has only that which comes from his Head.

The woman does not represent herself but she represents her husband, so when she puts on a head covering, she is not covering her physical head only but is symbolically covering her spiritual head - that is, her husband's head. When a man sees a woman with her head covered, it should remind him that Jesus covers his blemishes with the veil of His blood. When a man uncovers his head, he is uncovering his spiritual head, Jesus Christ, showing His perfection. When a woman sees her husband's head uncovered, it should remind her of the purity of the second Adam. The man uncovers his head to show restoration and a perfect life in Christ Jesus. Remember it was Adam's sin not Eve's. Adam is the disfigured image of God not Eve. Eve is the image of sinful Adam. Jesus is the perfect image of God. While the man remains without the Holy Spirit, he is the image of the

Walking in the Fellowship of Love

first Adam and his head is disfigured. It is proper to cover his head. After he received Jesus Christ and entered the Body, he is in the image of the Second Adam and Christ became the man's head, which he should not cover. Before Christ died, believers were alone. Now we have access to Him through the blood and remain in Him.

Why does the female need to cover the male's head to play out Yahweh's demonstration? He created Eve in the image of Adam. When Yahweh used a rib from Adam, he became her head. (No! He did not become her head after they ate of the fruit. God originally created her for Adam as an extension of himself and as a Helpmate.) The woman represents the man. With her head uncovered, she allows man's glory to rival God's glory. Remember, this is the logic Satan used to tempt Eve at the Tree of the Knowledge of Good and Evil: equality with God (Gen. 3:1-5). An uncovered woman's head has the spiritual message of mankind's mutiny against Yahweh's authority. The covered head of the woman represents the Church's submission to the authority of the Most High God.

The uncovered women of today represent the uncovered Church of today, who proclaim by their uncovered heads, "We are not under the authority of any head." The uncovered head of the woman portrays a Church who is rivaling Her maker. Combine it with men covering their heads and we have a people symbolically raising themselves above their Creator.

We must ask, "Is it possible that, by ignoring this teaching, the Church has a direct negative impact on the family?" Christians write much about the dismal state of the family of today and they blame the world's system. Many people work to rebuild the family framework. How can the structure stand if the foundation is missing? Christians must return to His thinking and admit they are part of the problem. If we pursue relationships between husband and wife that are contrary to marriage's original purpose and design, should the failing effort to restore the family surprise us? At the core of a healthy family is the proper relationship of Yahweh to His people. Ignoring the principles of headship leaves the man and woman denying their roles. The resulting spiritual message is chaos and frustration between the genders. Putting the head covering back on the woman and off the man reminds us of the foundation that we must build on.

Tree of Life

Why is the man's head uncovered?

His head represents Jesus Christ. When a man covers his head, he symbolically removes the Glory of God from the demonstration. We display something to the world one way or another. In the Bible, the Holy Spirit wrote the instruction for uncovering the man's head and we should obey Him. God is the head of Jesus Christ and He makes the Father known (1 Cor. 11:3, John 17:25). Jesus Christ is the head of the man and the man **is** to make Jesus Christ known. <u>The man is the head of the woman and she is **not** to make the man known, she **is** to **help** the man in making Jesus Christ known</u>. The woman represents the man and the man is nothing before the Lord. She should symbolically cover the man's head by physically covering her own. The man represents Jesus Christ who appears before Yahweh in our stead. We want Yahweh to see Jesus Christ, and therefore He will see us through Him. The man should symbolically uncover Christ's head by physically uncovering his own.

The result before God has the glory of Jesus Christ shining alone. And a Church, who is honoring her God by helping Him carry out His goal. A man with his head covered says he does not want to make Jesus Christ known. A woman with her head uncovered says that she wishes mankind to be prominently known, therefore ignoring Jesus Christ. A man with his head uncovered and a woman with her head covered are saying, "Don't look at us, but rather look at Jesus Christ our Lord." Which statement are you going to make as you pray before God? What message do you want Yahweh to hear you saying with your head?

Final Note:

Every relationship that is outside a proper marital setting is in opposition to Yahweh's message. Think about all the different messages about marriage sent by the world and the church today. Satan loves to have as many messages as possible because it makes the true message harder to find.

1) All relationships continuing in adultery and fornication cannot reveal the Message Yahweh needs to communicate. They represent false worship of false gods. Yahweh referred to Israel's worship of idols as adultery and fornication toward Him (1 Ch.

Walking in the Fellowship of Love

5:25, Jer. 2:20, and 3:1-11, Eze. 16:1-63 and 23:1-49, 1 Cor. 6:15-17). Man's adultery represents the false god who will never give True Life. The woman's adultery represents mankind's attempt to find spiritual life and fulfillment, while rejecting the plan God ordained for that purpose.

2) Homosexuals cannot symbolize the Message God needs to communicate. A man living with another man, as if they married, represents God being so involved with Himself that He ignores His people. Since we know that is not true, then it also represents Satan's selfish desire to take Yahweh's place. A lesbian represents the church centered on self and rejection of Yahweh's offer of spiritual union.

3) An abusive and controlling husband with an equally abusive and controlling wife represents leaders who, for their own selfish benefit, use a religious organization to control members. And a membership that fights with its leaders for control, resulting in division. It also represents the way Satan would rule, if given a chance.

4) An abusive and controlling husband with a loving and submissive wife represents the false religious leaders who mislead God's people for selfish gain. It represents false teachers who come in sheep's clothing but are full of evil. The membership looks for God to control the situation. It does not create a division by fighting the false teachers. It humbly stands on the Word and allows Yahweh to manage the situation.

5) A loving, selfless husband with an abusive and controlling wife represents the way the Church has treated her God down through the ages. He has always been faithful even when we did not deserve it. It represents a Church telling their God what to do. A church that is willing to accept all good and desirable things from God but give back nothing in return (Eze. 16). It speaks of the leadership continuing to lead, even if the membership does not care to follow. They continue to love their enemies who are misleading the rest of the flock.

6) A marriage license does not mean a proper married relationship. Living two separate lives and doing your own thing represents believers who want God to go His way so they can go their own way. They want to be the center of the relationship and

Tree of Life

manipulate God to their will. The marriage license gives the appearance of proper behavior when, in fact, the husband and wife live as if they where only roommates. This often leads to divorce, which shows how unreal the marriage was in the first place. It represents a Church that comes together for meetings only. They connect themselves loosely without much depth or oneness. The goals are man-centered ministries with many doing their own thing. Leadership is nonfunctional and separated from the membership. There are many, divided by their differences instead of united by their similarities.

7) The only relationship that can clearly declare the True Message Yahweh intends is a loving, selfless husband and a submissive wife. They represent a God who would willingly suffer for His people. They tell of His love for us. They remind us that Jesus Christ died for our sins when we were helpless. They remind us of a Church that lays aside the old life to take on her new life in Christ. The Church shares in Christ's death on the cross by submitting to Him. It talks of leadership that is tuned into the membership's needs and a membership following the leadership's example.

Please think about this chapter. Take it before the Lord. It is not a popular stand in Christianity today, but nothing that has merit ever is. This is about humbling ourselves before a Holy God in submission to His wishes. This is about the Message of Love that He wishes to explain through us. I pray that many of you lay aside everything you have ever heard and go back to the scriptures. May it be your wish to help your God tell His story His way.

May the Love Story of Yahweh be a Tree of Life to you!

Walking in the Fellowship of Love

Chapter 26

Jesus says, "My Sheep Hear My Voice."

To follow someone means to go where they go

I wonder how many readers I offended with the teaching about headship. I wonder how many readers I lost. I hope none. Our Lord used marriage to explain our alliance to Him. Jesus Christ tells us to enter by the narrow gate (Matt 7:12-14). I say, joining our lives to Jesus Christ is the narrow gate. Remember, we do not walk according to the wisdom of men but rather by the instructions issued through the Message. Marriage is not the only metaphor Jesus uses to explain our relationship to Him. He is the Good Shepherd who lays down His life for the sheep.

"Truly, truly, I say to you, he who does not enter by the door into the fold of the sheep, but climbs up some other way, he is a thief and a robber. <u>But he who enters by the door is a shepherd of the sheep</u>. To him the doorkeeper opens, and <u>the sheep hear his voice, and he calls his own sheep by name, and leads them out. When he puts forth all his own, he goes before them, and the sheep follow him because they know his voice</u>. And a stranger they simply will not follow, but will flee from him, because they do not know the voice of strangers" (John 10:1-5).

<u>*"I am the good shepherd; and I know My own, and My own know Me"*</u> *(John 10:14).*

My brother Tony says, "Sheep are the dumbest animals on earth." I know there are those who raise turkeys who might argue. Tony watched as his sheep strained to reach though the fence for the grass on the other side. However, if his sheep were to get out of their fencing, they would stick their heads back through the fence to eat the grass where they just stood. It reminds me of the saying "The grass is always greener on the other side of the fence."

My father has said to me more than once, "People are like sheep. If one fell off a cliff, the rest would follow." I have heard it said that in the slaughter pens, they use what they call the Judas Goat to help lead the sheep into the pens. The sheep's senses tell them that death is in front of them and they are unwilling to go in, but they will

Tree of Life

follow the goat into the pen of death. Spiritually, people are like sheep, in that we want what we do not have, hold in lesser regard what we do have, and follow others without asking why or where they lead us, even to our destruction.

Jesus Christ does not compel the sheep to follow Him. In fact, He claims that if sheep do not know His voice, they are not His sheep and they will not follow Him (John 10:1-5). Sheep will not follow a stranger. The Good Shepherd calls His sheep by name. A shepherd who knows each member of the flock well enough to tell them apart has spent much time with his flock. A part-timer or a hireling does not have the time to learn the differences between the sheep. Jesus Christ says something here that we must take time to understand. He knows us and He knows what makes our lives enjoyable or what makes our lives hard and discouraging. He lives with His people in the same intimate way a good shepherd spends time with His sheep. We do not flee Him because we know Him well enough to want to be with Him. The Good Shepherd leads us out and has no need to compel us to follow Him. In fact, if He needs to compel us, we are not His. This is how He knows we are His sheep: when we hear His voice, we follow Him.

Think about what the Holy Spirit is saying. He wants to live with us (John 15:1-7). He promises never to leave or abandon us (Isa. 41:17, Heb. 13:5, John 14:16-21). He wants to become one with us (John 17:9-25). Jesus Christ uses the illustration of the sheep and the shepherd to help His followers understand the relationship the Church has with Him. They follow the LOGOS of God because they recognize His voice and want to be with Him. They are not forced to follow Him under the fear of retaliation. Instead, He draws them by acts of love. His sheep know His voice. They claim Him as their Shepherd (Matt. 10:32-33).

This is not a one-way street where He proclaims Himself owner of the sheep. His sheep have entered an agreement with Him so they may be His sheep. If they did not enter such an agreement, they would flee when He called, because they would fear His voice. The people of Yahweh claim Him as their Shepherd, Master, Lord, Sovereign King, Father of their Spirits, and Friend. It is important that we take pride in our Shepherd. The more His people learn of Him, the more they value Him for being "WHO HE IS" and the more

Walking in the Fellowship of Love

He is owned by them. The more they own Him and take pride in Him, the more they want others to know and value Him also (Luke 12:1-10)

Enjoy being in the family of God, embrace it, and do not be reserved about your friendship with the Shepherd. It takes time to know Him. Guard your heart, be on the watch, and take care that you are not studying to "know about God" while missing out on "knowing God." There is difference. Many will come to Him and say, "LORD, LORD" and He will say to them, *'I never knew you; DEPART FROM ME, YOU WHO PRACTICE LAWLESSNESS' (Matt. 7:23).* (Read all of Matt. 7:13-23, and 25:31-46.)

Knowing about the things of God is not the same as having a friendship with God. Knowledge allows people to think that they are following Him, but they do so only when they want to and for a duration of their choosing. If there is a commitment between the Shepherd and the sheep, there is a true following. Off and on, here and there does not make a proper relationship.

If you want to know the Shepherd, you must experience the Shepherd. You cannot depend on someone else's stories, for they will always remain just stories. No matter how real someone else's walk with the Lord is, you cannot live with Christ through them. It must be between Him and you and between Him and you alone.

The Good Shepherd is not like the hireling

Jesus illustrates the difference of the thief and the hireling with the Good Shepherd (John 10:1-30). The thief comes to kill and destroy and the hireling will abandon the sheep as soon as a threat appears. The thief inflicts a cost onto the sheep. The hireling will not suffer a cost to him for the sake of the sheep. The True Shepherd of the sheep provides for the welfare of the sheep, at no cost to the sheep. The True Shepherd willingly lays down His life for the sheep (John 10:11).

The sheep that are not of the Good Shepherd's flock are without a True Shepherd. They are vulnerable to the thieves because they are led by a hireling. The hireling is not the owner of the sheep and does not know them nor does he care to know them. When he calls the sheep, they flee. Instead of leading the sheep, he must drive the sheep. He will keep the sheep in front of him because he must watch where they are going and redirect them if they are straying from where He wants them to go. He uses fear to force the sheep to comply with his will, and does not allow them to act according to their own will.

    The Good Shepherd is confident that His sheep follow Him because that is what makes them His. He does not need to force them to go where they do not want to go, for they will follow Him where He leads. What motivates the sheep is their wish to be with the Shepherd. They will go where they fear to go, for they trust the Shepherd. They believe He is taking them to green pastures and still waters (Psalms 23:2). The sheep have yielded their lives to the Shepherd and are dependent on Him for everything.

    Satan and the world around us are the thieves and hirelings who are driving the shepherd-less sheep by the influence they have over the world's system. They are not on the lookout for the sheep's best interest. Instead, they look to optimally benefit themselves. Satan is like the thief whose sole purpose is to destroy the sheep. False prophets are like the hirelings who guide the sheep but desert them when they are no longer interested or if something threatens them.

    The difference between the Good Shepherd and the hireling is Love. The Shepherd loves the sheep and the sheep love the Shepherd. We know we are the sheep of God because we know His Love, personally. His Love draws us to Him, and draws us closer to those who are also of the flock. We do not feel like we are losing ourselves by following our Shepherd. On the contrary, we feel like we gain more that we can repay.

Do two men walk together unless they agree? (Amos 3:3)

    Those who follow the LOGOS of God have an agreement with Him. It is an agreement that our God wants to make with His people from the start. He will be their God and they will be His people.

    The word which came to Jeremiah from the LORD, saying, "Hear the words of this covenant, and speak to the men of Judah and to the inhabitants of Jerusalem; and say to them, 'Thus says the LORD, the God of Israel, "Cursed is the man who does not heed the

Walking in the Fellowship of Love

words of this covenant which I commanded your forefathers in the day that I brought them out of the land of Egypt, from the iron furnace, saying, <u>'Listen to My voice, and do according to all which I command you; so you shall be My people, and I will be your God,</u>' in order to confirm the oath which I swore to your forefathers, to give them a land flowing with milk and honey, as it is this day." ' " Then I said, "Amen, O LORD" (Jer.11:1-5). (Read also Jer. 7:17-26, Exo. 6:1-8, Lev. 26:1-13, Joel 2:11-32.)

    Hearing His voice is not the same as listening to His voice. We must follow through with what He has taught us. Knowing the voice of the Shepherd is not enough. We must leave where we are spiritually in our lives and follow Him spiritually. Before Jesus Christ died on the cross, believers obeyed the voice of the Lord according to the old covenant, because they feared what would happen if they should disobey. They understood faith and forgiveness, but lacked confidence as they stood before the Law.

    Today, we obey the voice of the Lord because we trust His way is the right way. We obey because we believe in His promises. Our desire to be where He is draws us to obedience. Trying to keep the Law was a barrier between Him and us, but now He fulfilled the Law and removed the obstacle. We are free to obey according to Love and not according to fear. **The need for God's people to obey the voice of the Shepherd never went away.** The ability and motivation for obedience comes from another source. Obedience that comes from Love has no fear associated with it, for perfect (mature) love cast out all fear (1 John 4:18). We have the confidence to approach the Shepherd because we trust in His Love and not because we trust in our ability to obey His voice. We obey His voice because we trust in His Love and want to walk with Him and go where He goes. Obedience is the result of our trust in Him.

    If we do not agree to go where He goes and do what He does, how can we say we follow Him? If there is no agreement to walk together as a flock, how can there be companionship with one another? If we do not agree to work with the Shepherd, we will work against Him for He is Light and our true nature is darkness. We agree to follow Him when we accepted Him as Savior and Lord. Therefore, we need to fulfill the commitment that goes with that agreement. We want to go where the Shepherd leads. We want to be where the Shepherd is.

Being called a Christian does not make one a Christian! To be a Christian and follower of Jesus Christ, one must stop going his own way and yield to the leadership of his Shepherd. An agreement to follow Jesus Christ is a commitment to follow Him all the time. We once had a dog, Gabriel, who loved to go walking with us. He always went on ahead so he could take the lead. Gabriel did not care where we were going as long as he was in the lead. As soon as we turned right or left, or turned around, he ran as fast as he could to get back into the lead. Sometimes we are like Gabriel - always trying to get ahead of the Lord. If we get ahead of the Lord, it is possible to mistakenly take the wrong path. It may take months or years before we find out that we are no longer on the same path as Him. At that point, we find we are not holding to our agreement, for we are now off on our own.

We have a need to get together with Yahweh

How do people get together with God? We cannot go to His house and knock on His door. We can't go down to a physical place like the Potter's Field and meet at an appointed time, say 10 a.m., and physically meet Him face-to-face. How can people meet with an invisible God? (Rom. 1:20, Col. 1:15, 1 Tim. 1:17). He made our appointment before birth. Yahweh has been watching us and knows every detail of our beings.

> *LORD, You have searched me and known me.*
> *You know when I sit down and when I rise up;*
> *You understand my thought from afar.*
> *You scrutinize my path and my lying down,*
> *And are intimately acquainted with all my ways.*
> *Even before there is a word on my tongue,*
> *Behold, O LORD, You know it all.*
> *You have enclosed me behind and before,*
> *And laid Your hand upon me.*
> *Such knowledge is too wonderful for me;*
> *It is too high, I cannot attain to it (Psalms 139:1-6).*

Walking in the Fellowship of Love

For You formed my inward parts;
You wove me in my mother's womb.
I will give thanks to you, for
I am fearfully and wonderfully made;
Wonderful are Your works,
And my soul knows it very well.
My frame was not hidden from You,
When I was made in secret,
And skillfully wrought in the depths of the earth;
Your eyes have seen my unformed substance;
And in Your book were all written
The days that were ordained for me,
When as yet there was not one of them
(Psalms 139:13-16).

Our appointment with God is something He is arranging. We need to be aware of the times He has arranged for us to be with Him. We are not the ones looking for God. He is the one looking for us (Luke 15:1-10). He is the one who planned to communicate His Love to His people. He has always wanted the relationship that comes with His being our God and our being His people. He watched us and formed us in our mother's womb. We start to find God when we stop thinking we can arrange the meeting times and places. We must recognize that, as the Shepherd, it is His responsibility to cause us to know Him as Savior. It starts with trusting this saying about Jesus Christ. "He did not suffer on the Cross of Calvary to leave behind or abandon the souls that have put their destiny into His hands." He died on the Cross so any who put their lives into His hands He will save. He will not lose a single one (John 3:14-21, and 10:25-29). The Bible has made this statement about His Son: "If we believe that salvation has come through Jesus Christ, than we are saved" (1 John 5:7-13). Anyone who challenges that statement is in opposition to God the Father and all those who believe He gives the right to become Children of God (John 1:12).

Jesus Christ is where His people are, because they go where He is. Therefore, we know that our God is always present with us, waiting for us to notice Him. You will notice Him when you know what He has said to you. If you do not know His Word, you cannot

Tree of Life

know Him. If you do not know the people of His Word, you cannot know Him. For He has said that whatever you do to one of His, you also do to Him (Matt. 25:31-40). He and the people of His flock are one. The Body of Jesus Christ is waiting to know you and they want you to know them. Being known is a scary thought for some. They have been in the dark so long, the Light frightens them. You cannot walk in Jesus Christ's love and not be known and exposed.

The first step in the journey is to trust the Shepherd. The sheep must trust the Shepherd knows the path they should walk. When life gets difficult, they must trust that the Shepherd Loves His sheep and has already provided the solution to their difficulties. When life continues to be a problem, we trust and believe that He has used circumstances like these for our benefit. We need to come to a place in our lives where we can trust that He allows all events to happen and that they happen for a good reason (Rom. 8:27-29).

Trusting our lives to the Shepherd begins by trusting that "HE IS" the "I AM." If we do not believe that He exists, we cannot trust Him (Heb. 11:6). I mean we must treat Him in our thought life as if He is powerful, knowledgeable, capable, and present. We must trust the Holy Spirit is real and lives within our lives (2 Tim. 1:14, Eph. 4:30). Next, we must believe that He loves us always, even when we do not deserve His love. He wants to show us the length, breadth, height, and depth of His love (Eph. 3:14-19). If we trust He died for us when we were against Him and divided from Him, how much more we can trust His Love for us now that we are with Him? (Rom. 5:8-11).

Following Jesus Christ is not in the words we speak

And as they were going along the road, someone said to Him, "I will follow You wherever You go." And Jesus said to him, "The foxes have holes, and the birds of the air have nests, but the Son of Man has nowhere to lay His head." And He said to another, "Follow Me." But he said, "Permit me first to go and bury my father." But He said to him, "Allow the dead to bury their own dead; but as for you, go and proclaim everywhere the kingdom of God." And another also said, "I will follow You, Lord; but first permit me to say good-bye to those at home." But Jesus said to him, "<u>No one, after putting his hand</u>

Walking in the Fellowship of Love

to the plow and looking back, is fit for the kingdom of God" (Luke 9:57-62).

There are many in the world today who claim they are following Jesus Christ. They have their own places to go and accomplishments to perform. They want to follow but their lives get in the way (Luke 8:9-15). The LOGOS of God tells us the ways of the Kingdom are first (Matt. 6:31-34). Nothing should be more important than following and fellowshipping with the Tree of Life.

When someone said to Jesus that they would follow Him wherever He went, Jesus pointed to the life He was living as an example for He did not own a place to lay His head. There were no soft beds or comfortable couches. The work the Father gave Him to accomplish consumed Him. Jesus Christ did not spend His thought life seeking out pleasures or comforts. We may have comfortable couches and warm houses, but we are not to live a life consumed with plans on how to gain them. We are to seek first the kingdom of God and His Righteousness. The rest He has ready prepared (Matt. 6:33, Luke 12:31). Seeking the kingdom first is a 24-hour-a-day, 7-days-a-week, 52-weeks-a-year quest that lasts the rest of our lives.

In the beginning of time, before He created anything, He planned His plan. We can trust in His plan and we allow Him to complete the plan He has for our welfare in mind. We must trust in what the LOGOS of God displayed on the Cross of Calvary. The Shepherd's voice is calling His own and His own go to the One who calls. As we trust the Holy Spirit within us, the beauty of His character becomes more obvious, which will cause us to want to be with Him even more.

May the voice of the Shepherd be as a Tree of Life to you.

Tree of Life

Chapter 27

Sharing the Yoke of His Fellowship

Fellowship with our Husband is about sharing His burden

At that time Jesus answered and said, "I praise Thee, O Father, Lord of heaven and earth, that Thou didst hide these things from the wise and intelligent and didst reveal them to babes. Yes, Father, for thus it was well-pleasing in Thy sight.

All things have been handed over to Me by My Father; and <u>no one knows the Son, except the Father; nor does anyone know the Father, except the Son, and anyone to whom the Son wills to reveal Him.</u>

Come to Me, all who are weary and heavy-laden, and I will give you rest. <u>Take My yoke upon you, and learn from Me</u>, for I am gentle and humble in heart; and you shall find rest for your souls. <u>For My yoke is easy, and My load is light</u>" (Matt. 11:25-30).

Take Jesus Christ's yoke on and you shall find rest. Some of us can relate to this passage better than others. Life can be such a load to bear. Challenges and difficulties spring up and gather themselves at our feet looking for our attention. There is too much to do and not enough time to do it. The load that weighs us down most is from people's sin. Sometimes our load is from a sin that haunts us from our past. Perhaps our burden is sin committed by other people or it leftover residue of sinful actions of people we will never meet. It strains our relationships, makes our work environments difficult, steals our chance to walk down the street in safety, and creates health hazards in the air we breathe and the water we drink. Wars between governments and the fighting that takes place between individuals are results of sin.

We start life with the weight of Adam's sin and then we add our own. The Tree of the Knowledge of Good and Evil separated us from our Creator. The Law speaks to us about what causes the separation. Our sin left us unacceptable in His presence. We busy ourselves with trying to become acceptable, but the load slows us down and takes away our strength.

Walking in the Fellowship of Love

Jesus calls us to come to Him. He wants to give us rest. He directs us to join Him by taking on His yoke. When Jesus says, "I AM gentle and humble in heart," it creates for us a picture. Gentleness and humility are attributes that accompany the rest for our souls. It is God who is speaking when the Bible said, "Learn from Me, for I am gentle and humble in heart." How often have you pictured God Almighty as being gentle and humble in heart? Why should we learn from Jesus Christ - because He is powerful? No! It is because He is humbly all-powerful and gentle in His dealings with us!

Jesus Christ is calling for those whose burdens are weighing them down. He is not calling the well-to-do, well-put-together, self-made, man-about-town kind of person. It is the downtrodden and sick of soul that He wishes to assemble. He is not revealing Himself to the wise and intelligent but to those who come as babies (Matthew 11:25). He calls those who are aware that their lives are not in order. He is the doctor looking for those who are sick (Luke 5:30-32). He wishes to gather those who are weary and worn by the cares and troubles of this world (Isaiah 55: 1-3, Matt. 23:37). He wants to take off the heavy load we carry and replace it with a light one.

Since we admit we cannot carry our load alone, we are willing to exchange our load for His. He wants to share His yoke, which is laden with love, joy, and peace. When we take on His yoke, we take on a different burden. We take on the burden of His heart for His people.

His Yoke is about learning

Notice how much of what Jesus said in Matt. 11:25-30 is about revealing. "Take my yoke and <u>learn</u> from me." "No one knows the Father except the Son and whom the Son chooses to <u>reveal</u> Him to." "The Father hides these things from the wise of this world and <u>reveals</u> them to those He chooses to <u>reveal</u> them to." In 1 Cor. 1:20-31, the Holy Spirit, through Paul, uses the same theme. God <u>hides</u> from the wise what belongs to Him. He uses the foolish things of this world to shame the wise. Paul explains the foolishness of God is more intelligent than the greatest of the world's wisdom and His weakness is stronger than their greatest strength.

Tree of Life

Think of the marvels of science today. The wonders of the operations doctors can perform and how fast people are back to their daily lives. Science has discovered so much about DNA and how He put our bodies together. But the secrets of Life still escape them. The things of the Spirit confound scientists. What the world recommends is so different from what Yahweh teaches. He teaches that we must die to live and that we must yield control over our lives before we can gain it. To those of the world, this is such a strange teaching, but to us it is the power of God (1 Cor 1:18-21). The Cross is powerful because it joined our failed lives to His successful Life and changed our souls of spiritual death into souls of everlasting life.

The word "yoke" is the original Greek word, ζυγός **zugos** (Strong's numbering 2218g). The Bible uses it in Rev. 6:5 like a balance scale. Paul used it in Gal. 5:1 and 1 Tim. 6:1 when referring to the yoke of slavery. You might picture this yoke as a piece of wood carried across the neck and shoulders with two pails of water, one on each end. Peter uses ZUGOS in Acts 15:10 to describe the Law. He describes it as a load the Jews could not bear.

Compare what Jesus said here. Those who are heavy-laden (by their sin and the demands of the Law) can come to Him and He will give them rest. He is not saying that He will take away all possible burdens, only that the load He gives would be lighter, more restful. Before our new yoke, we were not strong enough to bear up under the load. It was like being loaded down with 150 percent of our capacity. The task we have now is to learn as we walk along the path with a humble and gentle Master. We share the load with Him so it is like carrying only 50 percent of what we are capable of bearing.

In Luke 14:19, Jesus uses the same Greek word ZUGOS when referring to a yoke of oxen, meaning a pair of oxen. I like to think the yoke He asks us to put on is the kind oxen would wear as a team - like a pair of horses in a harness pulling a plow. Jesus Christ would be one member of the team and we would be the other. Sometimes, we can sense Him personally working alongside to help us spiritually in a one-on-one friendship. Sometimes, He takes the form of another believer to encourage us and to help bear the load.

Walking in the Fellowship of Love

It is a shared load we carry

When we put on His double yoke and walk with Christ our Lord, we join Him in a relationship that becomes much more than following. We become a helper to Him. To work as a team, we must know our yoke-mate. Being a yoke-mate means it is impossible for us to go our own way, as we did before. We yield the right to leave anytime we want, for the yoke of the Holy Spirit connects and binds us to our yoke-mate. A team must agree on the goal and how to get there. Otherwise, they work against each other and make the task much harder than it should be.

Think about what we have said so far in this book. Before we joined Jesus Christ and took on the Yoke of the Holy Spirit, we carried the full weight of our sin and were free to go anywhere we wanted; but did not know where to go. Now the weight of our sin is gone and we are no longer allowed to carry the burden of our sin. We share His burden of Love for those who are forsaking life and choosing death. The Yoke of the Holy Spirit we share with Jesus Christ is His Life. He wants us to join Him as He reveals through us the same He revealed to us. He is using everyday circumstances in our lives to make the Father known to those who do not yet know Him.

Instead of the burden of righteousness we get because of the Law, we burden ourselves with Love for one another, as Jesus was also burdened when He went to the cross. Ours is not a load we carry on our own, but a shared load with the Master and with each of the called ones. We are to join **Him** while He carries **His** people's load. His work is a benefit to His people. We carry His work in us. We are to fellowship with Jesus Christ and learn from the Life we see Him live in us. What He wishes to teach us is not going to weigh us down, but will empower us to do good works for the right reasons. No one knows the Father except the Son and those to whom the Son desires to reveal. Fellowshipping in the Yoke of His Life is a necessary part of that revelation.

Jesus plans to make known the mind and heart of the Father to those who walk with Him by sharing His mind and heart. As we try to live our life as He lived His life, He allows circumstances to happen that give us the chance to love as He loved. This allows us to know Him better by sharing those moments with Him. We cannot

Tree of Life

know what it is to forgive a sin committed against us unless someone transgresses against us and we forgive them. We cannot love our enemies unless someone opposes us and we show concern for them. We cannot know what it is like to receive comfort in times of stress, unless difficult times happen to us and we receive comfort. We cannot know what it is to love unconditionally unless we know those who are hard to love.

We now live new lives that were unavailable to us before. We are coheirs of the inheritance Jesus Christ receives from His Father (Titus 3:3-9, Rom. 8:15-18, James 2:5). Nothing in our old lives compares with the richness of the life we gain in Christ Jesus. Before we can share in the riches we find in Jesus Christ, we must give up the life of spiritual poverty we now own.

We cannot walk in darkness and share in the light!

And this is the message we have heard from Him and announce to you, <u>that God is light, and in Him there is no darkness at all</u>. If we say that we have fellowship with Him and yet walk in the darkness, we lie and do not practice the truth; but if we walk in the light as He Himself is in the light, we have fellowship with one another, and the blood of Jesus His Son cleanses us from all sin (1 John 1:5-7).

In Him was life, and the life was the light of men. And the light shines in the darkness, and the darkness did not comprehend it (John 1:4-5).

The message the Disciples heard from the beginning of Christ's ministry was that God is Light, and in Him there is no darkness. It is impossible to walk sharing the same yoke as Jesus Christ and continue to walk in the paths of destruction. He is not walking in the paths of destruction. Therefore, we cannot walk there either. If we take on the yoke that Jesus Christ wears, we will always learn from Him what is Light and never learn what is darkness. As the Light of the Savior shines into our souls, the darkness of our souls goes away. He does not teach the thinking that results in sin and will not lead us into sin. He will allow us to face sin and overcome sin by the power of His Love.

Walking in the Fellowship of Love

Since He entered our daily lives, we became flooded with the Light of His Existence. In Him, there is no darkness. Therefore, any darkness that exists in our heart is from some other source that we are refusing to give up. Since the yoke connects us to our Savoir, we can no longer hold onto our destructive thinking. If we do, it is similar to yoked oxen that are trying to go in opposite ways. If life is not going smoothly in someone's spiritual life, maybe he is pulling opposite to his yoke-mate.

Jesus Christ is the LOGOS of God and expresses what the Father wishes to reveal. He changes the heart of men by putting "Life-Giving Thoughts" into their minds. We walk in the Light. The Blood of His Atonement washes away the stains of our sins. The Holy Spirit is searching the heart of Yahweh. Then He reveals it to us. He clarifies His thoughts by relating them to the "Demonstration of Love" Jesus Christ lived out on the cross (Romans 8:26-27 and 5:8-11).

As we walk in the light, we see things we did not see before. The things we have seen before, we see differently. We see things the way they are and become aghast we did not see it that way before. We were blind, but now we see. What we held in high esteem in our old lives is nothing in comparison to what we now have in our new lives. The Person we fellowship with replaces the false treasures we believed would bring us happiness.

We must agree with the Light about our sin!

To walk with Yahweh, we must come into agreement with His thinking. We are leaving the darkness for the Light. It becomes necessary for us to come into agreement with what the Light reveals. We cannot think as we want to think. We must take on His thinking and His ways. We are now yoke-mates to the all-knowing God. He intimately associates with us daily as He reveals Himself to us. As our thinking changes, our behavior also changes. We cannot walk in the Light of His Being and remain unchanged. We cannot walk in His Light and not reflect His Light.

If we say that we have fellowship with Him and yet walk in the darkness, we lie and do not practice the truth; but if we walk in the light as He Himself is in the light, we have fellowship with one another, <u>and the blood of Jesus His Son cleanses us from all sin</u>.

Tree of Life

If we say that we have no sin, we are deceiving ourselves, and the truth is not in us. If we confess our sins, <u>He is faithful and righteous</u> to forgive us our sins and <u>to cleanse us from all unrighteousness</u>. If we say that we have not sinned, we make Him a liar, and His word is not in us.

My little children, <u>I am writing these things to you that you may not sin</u>. And if anyone sins, we have an Advocate with the Father, Jesus Christ the righteous; and He Himself is the propitiation for our sins; and not for ours only, but also for {those of} the whole world (1 John 1:6-2:1-2).

John did not write his letter with chapters and verses. Men have divided his letter into chapters and verses. I prefer to allow the Holy Spirit's thoughts here to continue without interruption. As we continue our discussion, I want you to consider John 1:1-2:13 as one continuous thought. The Holy Spirit is making a point here and I think that if we divide His point into two separate parts, we confuse His meaning.

John's perspective of his reader is different in 1:1-2:13 than it is for the rest of the letter. When the Greeks of John's day wrote a letter, they could use their grammar to refer to time in the present (the time the writer wrote the letter) or in the future (the time the reader reads the letter). From 1:1 to 2:13 John speaks in the present tense to the reader as if he is still writing. He says, "I am writing to you." His reference is to the time of his writing. For this portion of his letter, we picture John sitting at His desk, pen in hand, writing his letter. Maybe he stops to think and then continues to write. In 1 John 2:14, he writes, "I have written to you." He writes as if he is no longer at his desk writing. He writes as if he refers to a point he made in the past. He is now refers to it in the past tense. We can picture him looking over the shoulder of his reader and explaining what he wrote in verses 1:1 to 2:13.

I believe the Holy Spirit led John to write like this for a reason, for this divides the letter into two parts. The second part from 2:14 to 5:21 is an explanation of the first part 1:1 to 2:13. It is like John is facing us, making his point step by step. Then, He finishes his point in 2:13, puts his arm around our shoulder, and begins to explain what he meant. Like someone who continues his thoughts in a private

Walking in the Fellowship of Love

conversation after his lecture is over, John is expanding on his original message. He is not introducing a new train of thought. He is explaining his reasoning in more detail. Therefore you should not separate what he said in verse 2:1-13 from verses 1:1-10. They are a continuous thought. When John writes that his purpose is *"that we may not sin"* (1 John 2:1), he is connecting it to what he meant when he said *"if we say that we have not sinned"* (1 John 1:6, 8, 10). Also, he explains what he meant when he says we are cleansed from sin and all unrighteousness (1 John 1:7, 9).

You see, we join Jesus Christ by placing onto our necks the Yoke of His Life and sharing His load. He is the righteous and pure demonstration of God the Father's Love. When we share a Life in which there is no darkness (sin/hate), our darkness becomes revealed. If we come into agreement (confess) with Him about our darkness, He promises to remove (clean) our darkness. If we say that we do not have darkness (sin/hate) needing removal, we remain in disagreement and call Him liar.

If we refuse to admit the truth He is revealing, then we continue to walk in the darkness and we cannot be in fellowship. We bear false witness when we claim that we walk in His yoke and yet do not confess our need for the Light of His Blood. If we do not change and sinful tendencies remain, we are unable to claim we walk in the Light. If we confess our need to have His cleansing work in our lives, then we know He will clean the sin from our lives. If we are, in fact, sharing the Yoke of His Life, it is not us but the Light of His Blood shining in us that makes us clean. If we change, and sinful tendencies do not remain, we know we walk in the Light. If we do not change, we are not walking in the Light.

The Holy Spirit creates in us the ability not to sin. We must want the ability to not sin to put on the Yoke of His Companionship. Love issued from a pure heart and a sincere faith is His goal (1 Tim. 1:5). When the Light of Love empowers our lives, sin becomes powerless over us, because knowing Him cleanses us from sin. Even after we join Him in His yoke, we remain vulnerable until He causes His Light of Love to shine in all parts of our lives. The longer we walk in unison with the Maker of Life, the more we learn to love as He commanded. There is no law written against Love and so therefore no violation of the law when we act in Love. As the Light

Tree of Life

of Love becomes our way of life, we will walk in the Light without sin.

Since it is no longer our lives we live, what happened in the old life is no longer our concern. Jesus Christ is now the one who answers to the charge laid before the throne. As He works in our lives, He removes our sin by conforming us into the sinless image of the Only Begotten Son of the Father (2 Cor. 3:17-18).

The privilege is ours

We now focus our attention on the wonderful privilege that is ours. He allowed us to join Him in His demonstration, while we still live this physical life. We join in the same manner as Jesus Christ and with the same attitude He had (Phil. 2:1-5). By doing so, we do not join as men enslaved to sin. We join as those He is changing daily into His likeness - not that we have already obtained His likeness (Phil. 3:8-16). We look forward to the day that we change in the twinkle of an eye and He completes us according to the will of Him who is doing the work (1 Cor. 15:51-57). It is true that we are not now as complete as we wish to be. He looks ahead to the time that He completes us and He counts us already complete.

Our focus is not on how complete we have become, for what He intends for each of us is different according to His purpose. We are to focus on His purpose. The person with the least honor before men may be the one who pleases the Lord most. The one who the Lord appears to bless the most may not be able to stand faithfully, unless he receives the blessing. Our focus must be on the success of the Holy Spirit within the Body as a whole. The Lord raises men according to His purpose. It is not to the man's credit. It is to the Lord's credit. The Light that shines belongs to the Lord and to no one else. When we honor and praise men for being faithful, we dishonor the Workman who gave him faith. A faithful man is only doing what is minimal and expected. No one receives praise for being average.

Since He treats us with compassion and grace, we are compelled to treat each other the same way for His sake. We should also look ahead to the day of our brethren's completion the same way Jesus looks ahead for us. We are not so complete that we can think of ourselves as better than another. He leaves us in our unfinished state so we might remain humble in our weaknesses, else we will become

Walking in the Fellowship of Love

prideful toward one another. We should not stumble in our estimation of another's weakness, but treat him as a colleague who wears the Yoke of the Holy Spirit. We are all weak like our brother. Any strength we have came to us through the Holy Spirit.

    We know we are His if we change. He removes sin from our lives and we change. The Light of Jesus Christ will shine out from us into the dark places of this world. He is spiritual and we are physical. We are not going to see His person in the flesh until we are able to see Him in the ones who also share His yoke. When we fellowship with those who share the yoke, we also see the Light of the One they share the yoke with. We see them as lamps giving Light to those in need of Light by the example He lives through them. The candle is not the Light. It is the instrument used to house the Light. He gives us the opportunity to share with others the same Light that we have had the privilege to share in (2 Cor. 4:3-7, Mat 5:14-16).

May the Light of the Yoke be a Tree of Life to you.

Chapter 28

The Yoke of His Fellowship is Love.

Back to the Greatest Commandments

My little children, <u>I am writing these things to you that you may not sin</u>. And if anyone sins, we have an Advocate with the Father, Jesus Christ the righteous; and He Himself is the propitiation for our sins; and not for ours only, but also for those of the whole world.

And by this we know that we have come to know Him, <u>if we keep His commandments</u>. The one who says, "I have come to know Him," and does not keep His commandments, is a liar, and the truth is not in him; <u>but whoever keeps His word, in him the love of God has truly been perfected</u>. By this we know that we are in Him: the one who says he abides in Him ought himself to <u>walk in the same manner as He walked</u>.

Beloved, I am not writing a new commandment to you, but an old commandment which you have had from the beginning; the old commandment is the word which you have heard. On the other hand, <u>I am writing a new commandment to you, which is true in Him and in you, because the darkness is passing away, and the true light is already shining. The one who says he is in the light and yet hates his brother is in the darkness until now. The one who loves his brother abides in the light and there is no cause for stumbling in him</u>. But the one who hates his brother is in the darkness and walks in the darkness, and does not know where he is going because the darkness has blinded his eyes (1 John 2:1-11).

Remember, in the last chapter, I said that we should not separate 1 John 1:1-10 from 2:1-13? The Holy Spirit is using John to make a connection. He is saying that Light is the same as Righteousness, which is the same as Love, and Darkness is the same as unrighteousness, which is the same as Hate. I believe Satan likes to divide 1:1-10 from 2:1-13 for it fits the teaching that comes from the Tree of the Knowledge of Good and Evil. To break His progression of thought - by dividing the chapter - is to take away the flow of the Holy Spirit's message. We make a mistake if we claim to

Walking in the Fellowship of Love

walk with the Father and walk in the darkness, even a little bit. If we claim to walk in His Light but fail to allow the darkness of hate in our lives then we are not walking in the Light. If we claim to confess our hateful sin while claiming to receive His cleansing and then hate another, we have yet to learn the truth about our sin.

    In John's letter, the Holy Spirit explains the Law of the Spirit of Life in Christ Jesus, which He mentioned through Paul in Romans 8. Notice, the Holy Spirit does not define sin in chapter one of 1st John. The Holy Spirit waits until chapter 2, verse 9 to define sin. The Holy Spirit's intent is to remove the darkness of hate from us. He does this through fellowship. Because God is Love, he who wishes to commune with Him must walk in His Love (1 John 1:5-7). Those who walk in His Love will have Love overflow onto those around them. Not that they Love as a work of goodness, but as a nature response to what they are receiving.

    In verses 1:1-10, John starts with a point well understood and agreed on by the followers of Jesus Christ. That is, God the Father sent Jesus Christ His Son to deal with mankind's sin. Those who come to Him are to repent of their sin and He will recreate them as a new creation. Behold all things are to become new (2 Cor. 15:16-20). The Holy Spirit uses John to remind us of the teachings He gave through Paul's writings (Romans 1-8). The Holy Spirit is now using those teachings to reveal new depth. Chapter 1 verses 1-10 represent the familiar portion of His teaching by which He compares the unfamiliar portion. The Holy Spirit takes what the believers understood and recognized as true in verses 1:5-10 and applies them to verses 2:9-13. What is true in 1:5-10 is also true in 2:9-13.

    In verses 2:1-8, the Holy Spirit connects the understood part and the point He is making. He shows the connection by making a word balance with His statement. The thinking in verses 2:1-8 is the fulcrum. The thinking in verses 2:9-13 equals the thinking in verses 1:5-10. If one is true, the other is equally true, like an algebraic equation. Verses 2:1-6 reminds the Christians that since they are clean, they must follow His commandments and walk as He walked. He reminds them that those who claim to know Him follow His teachings and those who follow His teachings have the Love of God in them (John 15:9 1, John 4:6-12). Verses 2:7-8 says the statement made in verse 2:9 is the same commandment that they have heard from Jesus Christ. The Holy Spirit reminds the reader of the two greatest commandments and uses them as the basis for His statement in verses 2:9-11. The followers of Jesus Christ have always heard that they are to Love one another. Now they hear that they are not allowed to hate. Look up Luke 10:23-36 to see a definition of a brother. Remember the Good Samaritan?

We cannot say we walk in the Light while hating those who God Loves. Our God loves the people He has arranged to be in our lives. We should remember that He displayed His Love for them the same way He did for us - by dying on the cross while they were yet His enemies. We are to join Him on the Cross of His Love by loving those who hate us and persecute us. We must be willing to die for the Lord's enemies the same way He was willing to die. This is what the Fellowship of Light is all about.

We are to walk as Jesus walked

The letter of John addresses a problem that is present even today. Many Christians believe that Love is the greatest commandment. They also believe that if they hate someone it is acceptable. John did not write his letter based on his own wisdom. It contains lessons that Jesus Christ taught during His ministry. Look at what He said during the Sermon on the Mount as recorded by Luke.

But I say to you who hear, <u>love your enemies, do good to those who hate you, bless those who curse you, pray for those who mistreat you.</u> Whoever hits you on the cheek, offer him the other also; and whoever takes away your coat, do not withhold your shirt from him either. Give to everyone who asks of you, and whoever takes away what is yours, do not demand it back. <u>And just as you want people to treat you, treat them in the same way.</u>

And if you love those who love you, <u>what credit is that to you?</u> For even sinners love those who love them. And if you do good to those who do good to you, <u>what credit is that to you?</u> For even sinners do the same. And if you lend to those from whom you expect to receive, <u>what credit is that to you?</u> Even sinners lend to sinners, in order to receive back the same amount.

<u>But love your enemies, and do good, and lend, expecting nothing in return</u>; and your reward will be great, and you will be sons of the Most High; for <u>He Himself is kind to ungrateful and evil</u>

Walking in the Fellowship of Love

<u>men. Be merciful, just as your Father is merciful.</u> *And do not judge and you will not be judged; and do not condemn, and you will not be condemned; pardon and you will be pardoned.*

Give, and it will be given to you; good measure, pressed down, shaken together, running over, they will pour into your lap. <u>*For by your standard of measure it will be measured to you in return*</u> *(Luke 6:27-38).*

These verses give us an idea of what Jesus was teaching His disciples. It may have taken John a whole lifetime before He understood the value of what Jesus was saying. How can we say we have fellowship with the Light if we are denying the Light of Love? Loving those who give a measure in return does not suggest a changed heart, for even the worst sinner does that much! Some hear this lesson and pass it off quickly. They tell us there are people who are difficult to love, that we have people in our lives that rub us the wrong way, but we still need to love them anyway. Well, get ready for a shock: Jesus is not talking about those who rub us the wrong way.

If we have a problem with someone, we must resolve it (Matt. 5:21-26). If we do not like someone who rubs us the wrong way, we are failing to live in the ever-present friendship of our God. If we have joined Jesus Christ on the Cross of His Love then we see the people who "rub us the wrong way" differently. Before Jesus Christ, we reacted to the people around us, but now we are react to the One who is inside us. This new viewpoint affects how we treat people around us. We see each other as Jesus Christ sees them and we see ourselves through the same eyes He sees us.

Let me put 1 John 1:1-10 into my words: "Anyone who says that he friendships with the Light and does not admit that he rubs people the wrong way is a lair and does not practice the truth." We know we can rub people the wrong way and we understand the difficulties of walking in this life without rubbing people the wrong way. Since we understand how hard it is for us to walk without mistakes, we ought to understand how hard it is for others to do the same. It is impossible to walk through life and not rub someone the wrong way and it is equally impossible to never have someone rub us the wrong way. Since we understand this to be true, we should have compassion on the poor soul who rubs us the wrong way. For it is unavoidable that someone will rub us the wrong way and he is the unfortunate person it has happened to."

Love is a compassion we feel when we know we rub someone the wrong way. We care that we rub them the wrong way. We may not be able to change the circumstances, but we can have compassion for him. We hope he can understand and forgive us and take the time to understand. If we could do it differently, we would. In Love, we should be willing to apply the same understanding we have for us to the people around us, who also may not be unable to help themselves any more than we can help ourselves (Romans 7).

Love those who oppose you

In this passage, Jesus Christ is not talking about the unavoidable "He is rubbing me the wrong way" people who are hard to like. His is talking about the "I hate you with everything that is in me" and the "I am going to trip you up and hurt you any way I can," people. These are the people who work at rubbing us the wrong way. If they know something irritates us, they do it all the more. They think of themselves as our enemy, so they actively oppose us. Jesus talks about having the love that wants the best for someone who wants the worst for us. Jesus Christ commands us to want good for those who want to turn our well-intended actions into something bad. He wants us to work on carrying out what is useful for them. We are to intercede in prayer for their well-being and so the Light may shine on them also. He wants us to lend to those whom we know will never return what they borrow. If someone assaults us, we should not fight back in anger, but have compassion for them (Matt. 5:38-42). We may need to protect ourselves, but our motivation is not hate or anger. We love those around us, which may require us to have conflicts with our enemies. Only our motives should be Christ-like and our goal should be Love from a pure heart (1 Tim. 1:5). We cannot avoid conflict, but our participation should reflect Love.

Remember that, in His heart, He grieves for those headed for an everlasting Lake of Fire. We should share in His grief, instead of taking it personally by selfishly focusing on our own problems. We should focus on how important that person is to our God. Jesus Christ suffered at the hands of men in Jerusalem. We were all there

Walking in the Fellowship of Love

in spirit, striking the blows and mocking Him. Yet He loved us unto death. We are to join Him in His death, by demonstrating Love for the one who lashes out against Him by lashing out against us. The Friendship of Love is about joining Him on the Cross and sharing in His Love for His enemies by loving those who hate us and use us. This is the yoke we share with Him.

As we fellowship with Him we see how hard He works for the person who acts so hatefully to us. After all, He did come for the ones who need a doctor (Luke 5:27-32). If our Lord is as important to us as we claim, then what is important to Him should also be important to us. He is working for our enemies' benefit and we put on His yoke and share in the work for our enemies' benefit. If we share in His Love we will be like Him.

Our only opportunity

This is the only opportunity we will have in all of eternity to join Christ in His Demonstration of Love. When others mistreat us, we should consider it with rejoicing for we have joined forces with Yahweh. He is working to display what He considers to be the greatest force of the universe: Love! We will not have many more chances to share His heart in such a violent world. We need to see all the situations we face from Jesus Christ's viewpoint - that is from the Cross of Love. We cannot understand how much He Loves the one who so willfully and hatefully strikes out against us until we understand His willingness to Love us when we were the same way. Remember, He paid the price for the right to love our enemy. If we love Him and have joined Him on the path He walks, then we will yield to Him and love them with the same Love that He loves them with.

If you are saying that loving your enemies is too hard to do, then you are on the right track. We must first admit that we are woefully inept compared to Yahweh. We must also admit that walking as He walked is vital to our relationship with Him and His people. We know we cannot do anything of this magnitude on our own and the work must be His handiwork. Fellowshipping with the Source of Life is the only way we can love those who willfully try to harm us. We cannot begin to love the unloving and hateful people of this world by our own strength. The first step is to admit that we are

Tree of Life

also full of hateful actions and full of the same thinking that expresses itself in hateful actions.

If we try to love our enemies by controlling our natural impulses, we will be doing a work that will not stand (Psa. 127:1, Matt. 7:24-27). Without the Holy Spirit's discipline, we are incapable of fulfilling His commandment. When we walk as He walks we fulfill His commandment without thinking about it. Love will be our natural response to whatever situation we are in. We won't have reached completion, but rather as we near completion, His image will shine from us more brightly (Philip. 3:8-15, Rom. 8:26-31, Eph. 2:10).

We must agree that we need transformation to His image. He is faithful and true to clean us from all unrighteousness. As we share His Life, His Light of Love fills us and drives the darkness of hate from us. Then, we will be the Children of Light and shine the same Light He shines, for it will no longer be us who live, but Jesus Christ living through us (Gal. 2:20). He will so ingrain us with His Love that we will show it without thinking about it. We may not be aware of how much His Love has changed us. We only know that our lives have improved.

May the Light of His Love be a Tree of Life to you.

Walking in the Fellowship of Love

Chapter 29

Following LOGOS is Not Easy

Love is the narrow gate we must enter
Enter through the narrow gate; for the gate is wide and the way is broad that leads to destruction, and there are many who enter through it. For the gate is small and the way is narrow that leads to life, and there are few who find it (Matt. 7:13-14).

There are many who have no particular spiritual place to go, so any road will take them there. Jesus said the road to destruction is wide to contain the many who travel it. Those traveling the road do not plan to arrive at a place of destruction, yet they do not try to avoid destruction. Going nowhere and doing nothing is all one must do to make destruction their destination. Humanity does not have the means to avoid such a path. Acts of selfish hate are always destructive. If we do not alter the course of current events, the acts of violent people will continue to get more violent. The character of hate leads its followers to the same conclusion, whether it is a small incident like telling a white lie or major one like mass murder.

To avoid destruction, we must listen to the Message of pure Love sent from Yahweh. To walk in His Love is wonderful and beautiful. To experience the power the Holy Spirit has over our situation is exciting and revealing. However, living within a Life of Love is not easy. Jesus compares our following Him to finding and entering a narrow gate. Very few will find it.

Many are glad for the benefits of love and receive them in a selfish, hateful way. They do not receive love in such a way that gives credit to the giver, but rather they view themselves as taking the advantage. In the end, they receive their selfish desires instead of the love offered. Love is just as self-sacrificial to receive as it is to give. To receive self-sacrificial love, one must do so in a self-sacrificial way. Love comes with a price - one must put others first. Jesus Christ gave Love to those who hated Him. Those who selfishly demand to do the work themselves cannot receive His selfless work. Men despise Jesus Christ's acts of Love because they expose their own inability to love. To accept the work of the Cross, one must accept his own inability to overcome the sin of hate. He must lay aside his own attempts at righteousness and accept Jesus Christ's righteousness.

Darkness hates the Light

Jesus Christ said the world hates Him because His goodness testifies that their deeds are evil (John 3:20 7:7). He warns us the world will hate us for the same reason (John 15:18-26). The narrow path the Shepherd leads us down causes Spiritual Light to shine in the lives of His followers. His thinking becomes their thinking. His actions become their actions. Humanity rejected Jesus Christ because His words of Love were Light in a dark world. He said the darkness of this world would hate those who are His, just as darkness hated Him (John 3:17-21). The ones who love darkness hate Him and hate those who have Him in their lives. They wish to silence Him by silencing His followers. They are willing to kill His followers if necessary. The narrow path that Jesus Christ follows is a difficult path because only by staying on the narrow path can we return good for the evil given us.

It's amazing to think people would oppose or hate a person who commits acts of love toward them. True Love shines like a light, exposing the darkness of hate and selfishness. They hate the light of True Love because it makes their imitation love visible for what it is part-time and incomplete. It hinders them from carrying out their agenda when others know the difference between real Light and the imitation illumination they call knowledge. Love acts according to the Demonstration of the Cross. It never returns darkness for darkness. True Love continues under all circumstances. Darkness does not accept the Light and hates the Light bearers (John 3:17).

The ones we counted as friends when we walked in the darkness will stop being our friends as the Light shines more and more in our lives. They will defend their own lifestyles by pointing out our failures to others or questioning our motives. They will claim the Light is evil or the Light bearers do good deeds for show. It is a humbling fact: we are only Light bearers and not the Light. It is a fact: we are failures. This gives our enemies plenty of material to work with. They will try to cause us to doubt the power of the

Walking in the Fellowship of Love

Message within us. They will work to cause others to doubt the Message of Love we bring.

The truth of our failure is that hindering the Message will hurt us deeply. It will cause us grief. It is good that we lament the ways we hinder the Message, but we must remain true in our confidence that He who is in us is greater than our failures and is able to overcome them (1 John 4:4). Yahweh drew up His Blueprint with full knowledge of our failures and predestined an outcome that uses our failures for His good (Eph. 2:8-10). Like a chemist who uses ingredients to make a chemical compound that will cause a given reaction, the Holy Spirit uses our interactions with others, knowing what the reaction will be. Our failures are to our shame but He uses them to bring praise to Yahweh.

We need to come to grips with our failures so our weaknesses do not cause us to stumble, but we must be careful not to concentrate too much on them. When we concentrate on our failures instead of the power of our God's faithfulness to make all works good, we begin to doubt the teachings of our God. If we admit to the truth of our failures and glorify our God by trusting in His successful administration of the promises He made, we grow in our confidence for He never fails (1 Cor. 13:8).

Darkness can cause us to doubt ourselves, but our confidence is not in ourselves. Jesus Christ has proved the power of Love and its ability to change men's hearts. Darkness cannot attack the Message of Love, which the Creator sealed for all-time in Jesus Christ. Darkness cannot modify it. Therefore darkness will attack the human messenger. If you are a Light bearer, you will become a point of attack. The goal of the attack is to separate the Message from the messenger and focus attention onto the messenger. Satan wishes to cause doubt in the minds of those who hear the Message and in the heart of the Light bearer. He will turn the conversation to the messenger's worthiness and ability to live out the Message.

We are all sinners and never stopped being sinners. Our goal is not instruction that leads to our goodness. It is to live according to the will of Love living in us (1 Tim. 1:5). Let us keep our eyes on the goodness of Jesus Christ and limit our boasting to His accomplishments (Jer. 9:23-24, 1 Cor. 9:16, Gal. 6:11-15). Let us applaud the work He has already done within His Church, so we may

Tree of Life

give glory to our Savior and King. Let not our failures discourage us. Trials come to everyone. Whenever something causes us to stumble and fall in our journey with the Shepherd of Love, He will pick us up and encourage us to continue in the way of Love.

At times when we feel dry or when we fall into temptation, is when we most need fellowship with other like-minded disciples. Jesus is the Good Shepherd. That tells me there are many of His sheep where He is. If we do not find ourselves in the midst of His sheep, maybe we have strayed and need to return to the flock (Heb. 10:23-25). Any attempt to remain in fellowship with our Shepherd, Jesus Christ, without fellowshipping with our brethren, can be dangerous. Alone and away from the flock, we become vulnerable to attacks by the enemies of the Light. Worldly thinking is all around us and is searching for those it can devour (1 Peter 5:6-11).

The path we follow is difficult because it is about Love for all

You have heard that it was said, 'YOU SHALL LOVE YOUR NEIGHBOR and hate your enemy.' But I say to you, love your enemies and pray for those who persecute you, so that you may be sons of your Father who is in heaven; for He causes His sun to rise on the evil and the good, and sends rain on the righteous and the unrighteous (Matt. 5:43-45).

Fellowshipping with Love is about loving all men all the time. This is a difficult path to take and not a popular one. Men will take advantage of any weaknesses and try to convince us that it is too hard to love as Jesus loved. They will be right as far as they go, for they are talking about our loving within our own strength. The road we travel with Jesus Christ, our King, may get difficult because the ones we love may turn against us. The ones we show love to will return selfish hate while calling it love. Loving those who act hatefully toward us is not an option - it is a commandment. Remember that Jesus Christ loved the ones that opposed Him and He loves to the point of death those who oppose us. He loved to the point of shedding His lifeblood.

Loving the ones who work at undermining us is hard to do. It takes much prayer and fellowship with the Light of Love. When you pray, do not pray that you might receive love, but intercede for the

Walking in the Fellowship of Love

one who opposes you, just as Jesus interceded for you when He died on the cross. Your Love will grow for the one you are interceding for. Don't give self-centered prayers but rather other-centered. Pray according to the Love of Jesus Christ. This is the good works that He prepared for you from the foundation of the earth. He predestined you to bear His image according to the likeness of His death (Eph. 2:10, Romans 8:26-30), even if it is only for the angel's sake and not noticed on earth.

In the Sermon on the Mount in Matt. 5, while teaching about loving your enemies, Jesus said, *"Therefore you are to be perfect, as your heavenly Father is perfect" (Matt. 5:48)* When Jesus said, "Be perfect," He was not saying that we must be without blemish. The Greek word used here is τέλειος **teleios** (Strong's number 5046) which means "having reached its end, complete, or mature." Jesus is telling us that we are to act spiritually grown up and mature (1 Cor. 13:9-13).

It is the goal of His instruction to convert us into the likeness of God, our Father. He loves the ones who oppose us, who lie about us, and hates us. Because the Father loved them enough to send his Son, who loved them enough to take their punishment, and because we are His sons and daughters, we should also love those whom He created. Jesus tells us in Matt. 5 that Love given to those who have earned Love is no different from the love given by the lost sinners of the world. All men will love as a payment returned for Love received. Some men will return hate for Love received. But only those who have the Spirit of God will return Love for hate received.

Why would the Children of God return Love to those who hate them? They love because they have received love from their God when they were living the same lifestyle. Yahweh recreates His people anew with the materials of Love. It is their nature to love because it is His nature to love. We know that we do not earn His love by acts of devotion. Instead, we know that we should have earned His anger. We are aware that God, the Creator of the universe, was within His right to destroy us because of what we have done. We know our enemies are also guilty and headed down the same road to destruction. We should feel how it grieves the Holy Spirit who is one with us. As we feel His grief and feel His compassion for those who are of the darkness, our hearts soften and the Love of God changes our feelings for our enemies.

Love on the cross is a valuable gift. It was a Love given based on the character of the one giving the gift, not on the one receiving the gift. If one gives Love in response to good deeds, then it is a payment based on the character of the one receiving the gift. Yahweh gives His Love as an outpouring of His character, with no thought of the receiver's worthiness. The Love we give to one another is also valuable, when given without thought of a return payment and based on our character and not on the receiver's worthiness.

The Love we give is a gift and not of works

For what does the Scripture say? "ABRAHAM BELIEVED GOD, AND IT WAS CREDITED TO HIM AS GOODNESS." Now to the one who works, his wage is not credited as a favor, but as what is due. <u>But to the one who does not work, but believes in Him who justifies the ungodly, his faith is credited as goodness</u>, just as David also speaks of the blessing on the man to whom God credits virtue apart from works: (Romans 4:3-6).

He considers our virtue a gift from Him to us and not as a product of our deeds. Similarly, God's Love is a gift and is not a payment for service rendered. If it is a gift and not earned, then He may give it to anyone! Likewise, the love we offer is not for someone to earn nor is it given as a reward for good behavior. It is a gift.

When the Bible speaks of this kind of Love, it used the Greek word ἀγαπάω **agapaō** (Strong's Number 25) and another Greek word derived from it, ἀγάπη **agapē** (Strong's Number 26). **agapaō** means to love without thought of return. This is different than the other common Greek word used in the Bible, φιλέω **phileō** (Strong's Number 5368), which means to return love for love given. We get "Philadelphia," the City of Brotherly Love, from this word. The Holy Spirit uses **agapaō** when the Bible talks of God's Love for us and our love for one another. **agapaō** Love is true to itself. Love does not change when the situation changes. Love's character is to seek the welfare of those around them. Love cannot act in any other way because it would stop being Love. This is why Jesus Christ loves those who hate Him because if He did not, He would stop being God.

Walking in the Fellowship of Love

As He transforms us by renewing our mind, we take on His image of Love (Rom. 12:1-2).

The ability to love one's enemies is not something that can be summoned from within. You cannot meditate it into being or conjure it up with prayer. It is a result of eating from the Tree of Life, which is a daily communion of thanksgiving with the Creator of the Universe. When we see people from Jesus Christ's viewpoint, we see them differently. We remove the barriers that exist between us, because we see their sin in context with ours. We see His Love for them in context with His Love for us. A mark of spiritual maturity is when we see others through His eyes.

The sign that we love the Father is that we love those the Father loves (1 John 5:1). If you love The Father, then you are happy because He is happy. You do not need something else to make you happy for His happiness is enough. When we can we see His Love for another person, we rejoice because we know He is rejoicing. We enjoy being around those whom the Father loves because we enjoy seeing Him enjoy them. If we can see how much He loves those who oppose Him, we begin to want reconciliation for them in the same way He wants the reconciliation. We begin to want what He wants and His Love begins to flow through us and toward those who hate us.

Love cannot tolerate sin

When others fall, we must be mindful of our own possibility of falling and help them stand without judging them. All are able to fall and all need the same grace to stand again. When Jesus Christ died on the cross for His enemies, He set the standard for helping the fallen. We must mimic His Love when we help to restore a fallen one.

When someone believes he is strong in the faith and trusts that he can stand, he may relax his reliance on the Holy Spirit (1 Cor. 10:12-13, 2 Peter 3:17). His attitude will begin to reflect his boldness and he may begin to tread along pathways that are harmful. Maybe he has much faith and he can safely travel alone on such a path, but what of those who might follow his example? (1 Cor. 10:23-24). For the safety of those watching, the Father may need to let the strong fall at the proper time. We must remember that what we do affects

Tree of Life

more than ourselves. Others have a vested interest in our lives as well. We must be careful in how we affect them. If we let our pride or selfish thinking replace our dependency on the Holy Spirit, we can expect our God will discipline us, for everyone's good.

When a shepherd has a sheep that leads others astray down unsafe passageways, he may have to discipline the one sheep for the benefit of the others, even to the point of death. One way he might do that is to break the leg of the offending sheep. The shepherd then carries the sheep around on his neck until the leg heals. He hopes the sheep becomes emotionally attached and reliant on the shepherd and does not want to leave his shepherd's side. If no other discipline works, the shepherd must kill the rogue sheep for the safety of the flock.

Jesus Christ is the Good Shepherd who intently watches over His sheep. He will do whatever it takes to get the entire flock of sheep home with Him (Luke 15:1-7). Be on the watch and remain dependent on the grace of God and do not relax your diligence over your heart and mind. Do not rely on your own understanding but place your confidence in your God (Pro. 3:1-8). Also, be mindful of one another. Pay attention to those the Lord has appointed to be your shipmates. All of us would be sheep gone astray if it was not for the Shepherd. So do not judge anyone when they fall or when they stand strong but act according to Love by treating all equally (James 2:1-8). Look to Him who is faithful to keep those who stand before Him standing and to restore those who have fallen.

We love as He loves when we look beyond the sin and see Jesus Christ's response to sin. He considered sin such an important issue that He became a man and died. The Holy Spirit is teaching that we must deal with sin. When we must deal with sin, we should follow Jesus Christ, who showed Love while nailed to a cross. In much physical pain, Jesus Christ prayed for those who were sinning against Him saying, *"Father, forgive them; for they do not know what they are doing" (Luke 23:34)*. It is possible for us to commit a sin against the sinner we are dealing with.

You will hear that you are to love the sinner but hate the sin. I say, no one ever loved the sinner while hating the sin. They always love the sin and hate the sinner. If they hated the sin, they would have removed it from their own lives. Instead they hate those who

Walking in the Fellowship of Love

sin, while loving their own sin. Whether the sin you deal with is yours or someone else, be careful not to approach it from a sense of virtue. Before correcting sin in another, be sure your attitude is true (Matt. 7:1-5, Luke 6 39-45). Pride always accompanies those who take onto themselves the authority to straighten things out.

Like the Law, Love cannot allow sin to continue. Unlike the Law, Love sees the results of the sin on the person doing the sinning as well as the one he sinned against. For sin always has a victim. Most of the time it involves someone else, but sin always has a victim in the person who committed the sin. If we look past the issue of what is right and wrong, we would see someone causing harm to himself. He cannot do better. Only those with the Holy Spirit have a chance to overcome sin. All others are helpless and without hope, like little children on their own or sheep lost and without a shepherd.

Jesus never got angry with sinners because they were sinners. He did get angry with those who claimed to have a righteousness that was absent in their lives. Remember, you also come from a life of sin and are no more able to overcome your sin than the sinner you are dealing with (Phil. 21-6). Always approach the sinner in Love as someone special to your God. As you confront the world about sin, you must hold in your mind that God has called you to join Him in a Demonstration of His Love, not of His holiness or of His goodness. If compassion does not move you toward the sinner, you will do more harm than good.

The damage we do through sin concerns Him more than failure to keep the Law. Keeping the Law is important to Yahweh because He wants what is good for us, not because He wants to control us. He wants good to be the norm for His people. He is not enforcing a law for the Law's sake. He is enforcing the Law for His people's sake. When you need to deal with sin, you must make the person more important than the Law. Stand up for the Law of Righteousness, by all means, but your purpose in doing so should be a goal of Love issued from a sincere heart of faith (1 Tim. 1:5). What good is restoring a fallen member of the Body, if you fall in the process? Hang on to a proper perspective of the goal and you will deal properly with sin in your life and in the lives of others.

Tree of Life

Love is a different language when God speaks it

If I speak with the tongues of men and of angels, <u>but do not have love, I have become a noisy gong or a clanging cymbal. Love is patient, love is kind and is not jealous; love does not brag and is not arrogant, does not act unbecomingly; it does not seek its own, is not provoked, does not take into account a wrong suffered, does not rejoice in unrighteousness, but rejoices with the truth</u>; bears all things, believes all things, hopes all things, endures all things. Love never fails... (1 Cor. 13:1 and 4-8).

To me, the verses above describe the power of the Lord our God. God is Love (1 John 4:8) so this description of Love is a description of God. Think about the meaning to the words "is patient" in context with God the Father, Jesus Christ His Son, and the Holy Spirit. He is waiting with His hands held out for those to come to Him (Isa. 65:1-2). He is the one encouraging them to come to Him while they push Him away.

The Godhead does not seek His own well-being, but looks for the betterment of all. The Godhead does not hold a grudge with a long list of wrongs committed years ago. He has forgiven our sins and separated them as far as the east is from the west (Psalms 103:8-14). God never deals with issues for His own sake but intercedes for His people's sake. We must also walk in the same manner as He walks (1 John 2:6). We need to think about His commandment to love one another. His Love is much higher and much more effective than the love the world has to give. You can only count on the love of the world while you have the approval of the world.

Our God has proven that He loves us even when we do not meet with His approval. He is teaching His people to love the same way He loves. We join His people in obeying His teachings by loving others in all circumstances. Loving all, under every circumstance, is not an easy road to walk. This is why He compares it to a narrow gate with a narrow little-used path, and why it is like joining Jesus Christ on the cross. He commands us to follow the narrow path by picking up our cross and following Him into the likeness of His death (Matt. 16:21-27, Mark 8:34-38, Luke 9:23-26).

May Love be a Tree of Life to you.

Walking in the Fellowship of Love

Chapter 30

Jesus says, "To Follow Me is Like Taking up a Cross"

To follow is to go where someone else is going

<u>The Son of Man must suffer many things and be rejected by the elders and chief priests and scribes, and be killed and be raised up on the third day.</u>" And He was saying to them all, "If anyone wishes to come after Me, let him deny himself, and take up his cross daily, and follow me. For whoever wishes to save his life shall lose it, but whoever loses his life for My sake, he is the one who will save it. <u>For what is a man profited if he gains the whole world, and loses or forfeits himself? For whoever is ashamed of Me and My words, of him will the Son of Man be ashamed when He comes in His glory, and the glory of the Father and of the holy angels</u>" (Luke 9:22-26).

And Jesus answered them, saying, "The hour has come for the Son of Man to be glorified. Truly, truly, I say to you, unless a grain of wheat falls into the earth and dies, it remains by itself alone; but if it dies, it bears much fruit. <u>He who loves his life loses it; and he who hates his life in this world shall keep it to life eternal. If anyone serves Me, let him follow Me; and where I am, there shall My servant also be;</u> if anyone serves Me, the Father will honor him. Now My soul has become troubled; and what shall I say, 'Father, save Me from this hour'? But for this purpose I came to this hour. 'Father, glorify Thy name.'" There came therefore a voice out of heaven: "I have both glorified it, and will glorify it again" (John 12:23-28).

In Luke, Jesus reveals to the disciples that the elders and chief priests will reject Him and crucify Him. He tells them that He will die and rise on the third day. Then He continues by comparing our following Him and our death on a cross. When Jesus says we are to follow Him, He means His predetermined will must happen while our secular wants go unfulfilled. We will face choices that pit the Lord's will against our own. When we yield to His will, we may feel like we are dying spiritually. If we never feel a personal loss because

Tree of Life

of the choices we make, then maybe we have never chosen His will of other-centeredness over our will of self-centeredness.

The path we follow in Christ will lead us to a good place: well lit, with green pastures, and still waters (Psalms 23). The path He blazed for us will take us back to the Garden of Eden by going through the Cross of Calvary. Jesus Christ already paid for the right to walk the path, but using that right cost us everything that we are. Only those willing to love to the point of spiritual death will navigate the path He has laid out for us. It is a path that lives out the saying there is no greater Love than to benefit another at your own expense (John 15:11-13). Our cost comes from the change we experience while following the path. Notice I did not say that using the path cost us all we have. It is much more personal than that.

Most likely, He is not asking us to hang on a literal cross. In a spiritual way, we must join Jesus Christ where He is (John 12:23-26, 14:1-12, and 17:18-26). "To be where He is," carries the expectation that we go where He goes. If we want to be where He is, we will need to follow the same path He took. That path puts us on a course to our spiritual cross and our part in demonstration. You see, what happened on the cross was between God the Father and God the Son, and then between God the Son and His people. What happened on the cross is so important that Jesus Christ makes it an integral part of our following Him.

You cannot be a follower of Jesus Christ unless you follow Him all the way. It is not possible to arrive at the destination that Jesus Christ arrived at if you do not follow the same path. There is a barrier between where we want to be and where we are now. We are unable to love each other as we should or live a life without sin. We must follow Him for He knows the way and we cannot find it on our own. However, the path is narrow and not well-traveled. The course leads to sacrifice and loss. We even lose the right to decide our course's direction. You see, followers must stay on the path set out for them. They cannot do their own thing. They must follow the instructions as given.

Say you want to find a house of a friend and you have never been to it before and you must follow direction. If you discard the directions and go about looking on your own you may not find it at all. If you go looking for the narrow gate, you will not find it. This is

Walking in the Fellowship of Love

because it is a way of life and Yahweh is the only one who knows what that way of life is. He designed and created life for a purpose. A successful life must align itself to that purpose. Any other effort will fail.

The Cross is like a seed planted in our hearts

In John 12, Jesus said that if He does not lay down His life, then He will remain by Himself. Jesus was willing to be the stock of wheat that died so we can be the harvest of wheat coming from His seed. He was one, but now He has become many. When a farmer sows corn seed, he expects to see corn growing. God the Father sowed the imperishable seed of Jesus Christ, the LOGOS of God, into the perishable lives of men. Then there were two, one life is life immortal and the other is ending in death. Jesus Christ planted His Love in the garden of our hearts. He is looking for His crop of Love to come from the seeds He planted. The thorns and thistles of hate and self-centeredness growing there are not useful to healthy spiritual living. He is weeding the thorns and thistles to make room for the seed to grow. After a while, there is only the one immortal life. The old makes room for the new.

We must be willing to trust that living a self-sacrificing life, symbolized by a cross, is worth more than living a life symbolized by ease, relaxation, and pleasure. Laying down our lives daily is painful and unpleasant. Weeding the garden is necessary. Without it, we cannot understand the LOGOS of God. The thinking of Yahweh must impregnate our being, like a seed planted in our souls. We need it to grow like a Tree of Life in the center of our garden.

Many paint a mental picture where following Jesus Christ is the end of our troubles and woes. Truth is, Jesus promised the trials and tribulations of life would happen to true believers as they do for nonbelievers (John 16:33). He promised that we would have companionship with Him in the midst of our trials and tribulations. He promised never to leave us or abandon us (Heb. 13:5, Matt. 28:20).

We have a daily intimate friendship with the Creator and the Ruler of all Creation. He shares His thinking of Love with us. He causes us to mature as the seed grows into the image of His Son (Rom. 8:29, 1 Cor. 15:49, Col. 1:15). His life was full of sorrows and grief, because of those who do not believe. How can we follow Him and not share His sorrow and grief for those who have yet to believe? The plant that grows in us is the image of His Love for His people.

Jesus makes it clear in the passages above, taken from Luke and John, that following Him is like losing our lives. Being a disciple of the Savior involves a personal cost to the one who wishes to follow. Jesus told us in Luke 14:25-35 that we must count the cost of discipleship. When we do, we must include the reward. As we count the cost to us, it is important that we also count the cost to Jesus Christ. We must remember that we would not have the opportunity to follow at all if He did not die on the cross and take on the responsibility and penalty for our sins. Truth is, we do not understand the depth of the cost He endured for us. We do not understand the depth of the cost He continually endures because of us.

He is the Father to all creation and He loves all those He has created. To watch His loved ones destroy themselves is extremely painful. He will love them forever and grieve the hell they live in. Yet Love cannot tolerate sin. Our God loves all those He has created. Therefore, He will separate those who would destroy Heaven from those who can live a life of Love in it. The LOGOS of God prepares us to live in Heaven according to His design.

Let us have the same mind that is in Christ Jesus

Jesus tells us we can know the ones who serve Him. They are the ones who are where He is (John 12:23-26). In Luke, He tells us that those who wish to follow Him must deny themselves, pick up their cross, and follow Him. He picked up His cross and led the way (Luke 9:21-26). Disciples are not greater than their Master, but can become like their Master (John 13:12-17 and 15:10-23). If Jesus Christ is the Master, then His disciples take on the same attitude that Jesus Christ has (Phil. 2:1-11). His Life grows in us, building up and upholding a quality of life worth living.

To understand Love's demonstration, our souls must understand the thinking behind the demonstration. To understand the thinking behind the demonstration, we must spend time with the one who performed the demonstration. To spend enough time with the one who performed the demonstration, we must continually fellowship with Him. We cannot be in continual fellowship with the

Walking in the Fellowship of Love

one who performed the demonstration unless we follow where He is going. He may ask us to love others to the point of feeling like we are dying.

If therefore there is any encouragement in Christ, if there is any consolation of love, if there is any fellowship of the Spirit, if any affection and compassion, make my joy complete by <u>being of the same mind, maintaining the same love, united in spirit, intent on one purpose</u>. Do nothing from selfishness or empty conceit, but with humility of mind let <u>each of you regard one another as more important than himself</u>; do not merely look out for your own personal interests, but also for the interests of others.

<u>Have this attitude in yourselves which was also in Christ Jesus, who, although He existed in the form of God, did not regard equality with God a thing to be grasped, but emptied Himself, taking the form of a bond-servant,</u> and being made in the likeness of men. And being found in appearance as a man, He humbled Himself by becoming obedient to the point of death, even death on a cross (Philip. 2:1-8).

The Holy Spirit said it all in Phil. 2. We are to have the same attitude the Master has. He does not ask us to do anything that God Himself is not willing to do. Jesus Christ is equal to His Father and the Holy Spirit in every way. He did not think the equality He had with the Father was more important than saving the creatures that He had created. He became submissive to His Father and allowed His Father to become His head, His authority. Jesus Christ did nothing that Yahweh did not example or command (John 5:30, 8:28-42, 12:49, and 14:10). He did not live His own life, His way, but allowed God the Father to lead Him. He did nothing on His own initiative but followed Yahweh's instruction. We are to follow His example and do nothing by our own initiative. The Holy Spirit is ours to explain and help us give exultation to Jesus Christ. The Holy Spirit does not draw attention to Himself (John 16:10). The Holy Spirit does not spend time revealing Himself, but reveals the Son of God.

The source of life found in the Son is the character of the Trinity. It is not a religion. It is a way of Life. Only those He incorporates into the Person of Jesus Christ have the source of Life in them, which springs up as a fountain of Living Water within them

Tree of Life

(Isa. 58:11). He is in us and we are in Him. We become so joined to Him that we do not know where He begins and where we end. We are not to consider the equality we have with each other as something to hang onto. We must consider each as higher than ourselves (Philip. 2:3).

What is the cost? Is it a great cost or a minor cost? The value of the gain is so compelling, the cost appears to be little. Jesus Christ is telling us the cost for what He is offering is everything we have, even ourselves. We can hold onto nothing and take it with us into the new life. He will not allow anything to come between Himself and His people. He is driving a hard bargain, but He needs to. He is protecting something that is more valuable than His own Life.

May the cross you bear with Jesus be a Tree of Life to you.

Walking in the Fellowship of Love

Chapter 31

Oh Death, Where is Thy Sting?

Death changes our outlook on life

I would like you to think about something. What if the next time you visit your doctor, he said that you had advanced cancer and would most likely not survive the rest of the year? I would like you to play out this scenario, thinking about what you would say to your family and close friends. You would need to go home and tell your family, friends, business associates, and others that you are dying. What would that mean to you? What would you say? What kind of confidence would you have at the threshold of death?

Do you see yourself resting spiritually because you have put your life into the hands of your Lord and God? Will He be Master over your life or will you be in a crisis of faith? Stop and think about what you would say. What would your life be like if you knew death was at the door? We'll wait. La-Dee-La-Di-Dah La-Dee-La-Di-Dah. No, I mean it. I want you to think about what life would be like when you are on the short end of the stick. We'll wait. La-Dee-La-Di-Dah La-Dee-La-Di-Dah.

So, what will the theme of your message be? What do you plan to give those left behind? Will the prospect of being face-to-face with Jesus be a joy or a horror to you? How real will your faith appear at the time you face your last moments? Will your words and actions speak of trust that you are going a better place? Or will they show that this physical life is more valuable to you than the next? Will you be resting in the Lord or will you be hanging onto your old life with everything you have?

How would you handle your spouse or child or someone else close to you being the one who dies? Maybe it would be easier to face your own death than lose someone else. What would be your theme in the time of your loss? If you uphold your faith during a time of great grief, it will comfort those watching to see that you believe what you say. They gain comfort because the satiability of your faith gives them hope. If your faith falters, it looks like everything you said about your God is not true.

Tree of Life

Death is nothing more than a transition from our temporal existence into an eternal existence. Maintain your faith and you declare His faithfulness with something louder than words. Christians can make a positive impact on those around them by the way they face death. I hope that you prepare your heart to be a good witness during the last moments of your life.

Between you and Yahweh

Now let's continue our scenario by going back into the recesses of your mind, where it is just you and Yahweh. What will you say to Him? Would you be resting in Him, thanking Him, trusting Him? Would you tell Him how unfair He is? Would you believe that He has a purpose behind what He is allowing to happen?

How we perceive the things around us changes when we know the end is near. Our priorities change. We become bolder. We have less to lose. And we have no time left to do what we always wanted to do. As followers of Almighty God, we should live right now the same way we would live if we only had a month left. You do not know the day that you will die! Tomorrow, you could die in a car accident. It may not your fault, but you will still be dead. You could find out that you have cancer that is too advanced to cure. The timing and circumstances resulting in your death are not yours to choose. You cannot add one second to your life span (Luke 12:13-26).

The idea of death is scary to those who lack confidence in the saving grace of Christ's death. We lack confidence when we do not trust Him. We do not trust because we do not know Him. We do not know Him because we where to busy with our temporal existence. Our lives are not our own. He bought us with an incredible price (Acts 20:28, 1 Cor. 6:18-20 and 7:20-24). The life we now live we do not live for our sake.

We understand that every situation He puts us through is useful for the Body of Christ. Maybe it benefits us directly, but it could be for someone else's benefit - maybe someone we do not even know. We may never know why things happen the way they happen, but we can trust in the wonder and beauty of the person of our God and Savior, Jesus Christ. Can we accept every event that we face as being from the Lord? Can we trust He knows what is happening and allows the circumstances to develop? Can we trust He would not let

Walking in the Fellowship of Love

us go through any situations that He did not feel we could handle? We can rest in His power as God, believing He knows all and plans all for the good (Rom. 8:25-31). Knowing that all things are thought-out and planned by Yahweh gives a larger meaning to what we face each day. We are not alone to face life nor are we alone to face death.

What is in the treasure chest of your heart?

"<u>The good man out of the good treasure of his heart brings forth what is good;</u> and the evil man out of the evil treasure brings forth what is evil; <u>for his mouth speaks from that which fills his heart</u> (Luke 6:45).

For no man can lay a foundation other than the one which is laid, which is Jesus Christ. Now if any man builds on the foundation with gold, silver, precious stones, wood, hay, straw, <u>each man's work will become evident; for the day will show it</u> because it is to be revealed with fire, and the fire itself will test the quality of each man's work. If any man's work which he has built on it remains, he will receive a reward (1 Cor. 3:11-14).

Imminent death discloses the true treasures of your heart and the truth about the value of what you store in your heart. Let me ask you another question. If your house were burning, what would you risk your life to save? All too often, we do not take a spiritual inventory of what is in our lives. It is not until something takes away what we value that we recognize the important things. It may take misfortune or death to see what we are missing and what we value. It is better to learn the real value of what is in our lives by learning to Love now. Why wait for something tragic to force you to reevaluate your life? Love puts people and things into a proper perspective. Love allows us to be thankful for what we have and to enjoy what is around us today.

In 1 Cor. 3:11-15, we find out the clutter of our actions and decisions will burn in the fire. It will expose what we have stored up. Are we putting effort into things we will not value after we are dead? Things we build that are not on the saving grace of Jesus Christ are like wood, hay, and straw - common articles of no lasting value. Big boats, high-powered cars, good looks, recognition, attention from the

Tree of Life

opposite sex, money, what money can buy, and material possessions are valued by the walking dead and are all wood, hay, and stubble.

If we share in a work done by the Master Carpenter, we share in gold, silver, and precious stones. They are not the common things of this world, which have value that fade with time. They are eternal, with eternal value that never fades. Our earthly lives are a few precious moments in which we may walk and work with our Lord in faith. Death will put a stop to the time allotted in which we place the gold and silver and precious stones on the pile. Friends, fellowship of the cross, kindness, time spent with loved ones, prayer, and the like are eternal and continue after death.

Death is not about dying. It is about living and it is about how we lived. Death stops the physical life of a material body. But for the soul, dying is about change. We will change from the limited physical existence we know to an existence we have heard about but do not know. Change is always a little scary. Death is about the treasures and privileges that we will lose and about the treasures and privileges that we will gain. We lose a walk by faith and gain a face-to-face walk with our God. You see, after you die, the only thing that matters is what has happened between you and the Master and how that relationship affected others.

We can only speculate about the treasures and privileges we might gain by dying. We can know the treasures and privileges we will lose by dying. Many have lives that have already lost the treasures and privileges that matter most. They may not wake up to the finer things in life until they face death. In this life, we have a privilege that we cannot have after we die. That is, we can have faith in a God whom we cannot see. When we see God face-to-face and know Him as He is, we no longer need to have faith to believe that He exists. In this life, we must trust that the One we cannot see is active in our lives. We sense His presence and know He is there in the same way we know the breeze when it touches our face. We cannot see the wind, but we know it exists (John 3:8).

How we face death has a lot to do with how we faced life. Our perception of death changes once we comprehend that our lives are an irreplaceable privilege. We walk with God in a way not available in eternity. Do you treasure your life as a "once-in-an-eternity experience"? After you die, everything will be different and

Walking in the Fellowship of Love

the chance to stand firmly in the face of opposition will be gone, for the opponents will be gone. No more martyrs will need to burn at the stake. Believers will not be cast out of their families because of their faith. And no longer will anyone need comfort in times of trouble. Faith in what is unseen is replaced by knowledge of the seen.

Angels are watching to learn something that they cannot learn on their own. We place our hope in someone we cannot see. We hold onto something we cannot touch. We walk with God as equals although there is no way we can be His equals. Friend, think about the privilege that is ours and begin to enjoy it. Enjoy the troubles of this life, for it is the only chance we will have, in all of eternity, to walk a walk of faith during a great trial.

How are you living out the rest of our life?

Humans have a privilege to walk with our God, like no other creature. Mankind alone has the opportunity to die for a faith in a God they cannot prove. We have the freedom to die to self and live for Christ. Our physical death is a privilege we will not have again. How we die is as important as how we live. How we die puts a final stamp on everything we did. Our God has already reached out to us by associating Himself with us. We are called to fellowship with Him and with those who are His. We should never take the relationship we have entered for granted. We should never lose sight of our privilege.

This brings me back to the scenario I discussed in the beginning. What do you want the conversation among your friends and coworkers to be like after you tell them you are going to die? How would you like to live out the rest of our life? How would you like them to remember you after you are gone? How do you want Yahweh to remember you after you die? Do you want Him to think of you as a good worker? Would you rather have Him think of you as His precious jewel? How you live influences the meaning of your death. How you die confirms the life you live. How you handle the daily events you face will dictate what people think of you and, more importantly, what your God thinks of you. Paul did not consider his actions important, but instead considered them rubbish because of what Jesus Christ did. It is what Jesus Christ does through you that gives worth to the life you live.

Tree of Life

Well, you are going to die. Almost everyone is going to die a physical death. The question is, "Do you believe in Life with Christ?" Those who have fellowship with the Life have life within them. If you are fellowshipping with Life, a physical death is like moving to another state, closer to the one you love. You will miss those whom you are leaving behind, but you will look forward to your new life. If you walk in the Light as He is in the Light, you also treasure the privileges you experience with Him. These are experiences that angels cannot experience and you will no longer be able to experience when life is over.

The privilege we treasure is not in the suffering, but rather in trusting and resting in faith while going through the suffering. The privilege is believing in the trustworthiness of our God, even when all earthly reasoning points elsewhere. The privilege is not witnessing, but in a relationship so powerful that we cannot keep it to ourselves, so we witness. The privilege is not a walk through the Valley of the Shadow of Death. It is to walk through the Valley of the Shadow of Death and fear no evil, for He is with us (Psalms 23). Treasure the time that is at hand and do not shy away from it. Embrace all as from the Lord and rejoice that you are able to walk with Him in all situations of life. From the treasure of your heart, you will bring out good treasures (Luke 6:45 and12:30-34 and 2 Cor. 4:5-7). Your death could be to His glory.

May the time spent with the Lord be a Tree of Life to You.

Walking in the Fellowship of Love

Chapter 32

The Modern Day Martyrs

The Martyr makes a statement

Who among you is wise and understanding? <u>Let him show by his good behavior his deeds in the gentleness of wisdom</u>. But if you have bitter jealousy and selfish ambition in your heart, do not be arrogant and so lie against the truth. <u>This wisdom is not that which comes down from above, but is earthly, natural, demonic</u>. For where jealousy and selfish ambition exist, there is disorder and every evil thing. <u>But the wisdom from above is first pure, then peaceable, gentle, reasonable, full of mercy and good fruits, unwavering, without hypocrisy. And the seed whose fruit is righteousness is sown in peace by those who make peace</u>.

<u>What is the source of quarrels and conflicts among you?</u> Is not the source your pleasures that wage war in your members? You lust and do not have; so you commit murder. You are envious and cannot obtain; so you fight and quarrel. You do not have because you do not ask. You ask and do not receive, because you ask with wrong motives, so that you may spend it on your pleasures. You adulteresses, do you not know that friendship with the world is hostility toward God? <u>Therefore whoever wishes to be a friend of the world makes himself an enemy of God. Or do you think that the Scripture speaks to no purpose: "He jealously desires the Spirit which He has made to dwell in us"</u>? (James 3:13-4:5).

There is a wisdom that comes from Yahweh and a wisdom that does not and is earthly, natural, and demonic. There is His wisdom of other-centered Love or the wisdom of self-centered hate. The first is the principle that He designed Creation to function by. The second is the principle that works to destroy it. Hear what Yahweh teaches here! Those who claim to have understanding, let them show by their behavior the understanding that they have. Those who claim to be wise, but are not, will act with selfish ambition and jealous hate. Those who have the His wisdom are clean, harmonious, tender, levelheaded, full of forgiveness and good fruits, determined, and without double-standards.

Tree of Life

True wisdom shines most brightly when the darkness attacks and the cost is great. Some of us will be led by the Lord to display His wisdom as a martyr. We are not martyrs if, during the attack, we act according to the ways of darkness. There is a right way to respond to the evil around us and a wrong way. Our attitude in life will govern our response to evil. We must understand that living or dying in un-Christ-like fashion, is lying against the truth. It is just another form of good works done for the wrong reason. We must accept what happens to us as from the Lord. So in the midst of whatever event we might be in, we can display the image of our Lord. Even our death is an event we take part in to glorify our Lord.

Remember, martyrdom is never about the person. It is all about the message. No one kills another just because they are good. It is because of the Message they bear. By staying true to the Message all the way through death, the martyr declares his agreement with the Message in ways far louder than words. Martyrdom is not about staying true to a principle. It is about staying true to a personal relationship with the God of the Universe. The faithful death of the messenger, when it comes about because of the Message, always causes the Message to be more real and accepted by those who witness the martyr's death. There is no more honorable way to die than for the Message that Jesus Christ died to deliver.

The proper attitude for a Martyr

Notice: the one who makes peace plant seeds of peace. The attitude of a martyr is one of mercy, gentleness, and good fruits (Gal. 5:13-26). A martyr's job is first and foremost to be a reflection of the Holy Spirit who lives within. Darkness will attack the Light. The Light is to return Love issued from a pure heart. Unreasonable anger, revulsion, loathing, and disgust toward the enemy reflect the image of the enemy and are signs of hate that fly in the face of the Message. No matter how virtuous the case or noble the conflict, if we enter with the wrong attitude, we commit sin before our Lord and bring disgrace to His Message. There will always be conflict between those who walk in the Light of Truth and those who walk in the darkness of ungodly thinking. Returning evil for evil is never an acceptable action for a believer. Evil people will do evil, hateful things to the

Walking in the Fellowship of Love

people of the Light. They wish to draw out an unloving response. We must respond to provocation with the attitude that Jesus Christ has (Philp. 2:5-8, Isa. 53:1-10, John 19:10, Luke 22:66-71). We can only do that if He builds His attitude in our souls.

Jesus Christ did not seek out His enemies to incite a quarrel. Therefore, we are not to seek a confrontation. When someone incites a quarrel with the enemy, he usually does it for personal reasons and without Love. Those looking for a fight will only bring disgrace on our Lord (Matt. 26:52). Such quarrels always start in the innermost place of a person's heart. Quarrels brew over time by focusing on what is wrong and how to correct the wrong. Quarrelers seldom focus on what is right, good, and loving. The conflict is not ours. It belongs to the Lord (2 Chr. 20:15). We will join him in His conflict soon enough.

The conflict is never about the martyr personally. The enemy will wish to make it personal to keep men's eyes away from the Message by focusing attention on the messenger. His real motive is to silence the Message not the messenger. Do not help him by losing your own focus on the Lord's worthiness and allow him to focus attention onto a defense of your worthiness. Do not let him focus your attention on the merits of the debate. We want the Law of Love to govern us during the debate! We should always bring the focus back to our Creator and what He thinks, based on the Scriptures. Our goal is instruction leading to love.

When someone comes to us and begins conflicting with the Holy Spirit, it is easy to enter the quarrel on a personal basis. Our concern for the other person maybe replaced by a wish to defend one's self. The more forceful the defense of self, the more darkened our affirmation of the Message becomes. Unchecked, our defense will promote the world's viewpoint rather than Yahweh's. We should remember that we are only the messenger and not the Message. We are not the Light - we *point* to the Light. The debate is not about what you believe. It is about what Yahweh has said and what He expects. Darkness hates the Light, so it is unavoidable that it will conflict with the Light that is in us. It is important that our response does not take away from Yahweh's Message.

Those around us are watching to see if what we say is true. They are evaluating us to see how we counter such aggression. We

Tree of Life

cannot hide the truth that lives in us, for conflict will bring out for all to see what we have stored in the inner reaches of our hearts. There may be good or there may be bad. It is hard to keep a false appearance in the midst of a heated situation. The fortitude with which we properly debate is in us long before the conflict started. In the midst of battle, it is too late to train or build up the spiritual stamina needed to act properly. The Holy Spirit is now training His disciples in the art of Love for one another and the art of Love for their enemies. They share it with those they meet. They speak with actions that reflect the image of Jesus Christ. They sow the Seed of Wisdom in peace. They who sow the Seed show the value they place on the Seed by the way they sow it. The Message is peaceable, gentle, reasonable, other-centered, long-suffering, understanding, and full of mercy. Our attitude should reflect it while we share the Message. Our love toward the one conflicting with us should be unwavering in Christ-like Love.

The motive, by which we share the Message will mimic the walk we have with the Message. Our actions are to contrast with the motives that James gives for quarrels and conflicts. It is not easy and we will fail, but we must pick ourselves up and continue the journey. The battle starts with our mind. It is the first battle that the Holy Spirit must help us win. We do so by taking each thought captive (2 Cor. 10:3-5).

The One who taught us to turn the other cheek is now enables us to care emotionally for the one who strikes us. It may appear that turning the other cheek empowers those who strike. It may become depressing that people see our example as weakness. Remember, the greatest act ever performed by a human being was just such an act. Jesus Christ set the example. He put aside Himself, responded with Love to those who hated Him, stood up for the truth of the Message until death, and carried out the task given to Him by His Father. Jesus Christ stayed true to His relationship with the Father even when they became separated. The evil one wishes to break your relationship with your Father and cause you to doubt His Message.

When the battle is thrust on us, we should not add to the conflict through poor behavior. It is our behavior that wins the battle. Logic and thoughtful debate tactics will never make the Message easier to understand. Rather, it is Love shining in the midst of hate

Walking in the Fellowship of Love

that clears away the darkness. Love for our Creator is first followed by Love for one another. This means that we are not to continue in the conflict by continuing the conflict in the solitude of our thought life. As we think the matter over we must talk with the Holy Spirit and allow His thinking to become ours. We need to see the conflict from the vantage point of the Cross. We need to remember that we are trying to win people to Christ and not trying to win the debate. Our prayers should reflect our love for the person who is in conflict with the Light.

In this portion of James, the Holy Spirit said, "Those who make peace sow the Seed, whose fruit is righteousness in peace." The first place for peace to reign is inside the temple of our souls, in a place where no one else can see. This is something that must happen between the Shepherd and the sheep.

We do not control conflicts and quarrels, only our part in them

Conflict and quarrels will exist in our lives regardless of the purity of our heart. Even our Lord had conflicts with the Pharisees and Sadducees. The conflict always originated from jealousy and selfish ambitions of the religious leaders. Those who travel the course laid out by the Shepherd of Life avoid needless conflicts and debates. But conflict will happen and we need to live in Love through it.

We never need to force the thinking of the Holy Spirit on anyone. We only need to make the path to the LOGOS open for them to see. Those called by the Holy Spirit will respond to His leading. Those who hear the Holy Spirit will recognize what they see and want more of it. We who are of the Light must walk in the Light and fellowship with the Light. As we walk in the Light and share the teachings of Light, we will also reveal the false teaching of men, without trying to. We combat the wrong lessons by teaching the merits of Yahweh's thinking and not by debating the merits of men's thinking.

We can identify those who claim to walk in the Light but are of the darkness by their need to control the battle. They play their conflicts, battles, victories, and losses over and over within their mind, which is obvious by their conversations, which revolve around strategies for the conflict. Their purpose is to win the debate. They

Tree of Life

set traps and use every opportunity to bring in the advantage so they may show that they are right.

Those who walk after the Good Shepherd have already yielded control to Him and allow Him to control the conflict as He sees fit. They avoid the debater for he does not care for the truth, only the glory of the fight. Those who speak openly about the truth cannot stay out of the battle. They must prepare to meet opposition from friends, family, acquaintances, and from Satan. The opposition we receive should not discourage us, for the Holy Spirit is near to encourage. Let Love be the dominating factor in our dealing with the world.

It is Jesus Christ in you that the world hates so much

When you face conflict, think about the conflict Jesus faced from the religious leaders of His time. Compare His way of handling conflict with the way you handle conflicts. Jesus Christ never consulted His disciples about how to combat the influence religious leaders had over the people. He never changed His course or modified His teachings based on what the religious leaders would think. Jesus stayed on the course given to Him by the Father, never avoiding or starting conflict with anyone. Conflict came to Jesus Christ because others opposed His teachings. The negative reaction to His obedience to the Father had no impact on His walk. Jesus was not planning to affect human opinion. He planned to affect the course of human history.

On the other hand, the Pharisees, Sadducees, and Scribes where constantly taking counsel from one another on what to do. They counseled among themselves to devise trap questions to spring on Him while the people looked on. Their plan was to trip Jesus up and become authoritative over Him. They thought they knew all the possible answers and prepared to take the advantage, no matter how He answered. They worried about public opinion. The truth never interested them. Their open opposition to Christ's teachings was intended to keep people from listening to Him. They traveled to where Jesus was teaching, to find fault with Him. They looked for anything they could use to raise doubts in the minds of the people.

They were not looking for the truth. They only wanted to decrease His popularity. They did not know their God and His

Walking in the Fellowship of Love

thinking. Therefore, they were wrong in their thinking about Jesus. He answered their questions with the Truth, which caught them off guard and turned their trap back on them. They did not have a good reply because they knew He spoke true words. His thinking was so different from theirs that they did not have an answer. Yet their desire for popular opinion blinded them. After a while, they stopped questioning Him altogether for fear of looking inept.

Jesus' answers confused religious leaders because His eyes were on the Father. Their eyes were on the people (John 14:10, 16:13). Our purpose is not to win the minds of the people around us. It is to walk honestly in true friendship with our God, speaking as a witness of the truth that we have regarding Him. Those with ears to hear will listen, but we may never know they heard and we do not need to know who heard.

We are not so well put-together as our Lord, for we do not spend as much time in the Light as we should. We may fail in debates with religious leaders. This is because they spend so much time thinking through each argument and coming up with a retort. We will never fully win the debate on their terms. It is not our job to take on the false prophets. It is not our mission.

The Holy Spirit will provide the words we need in the day and the hour of the conflict. We should never spend time preparing for the debate, for if we do, we will enter it with our strength only. To do well in the debate, we must research the Knowledge of Good and Evil. Then we would study to increase our knowledge about Yahweh instead of _knowing_ Yahweh. That is a trap Jesus never entered, and neither should we. We need to see from a different viewpoint and not debate using the terms of the world. For example, Our God and His Law came first, so any conflict the world has with His commandments is a conflict with Him. We do not debate the wisdom of His commandments. We declare the trustworthiness of the one who gave the commandment.

We know the Creator stands against abortion because we know that killing innocent babies is in opposition to His giving them life. He knitted them together in the womb and knows every part of them (Psalms 139). Because God is Love, we must understand He would be against killing for such a self-centered reason, as given by pro-choice supporters. Those who promote abortion oppose Yahweh

Tree of Life

Himself and we should be witnesses to their opposition to the Creator. We should not debate the correctness of what Yahweh commands but point out the opposition to His commands. The debate is on the truth that there is a Creator and not on who has Constitutional rights over whose body. Those who stand with Yahweh must also oppose abortion or they stand against Him. It is not our decision to make. The debate is not about what men think. It is about what Yahweh is going to hold us accountable for. We are either for the Creator of Life or we are against Him!

The debate of evolution vs. creationism is not about how the universe came about. It is about the existence of a Creator. The real purpose of the debate is to cause doubt in the existence of God. If we debate scientific findings, we debate on the world's terms. Instead of debating fossil records, we must bring the true issue to the front and ask, "What will the Creator think when you tell Him that He does not exist?" We need to bring the debate back to the existence of a Creator who holds us accountable to the Message He sent in His only begotten Son.

We should prepare ourselves for the day of conflict by knowing Yahweh's thinking and by accompanying Him on His travel. His thinking should be our thinking. On the day of conflict, the Holy Spirit shall use what is in us to defend the faith through us. Our job is to discover the mind of God and trust the outcome will be according to His plan. The outcome is not our first mission. Yahweh has already taken that into consideration. Our first mission is to maintaining our relationship to our God through the obedience of Love. We should never doubt Him because of how well the debate went or how bad the situation looks. The Triune God has the victory already and we should rejoice. We have a privilege to share the same martyr experience Jesus Christ experienced.

Who will the Martyrs be?

This is My commandment, that you love one another, just as I have loved you. <u>Greater love has no one than this, that one lay down his life for his friends</u>. You are My friends if you do what I command you. No longer do I call you slaves, for the slave does not know what his master is doing; but I have called you friends, for all things that I have heard from My Father I have made known to you. <u>You did not</u>

Walking in the Fellowship of Love

choose Me but I chose you, and appointed you that you would go and bear fruit, and that your fruit would remain, so that whatever you ask of the Father in My name He may give to you.
   This I command you, that you love one another. If the world hates you, you know that it has hated Me before it hated you. If you were of the world, the world would love its own; but because you are not of the world, but I chose you out of the world, because of this the world hates you. Remember the word that I said to you, 'A slave is not greater than his master.' If they persecuted Me, they will also persecute you; if they kept My word, they will keep yours also. But all these things they will do to you for My name's sake, because they do not know the One who sent Me. If I had not come and spoken to them, they would not have sin, but now they have no excuse for their sin" (John 15:12-22).

   We do not look for conflict - it finds us. If we walk in the Yoke of Fellowship, the darkness will want to destroy us when it tries to destroy the Light. If they listened to Jesus Christ, then they will listen to us, or else they will hate us the same way they hated Him. We are to Love those who oppose us. They oppose not only us but also their Maker and Master. We are the visible representation of the One they hate so much. Our job is to represent the Love our God has for His enemies. When Jesus tells us the world will hate us, He is talking about their hating our Love for one another and our intimate relationship with Him. We are His friends because He is revealing the Fathers thinking to us (John 15:12-17).

   If the world enters conflict with us because we attacked them, we deserve what happens to us (1 Peter 2:18-21, 3:8-18, and 4:12-19). If the world conflicts with us because we are friends and associates of the Creator, then we have a chance to join Him on the cross and learn more of "WHO HE IS." If you read about the martyrs of the past, you will find that they only wish to speak according to their beliefs. Others opposed their convictions strenuously and the conflict resulted in their deaths. The martyrs never personally threatened or killed their opposition. Religious leaders, motivated by selfish ambitions and jealousy, were afraid they would lose followers so they tried to silence them. Since religious leaders relied on

Tree of Life

themselves and their success was all about them, anything the martyrs did took away from their prestige and that was a threat.

The followers of the Light fear not the teachers of darkness. Darkness fears the Light. The false teachers fear one another and compete with one another. The followers of the Light compete with no one. They know that those who have spiritual ears will hear what the Holy Spirit is saying. In Matt. 22:14, Jesus says that He calls many but He chooses few. We accept that only a few will hear and start out on the walk.

Although abortion is in opposition to the stated will of God, He has not rained down fire and brimstone onto abortion clinics. Anyone who approves of destroying a clinic or killing doctors in the name of God is listening to the teachings of men and not the Heart of God. In this is truth: the day will come when He will clean this earth with fire. On that day, He will deal with the sin of this planet. We are to look ahead expectantly for the day of His judgment and warn others of its coming. However, it is not our place to overcome sin by taking matters into our own hands. We are to reveal His Message. By doing so, we point out what is wrong with this world. Jesus Christ did not come to battle the sinners, but rather to save them. Unbelievers battle His effort. They will try to stop Him. He leaves them to their own and they create their own futures.

Study the life and death of Jesus Christ, for He is the example of how we are to act on the day of conflict. Remember, the Good News has always benefited from the death of the Believer. Even if you do not die a physical death, you must die a spiritual death with the same mind of as the martyr.

May the way that Jesus gave His Life
**   for His people be a Tree of Life to you.**

Walking in the Fellowship of Love

Chapter 33

Treasure the Right Things in Your Heart

I count all as lost for the sake of Christ
But whatever things were gain to me, those things I have counted as loss for the sake of Christ. <u>More than that, I count all things to be loss in view of the surpassing value of knowing Christ Jesus my Lord</u>, for whom I have suffered the loss of all things, and count them but rubbish so that I may gain Christ, and may be found in Him, not having a righteousness of my own derived from the Law, but that which is through faith in Christ, the righteousness which comes from God on the basis of faith, <u>that I may know Him and the power of His resurrection and the fellowship of His sufferings, being conformed to His death; in order that I may attain to the resurrection from the dead</u>.

Not that I have already obtained it or have already become perfect, but I press on so that I may lay hold of that for which also I was laid hold of by Christ Jesus. Brethren, I do not regard myself as having laid hold of it yet; but one thing I do: forgetting what lies behind and reaching forward to what lies ahead, <u>I press on toward the goal for the prize of the upward call of God in Christ Jesus</u> (Philip. 3:7-14).

When it comes to having what men regard as important, we have to consider Paul's a successful career. In earlier verses of Philip. 3, Paul lists off his credentials, an impressive list for his day. He was a Jew, not a gentile. Born a Hebrew of the tribe of Benjamin, not a convert. He had religious achievements, was educated as a Pharisee, and was most likely well off materially. He claimed that his integrity according to the Law was untouchable and that no one could find fault with his adherence to the rituals of his people. Paul mentions his zeal as a Pharisee in persecuting the Church. He could have mentioned his zeal as a servant to the Church. He could have mentioned his influence over the Church as their spiritual father.

It would be understandable, if Paul had thought "My life has value." Certainly there are others who believe that Paul's life was of great value. For example, listen to the preaching in the Church today about Paul. See if you agree that they consider Paul a special Christian. He was the appointed Apostle to the Gentile Church and they quote his writings often. It may be that Paul is quoted more than Jesus Christ in sermons of this modern era. Much of what the Church understands about governing the Body comes from his teaching. Yes, men hold Paul up as an example of what a successful Christian life looks like.

When men evaluate Paul as a successful person, they look at it all wrong. Men evaluate success by how grand the ministry and how influential it is over the Christian community. Paul is one of the most successful Christian ministers of all time. Paul was a successful Pharisee, a respected leader of the old school of thought. And he was also a successful Christian, a respected leader of the new school of thought. If any man had something to boast about, it was Paul (Gal. 6:14, Eph. 2:1-10, Rom. 4:1-8, 1 Cor. 1:26-31 and 3:16-21).

Take time to read 2 Cor. 11:16-12:12 and you will find another list that Paul has put together to prove the reason he might have for boasting. If you research the related scripture verses, you learn that Paul did not consider this additional information valuable, for the list has no value anywhere but on earth. Here is arguably the most influential man in Christian history counting as rubbish what most Christian leaders are striving for.

Paul found something else more important that made him feel special. He does not want to point to himself. He wants to point to His God. He regards his relationship with Jesus Christ as special. Paul considers his own life as an embarrassment to Jesus Christ, one which he will never live down as long as he lives (1 Cor. 15:9). If you asked him about miracles, he would tell you that he did not have power to perform miracles. It was the Holy Spirit within him who performed the miracles (Gal. 2:18-20). Paul wished only to boast of his knowledge of Jesus Christ and Him crucified (1 Cor. 2:1-2). Jesus Christ is what Paul offered others.

Paul did not treasure what he did. The self-centered thinking found in so many teachers today was not his thinking. Look at the character of other well-known people in the Bible stories and you will find people with a heart desiring to know the Lord. When you read about Abraham, Moses, David, Daniel, Samuel, Job, and others, you can see that what they have is more than obeying a system of

Walking in the Fellowship of Love

laws. They longed for someone and that relationship was more important than their lives.

Our walk is not with flesh and blood. Our walk is with the Holy Spirit. We cannot see Him with physical eyes. We cannot point to Him and show others. We must see Him with the spiritual eye of our hearts and mind. With faith, we see the work He is doing in our lives, in the lives of those around us, in the true Body of Believers, and in the world in general. <u>This is the treasure we seek.</u>

Companionship of the Light is about change and renewal

I am the true vine, and My Father is the vinedresser. Every branch in Me that does not bear fruit, He takes away; and every branch that bears fruit, He prunes it, that it may bear more fruit. You are already clean because of the word which I have spoken to you. Abide in Me, and I in you. <u>*As the branch cannot bear fruit of itself, unless it abides in the vine, so neither can you, unless you abide in Me.*</u> *I am the vine, you are the branches;* <u>*he who abides in Me, and I in him, he bears much fruit; for apart from Me you can do nothing.*</u> *If anyone does not abide in Me, he is thrown away as a branch, and dries up; and they gather them, and cast them into the fire, and they are burned. If you abide in Me, and My words abide in you, ask whatever you wish, and it shall be done for you (John 15:1-7).*

The word translated "abide" is the original Greek word, **μένω menō** (Strong's numbering 3306g). It means, "to stay in a given place or state or relationship or expectancy." A successful Christian life is not a series of spiritual conquests or the number of conversions made after a gospel message. True, we want others to share in the fantastic Life available to those who know Christ. But what advantage are the conquests to the one who does not **know** Christ because he was too busy talking **about** Him to be **with** Him?

Like Paul, what we do should be a natural outpouring of our friendship with the Light of Love. The treasure that pleases us should be the friendship we have with the Light. The effect the Light has on us is not a reflection of who we are. It is a reflection of who "HE IS." We are the craftsmanship of His hands (Eph. 2:10). We did not lift ourselves up by the bootstraps and triumph over sin. Instead, He saved us through His grace (Eph. 2:8). It is time to treasure our

Tree of Life

weakness and glory in His strength. If we rejoice in the companionship we have with Him, others will learn to treasure Him also.

In John 15, Jesus tells us that we can do nothing apart from Him. We are the branches and He is the vine. The fruit of the vine comes from the fellowship of Light. It is not the branch that is producing the fruit. It is the Vine producing through the branch. The Vine teaches from the Tree of Life and the results within the student will reflect that teaching. If fruit results from being in the Vine, the branch does not take credit for the fruit it bears!

The Vine Dresser, the Holy Spirit, is the one who decides what the Vine needs and His purpose is to cause more fruit to appear. He strengthens weak branches so they can bear much fruit. When the Vine Dresser finishes pruning, it may look like He cut the branch too short and left nothing to bear fruit. But what grows back is far more capable of bearing the fruit than what was there before the pruning. We should treasure the time of our pruning. Even if it looks like He took everything away. What is important will return and the branch is better able to bear much fruit. Feed on the knowledge that comes with the Tree of Life and you will bear much fruit. Jesus promised it and it will come to pass.

We should relish the privilege of being a branch. Our glory is in the work done through us by the Vine. We must begin to see the need for the pruning and, as painful as it may be, we must embrace it as good. What is in us, which cannot belong to the vine, He will trim away to make room for what is in the vine.

We must treasure the circumstances He allows in our lives, as something good for the Body of Christ and for production of the Fruit of the Spirit. We should be careful that we do not treasure useless controversies and worldly thinking, and thus fight the pruning. We need our old useless ways of thinking removed, for they cannot bear the fruit of the Tree of Life.

But the fruit of the Spirit is love, joy, peace, patience, kindness, goodness, faithfulness, gentleness, self-control; against such things there is no law. Now those who belong to Christ Jesus have crucified the flesh with its passions and desires. If we live by the Spirit, let us also walk by the Spirit. Let us not become boastful, challenging one another, envying one another (Gal. 5:22-26).

Walking in the Fellowship of Love

Remember Love issued from a pure heart of faith is the goal of the Holy Spirit. The Holy Spirit will use tough situations that prune the false teachings and rituals of worldly religion and prepare new growth of True Life in Christ Jesus. How do I know there are situations coming that He will use to prune us? Because that is what the Vine Dresser's job is: to prune the branches of the Vine in preparation for the Fruit of Love.

For where your treasure is, there your heart will be also (Luke 12:44).

What is it that you treasure right now? Where do you spend most of your time? How much time do Yahweh and His people get? Are you looking back on your life and wishing you made different choices? You cannot go back and change what you have treasured in the past. That is water over the dam. You can make new choices and treasure what is good in your life, which are a part of walking in the Light. You can choose the important things from the Tree of Life. Your treasure is what you spend your time on. Does your treasure have eternal value?

Fellowshipping with the Shepherd and fellowshipping with those of His flock are two treasures that we keep through eternity. They are of the lasting kind. I encourage you to find and fellowship with those who value their God and bring into remembrance His works.

Then those who feared the LORD spoke to one another, and the LORD gave attention and heard it, and a book of remembrance was written before Him for those who fear the LORD and who esteem His name. "They will be Mine," says the LORD of hosts, "on the day that I prepare My own possession, and I will spare them as a man spares his own son who serves him." So you will again distinguish between the righteous and the wicked, between one who serves God and one who does not serve Him (Mal. 3:16-17).

May the Lord you treasure be a Tree of Life to you.

Tree of Life

http://www.hecomesfirst.com

www.ingramcontent.com/pod-product-compliance
Lightning Source LLC
LaVergne TN
LVHW051622080426
835511LV00016B/2124